NO ONE HAS TO DIE

INSIDE THE LONGEST ARMED STANDOFF IN THE HISTORY OF THE U.S. MARSHALS

STEVE MONIER

CONTRIBUTIONS BY
GARY DIMARTINO

AND
DAVID DIMMITT

Genius
Book Publishing

Published by:
Genius Book Publishing,
PO Box 250380
Milwaukee, Wisconsin 53225 USA
https://GeniusBookPublishing.com

ISBN: 978-1-958727-46-1

240924 Trade

CONTENTS

On February 28, 1993, agents from the Bureau of Alcohol, Tobacco, and Firearms (ATF) attempted to serve search and arrest warrants at the compound belonging to the religious sect of the Branch Davidians near Waco, Texas. David Koresh was their leader. The group was suspected of stockpiling illegal weapons, and the ATF obtained warrants for the arrest of Koresh and a few select leaders of the Davidians' members.

An intense gun battle ensued, where four ATF agents were killed, and sixteen were wounded. Six members of the Davidians were killed. A fifty-one-day standoff followed involving hundreds of FBI and ATF agents, members of the National Guard, and U.S. Armed Forces.

In order to end the standoff, the FBI launched an assault on April 19th using a tank to insert tear gas into the compound. A fire broke out. Seventy-six Branch Davidians, including twenty-five children, two pregnant women, and David Koresh died in the fire. The Waco siege and the 1992 standoff at Ruby Ridge in Naples, Idaho, which lasted eleven days, became a rallying cry for Sovereign Citizen and militia groups around the world.

FOREWORD BY MIKE EARP

ASSOCIATE DIRECTOR FOR
OPERATIONS, U.S. MARSHALS
SERVICE (RET.)

In 2007, I was in my twenty-ninth year in law enforcement and my twenty-sixth with the United States Marshals Service (USMS). I was the assistant director of the Investigative Operations Division, which oversaw all investigative operations throughout the ninety-four judicial districts in the country, and all the violent fugitive task forces nationwide.

While the USMS and its task forces arrest more than 120,000 criminals each year, there are incidents during some of these arrests that require review for lessons learned and things to avoid or overcome in future operations.

President George Washington established the U.S. Marshals Service in 1789, following the passage of the Judiciary Act. The USMS is the first and oldest federal law enforcement agency in the country. During this nation's history, the Marshals Service has had several incidents involving anti-government groups that do not recognize the U.S. government or its laws. Throughout its storied 235-year history, the USMS has dealt with many of them. When serving warrants, the USMS and the U.S. Department of Justice (DOJ) have tried to adopt strategies to avoid armed standoffs with the wanted persons or their supporters.

On January 12, 2007, Ed and Elaine Brown of Plainfield, New Hampshire, failed to appear for the continuation of their trial in the U.S. District Court in New Hampshire on felony charges of failing to pay income taxes over a ten-year period. They retreated to their 110-acre fortified hilltop property in Plainfield. That same morning, heavily armed members of the U.S. Constitution Rangers, a militia group, gathered at the end of the Browns' long driveway. They were there to prevent the Marshals from arresting Ed and Elaine. Ed was the leader of the Constitution Rangers. Elaine returned for the continuation of the trial, but Ed refused and vowed to violently resist his arrest by the Marshals. The jury found Ed and Elaine guilty on all counts. Elaine was ordered to stay with her son until sentencing but a month later cut off the electronic bracelet when she returned to the Plainfield compound to rejoin her husband. In April of 2007, Ed and Elaine Brown were sentenced in absentia on those felony tax violations. Both vowed they would not be arrested.

The USMS and the DOJ were concerned a scenario would develop similar to the 1992 Ruby Ridge, Idaho, incident with Randy Weaver and his family, and supporters of the 1993 Waco, Texas, incident involving David Koresh and the Branch Davidians.

After federal ATF warrants were issued in 1992 for Randy Weaver on weapon violations, the USMS attempted to surveil and eventually arrest Weaver and anyone who interfered with them. During the surveillance of the Weaver property, a dog alerted Weaver and his group to the USMS presence, and an exchange of gunfire ensued. A decorated deputy U.S. marshal and Weaver's son were killed. The FBI took over the standoff, which resulted in Vicki Weaver being killed.

In February 1993, ATF obtained arrest warrants for David Koresh for stockpiling weapons at their compound outside Waco, Texas. The

ATF had planned a predawn raid on the compound but discovered that someone had advised Koresh and his followers the ATF were coming. In an initial exchange of gunfire, four ATF agents were killed, along with several of Koresh's followers. A fifty-one-day standoff ensued during which the FBI took over operational control. In April, the FBI launched its entry into the compound. A fire ensued, leaving some seventy-five people, including twenty-five children, dead. In all, eighty-two people died during the armed Waco standoff.

After these prominent incidents, and during numerous anti-government protests over the years, both the DOJ and the USMS emphasized operational arrest plans to avoid armed standoffs.

Marshal Steve Monier was a former chief of police and longtime law enforcement officer. Gary DiMartino was a well-seasoned chief deputy marshal, a former instructor at the USMS Academy, and a former member of the USMS elite Special Operations Group (SOG). These deputies were the SWAT (Special Weapons and Tactics) operatives, trained in both rural and urban settings.

Marshal Monier had the pulse of the community and state. The Browns surrounded themselves with armed supporters and other people attracted to their anti-government rhetoric. While many people in New Hampshire were encouraging a non-violent end to the standoff as it continued, others were telling Monier to end it quickly. Numerous anti-government sympathizers, tax deniers, and militia members were regularly visiting the compound. Marshal Monier and Chief Gary DiMartino developed a plan to enlist local law enforcement support and had individuals providing information about the visitors and weapons on the compound.

Some Brown supporters were staying at the compound and using the internet to promote the Browns' cause. Several key supporters were bringing them additional firearms and, eventually, bomb-making materials. Steve and Gary agreed that they needed the element of surprise and the right conditions to arrest Ed and Elaine, who continued vowing they would kill all law enforcement personnel before surrendering.

After careful planning, the district advised me they wanted to introduce undercover personnel into the compound. I was meeting weekly with Acting Deputy Attorney General (DAG) Craig Morford and his staff to brief them on our operational plan to safely arrest the Browns without incident. The DAG approved this plan.

To achieve a successful conclusion to the standoff, and to slow or stop the flow of visitors to the compound, the district moved forward in September with the simultaneous multi-state arrests of four of the Browns' most culpable supporters. This carefully coordinated operation achieved its goal of stopping most other supporters from visiting the Browns.

Given information available, I next recommended we use select members of the Southeast Regional Task Force (SERTF) to travel to New Hampshire, pose as sympathizers, and insert themselves into the Brown compound. The SERTF had dealt with anti-government sympathizers on several occasions, and HQ believed they were best positioned to surreptitiously gain access to and affect the arrest of the Browns.

Marshal Steve Monier and Chiefs Gary DiMartino, Billy Sorukas from HQ, and Dave Dimmitt planned their briefing of the task force undercovers and used their cooperator to introduce the deputies to the Browns. Within days, this small team of marshals pulled off the ruse and were able to arrest Ed and Elaine Brown at their compound without incident. To quote Marshal Steve Monier after the arrests, "They invited us in, and we escorted them out." Booby traps and nearly one hundred IEDs were located and disabled after the arrests.

The way the District of New Hampshire planned, developed, and executed this operation became the go-to, or gold standard, for similarly difficult and potentially deadly cases. In all operations, the USMS goal is to safely arrest wanted felons while ensuring the safety of our communities. That is exactly what Steve Monier, Gary DiMartino, Dave Dimmitt, Billy Sorukas, and other brave and dedicated marshals were able to do in ending a 266-day armed standoff in the scenic hills of Plainfield, New Hampshire.

—Mike Earp

PREFACE

The modern American Sovereign Citizen movement can be traced back to the rise of far-right groups such as the Christian Identity movement, Posse Comitatus, and the constitutionalist wing of the militia movement. This movement can best be described as a loose grouping of primarily American activists, tax protesters, anti-Semitic Christian Identity followers, and conspiracists who claim they are only answerable to their common law beliefs. Most notably, sovereign citizens believe that state and federal laws don't apply to them, and the courts don't have any jurisdiction over them.

Some sovereign citizen groups assert their own right to issue arrest warrants and their own form of currency. They believe their legal rights derive not from federal or state government, but from their own interpretation of the Constitution, Magna Carta, Bible, Common Law, and the Articles of Confederation. They do not recognize the legitimacy of the federal courts or federal law enforcement.

Most believe that the county sheriff is the only authorized law enforcement officer or agency/department of the United States. Accordingly, when a sheriff has been notified of an "unlawful act" and fails to take action, some sovereign citizens believe they have the "lawful right" to enforce and protect "local jurisdiction."

One group formed in 1977 was the U.S. Constitution Rangers. The founder, Lawrence "Pappy" Robertson, was born on April 11, 1924, in Kentucky and served in the U.S. Army from 1942 to 1945. Following his beliefs that "We the People…" meant that each citizen is sovereign, he formed and chartered the organization. A copy of the charter of the U.S. Constitution Rangers was recorded in the Library of Congress. Pappy Robertson then began to "commission other Americans, under oath, into the ranks to protect and defend the Constitution Republic of the United States of America."[i]

The members of this group viewed themselves as the "law enforcement branch" of the Sovereign Citizen movement. Their members identified as self-appointed protectors of the U.S. Constitution. Some carried badges identical to a brass badge Pappy Robertson stumbled upon in the White House basement, where he served for a time as a military police (MP) officer in 1943.

"The brass badge was a five-pointed star with a ring halfway up the points of the star. On the ring were the words 'United States Continental Congress…' In the center of the badge was the scale of justice."[ii] Many of the "Commissioned Rangers" wore the badge and openly carried firearms.

Various incidents involving federal law enforcement agencies have caused membership in the U.S. Constitution Rangers chapters to grow over time. This includes, but is not limited to, the U.S. Marshals Service (USMS) attempt to arrest Gordon Kahl, a Christian Identity follower in Medina, North Dakota, on February 14, 1983; the FBI raid of The Covenant, Sword, Arm of the Lord compound in Arkansas on April 19, 1985; the USMS & FBI attempt to arrest Randy Weaver at Ruby Ridge in Naples, Idaho, on August 21, 1992; and in particular, the Alcohol, Tobacco and Firearms (ATF) raid and FBI attempt to arrest David Koresh and some of his followers of the Branch Davidian

compound in Waco, Texas, on April 19, 1993. The Waco standoff
lasted fifty-one days and led to the deaths of some seventy-five people,
including twenty-five children.

Other than rendering a group charter or chapter recognition, and
disseminating anti-government and anti-tax materials, however, there is
not a strong central structure to most sovereign citizen factions or
militia groups. As a result, some members rise to local, regional, or
national prominence. By espousing their radical beliefs, they are also
likely to draw the attention of state and federal law enforcement
agencies.

Edward Lewis Brown, who lived in Plainfield, New Hampshire, was
one such person. Plainfield is a pastoral farming and artists' community
situated along the Upper Connecticut River Valley in northern New
Hampshire. In the aftermath of the raid on the Davidian compound in
Waco, Texas, Brown, a self-described "retired exterminator," became
very active in the militia group, the U.S. Constitution Rangers.

Touting himself as the leader of the national organization, Brown
had followers in New Hampshire, Vermont, New York, and other
states, whom he invited to "training sessions" in Plainfield, New
Hampshire, and with whom he stayed in regular contact. His wife, Dr.
Elaine Alice Brown, was a dentist with a thriving dental practice
located in the commercial building they owned in the neighboring
town of Lebanon. In the mid-1990s, both the Browns were in their late
fifties.

Because of his public statements, expressed beliefs, and activities,
and the "training" meetings he held for his Constitution Rangers in
Plainfield and Lebanon, law enforcement noticed Ed Brown. He gave
media interviews, and he liked the attention it brought him.

Amongst their many conspiratorial beliefs about the "corrupt"
federal government, many Constitution Rangers, sovereign citizens, and
tax deniers believe that the graduated federal income tax is illegal. Tax
deniers cite many reasons for this, but prominent among them is an

argument that the Sixteenth Amendment to the U.S. Constitution has never been properly ratified.

Despite numerous and spurious challenges in the federal courts to the federal income tax laws since the Sixteenth Amendment's ratification on April 8, 1913, *not one* has prevailed.

In an interview published in the *New Hampshire Sunday News* in October of 1994, Ed Brown claimed President Clinton, Mikhail Gorbachev, the Council on Foreign Relations, the Illuminati, the Jesuits, the ABA, FEMA, and the Freemasons are all part of a conspiracy to deprive citizens of life and liberty. The *New Hampshire Sunday News* reported that Brown had stockpiled food, weapons, and ammunition in the belief that the federal government would "take over property, utilities, and the media."[iii]

The stockpiling took place at the Browns' Plainfield home, where they built an oddly shaped, castle-like structure complete with a three-story watchtower facing a long driveway. The house was strategically situated on a hill on a sprawling, 110-acre compound on their mostly wooded property. They had solar panels and a windmill installed and could live off the grid. There was a secret bunker and an escape tunnel built in.

Brown and his wife were well armed and well supplied at home. And they were armed whenever they went out. Ed carried a loaded .45-caliber semi-automatic pistol in his waistband. An M1 carbine rifle was tucked between the front seats of his truck. Dr. Brown carried a semi-auto handgun in her shoulder bag.

What was not known in 1994 was that Ed and Elaine Brown would stop paying their federal income taxes in 1996. By 2006, the Browns were liable for taxes of more than $625,000, plus penalties and interest. After repeated attempts by the IRS to get them to settle back taxes, the Criminal Division of the IRS executed a search warrant for Elaine's dental office in Lebanon, New Hampshire, in 2004.

There, Ed Brown, wearing his "United States Continental

Congress" Ranger badge, confronted the IRS agents and said that, with just one phone call, a group of heavily armed Brown associates and rangers could be there within minutes to support him. Owing to back up from the Lebanon Police Department, and the New Hampshire State Police, a potentially deadly encounter was avoided. But the IRS agents were worried about confronting the Browns at their heavily fortified Plainfield property. Prosecutors presented evidence to a grand jury in April of 2006 for felony violations of federal tax laws, and they were indicted.

The IRS investigators knew of Ed Brown's leadership in the U.S. Constitution Rangers and of his disdain for federal authority. Having successfully worked with U.S. Marshals on a 2001 case, where again heavily armed tax deniers were involved, the Criminal Investigative Division of the IRS approached New Hampshire District U.S. Marshal Stephen Monier and Chief Deputy Gary DiMartino with a request.

The U.S. Marshals Service (USMS) Joint Fugitive Task Force worked well with the IRS on a prior warrant under similar circumstances, they said. "Would you again take the lead on these arrests?" the supervisory agent asked. The marshal and chief agreed.

With the assistance of the Lebanon Police Department, a team of deputy U.S. marshals successfully executed a carefully planned ruse, Operation Joint Trust, on the morning of May 24, 2006. They arrested both Ed and Elaine Brown in the parking lot of Elaine's dental office. It was a classic U.S. Marshals Service ruse that reduced the risk to the law enforcement officers involved and minimized the possibility of an armed confrontation with either of the Browns.

Despite the recommendations of the lead assistant U.S. attorney handling the tax case to detain Ed Brown at arraignment in U.S. district court, both Ed and Elaine were released on a number of conditions.

The subterfuge to arrest them was successful. Their subsequent release on conditions was not.

Their trial began on January 9, 2007. Initially, they both appeared for that trial, but on the fourth day, January 12th, they both failed to return to court. In the interim, the Marshals had become alarmed at what internet chatter was developing amongst Ed Brown's supporters in the Constitution Rangers and other extremist groups. The trial judge issued warrants for failure to appear.

Heavily armed supporters of the Browns gathered at the end of the Browns' driveway in Plainfield the same day they failed to return to court. Chief Deputy Gary DiMartino immediately opened communications with both the Browns in an attempt to get them to return to the court for the continuation of the trial.

What followed was a tense, nearly nine-month-long armed standoff with militia members, tax deniers, and other "hangers-on," including members of the "Free State" movement, all in the scenic hills of the "Live Free or Die" state of New Hampshire. Lasting 266 days, it was the longest armed standoff in the 234-year history of the U.S. Marshals Service.

The Browns and their armed followers threatened to hang the judge and prosecutors handling the tax trial. They made frequent threats of violence toward the U.S. Marshals and any law enforcement that attempted to arrest them. They used social media, national internet radio shows, and chat rooms to spread their beliefs and calls for violence. They made frequent references to Ruby Ridge and Waco.

The local, regional, and national media all covered the armed standoff. Randy Weaver, of the siege at Ruby Ridge infamy, visited the Browns and held a press conference with Ed and Elaine on their front porch. People in Plainfield, New Hampshire, and around the nation asked, When and how will this end? Would Plainfield be another Waco?

What ensued was a heroic and determined effort on the part of a remarkable team of U.S. Marshals Service employees to bring the armed standoff to a peaceful conclusion. It was a winding path, filled with instances of extreme volatility, danger, and constant pressure to end the saga.

It concluded with one of the most successful modern-day "Trojan Horse" operations in the long and storied history of the U.S. Marshals Service.

This is the true, previously untold, inside story of that operation...

CHAPTER 1
NOT JUST ANOTHER DAY...

U.S. Marshal Stephen Monier arrived at his desk at approximately eight a.m. on Friday, January 12, 2007. This was going to be the fourth day of the trial for Ed and Elaine Brown of Plainfield, New Hampshire, on felony charges for conspiracy to commit federal income tax violations. The government had a very strong case, and the Browns were representing themselves.

A friend sympathetic to their cause, Michael Avery, from the suitably named Outlaw Legal Services of Florida, was serving as a "paralegal." He had helped Ed and Elaine prepare all their pre-trial motions. He was seated at the defense table to "advise them." The Browns had rejected any representation by an attorney.

It wasn't going well for the Browns. Ed Brown's spurious arguments against having to pay federal income taxes were rejected by the court, and his theories on the federal tax laws were shut down by presiding Judge Steven McAuliffe at several points. The government's witnesses were showing that Ed and Elaine had stopped paying their taxes in 1996 and owed more than $625,000 in unpaid income tax. They were also charged with structuring, the intentional manipulation of financial transactions to evade reporting requirements.

As was his custom on getting to the office, Marshal Monier checked in with the control room upon arrival and spoke with the two court security officers manning the cameras and other systems monitoring courthouse activity that day. All was quiet, they said.

Marshal Monier and his chief deputy, Gary DiMartino, were both concerned about this trial. The U.S. Marshals Service (USMS) had deemed that the trial was "high risk" given that Ed Brown, a self-described "retired exterminator," had become a leader in the militia group, U.S. Constitution Rangers. Membership in the rangers had grown in the aftermath of federal law enforcement's attempts to serve arrest warrants at Ruby Ridge in Idaho and at the Branch Davidian compound in Waco, Texas. Chief DiMartino and Inspector Brenda Mikelson had ordered extra courtroom security and intelligence gathering for the trial. They had ensured that court security officers were being extra vigilant in screening people involved with, or attending, the trial in the U.S. District Court in Concord, New Hampshire.

Marshal Steve Monier and Chief DiMartino had worked together for the past five years in the District of New Hampshire. Chief DiMartino was a career deputy U.S. marshal who had risen through the ranks to become a chief deputy in the Marshals Service, the number two person in every one of the ninety-four district offices of the USMS.

Deputy U.S. marshals are highly trained federal law enforcement officers, not unlike career FBI, ATF, and IRS agents. They apply for open positions in the Marshals Service, take written and physical exams, and are subjected to background investigations prior to being hired. They attend, and must successfully complete, the USMS Academy and other advanced training programs throughout their career.

Gary DiMartino began his law enforcement career in a Rhode Island police department before applying for, and beginning, his calling with the USMS.

Because he had served in several supervisory positions on both the

East and West Coasts during his long tenure with the agency and had taught at the Federal Law Enforcement Training Academy in Glynco, Georgia, he was a highly respected and well-known chief in the USMS. Marshal Monier considered him a very qualified, competent, and professional member of the service and was pleased that when President George W. Bush had nominated him to become the U.S. Marshal for the District of New Hampshire, Gary was his chief deputy.

Unlike the deputy U.S. marshals, who form the corps or "backbone" of the USMS, each U.S. marshal (USM) who heads the district offices of the USMS is nominated by the President of the United States and must be confirmed by the U.S. Senate before taking the oath of office. This has been the case since the U.S. Marshals Service was created in 1789 by the 1st Congress of the newly formed United States government.

When the 1st Congress of the United States stood up the federal judiciary, they realized there was no agency to enforce court orders, apprehend offenders, or help run the court system. In the Judiciary Act, the 1st Congress created the United States Marshals Service, with each marshal in each district to be appointed by the president with the "advice and consent" of the United States Senate.

President George Washington swore in the first thirteen U.S. marshals, including the first marshal of the District of New Hampshire, in 1789. The U.S. Marshals Service is our republic's oldest federal law enforcement agency, with the broadest of authority in enforcing federal law and orders from the U.S. courts. For over 234 years, the U.S. Marshals have done everything from protecting the courts, to taking the census, to protecting the President of the United States.

In the twenty-first century, their core mission is the protection of the U.S. courts, enforcing court orders, apprehending fugitives, running the witness protection program, finding missing or abducted children, and taking the lead on enforcing the provisions of the Adam Walsh Act to track and monitor convicted sex offenders.

Congress and the U.S. Department of Justice made several legislative and administrative changes to how the work of the USMS was conducted over the decades, and in particular, in the twentieth century. Originally, each U.S. marshal could appoint his own deputies as needed, to carry out orders from the court.

As David S. Turk, the official historian of the Marshals Service, noted in his seminal work titled *Forging the Star*, "[L]ong after gaining their Old West reputation with personnel such as Seth Bullock, Wyatt Earp, Bass Reeves, Bat Masterson, and Heck Thomas, U.S. Marshals and their deputies followed a winding trail of transition."[i]

At approximately nine-thirty on that Friday morning, Chief DiMartino stuck his head into the marshal's office and said, "Marshal, Ed and Elaine failed to show up this morning for the continuation of their trial."

It was a decisive moment in the long run-up to this point in the case of the *United States v Edward L. Brown & Elaine A. Brown*. Their failure to appear was long feared by both Monier and DiMartino.

Both had had uneasy feelings about this case, since the district court's magistrate judge released them on conditions, at their arraignment on May 24, 2006, on the income tax and other charges.

Among the conditions of release were that the Browns surrender all weapons to the USMS and the U.S. probation officers who would accompany them back to their Plainfield home. Further, they were to cooperate with, and report regularly to, the U.S. probation officers at the U.S. district court and appear at all future court proceedings.

Deputy U.S. marshals and U.S. probation officers drove Ed and Elaine back to their home in Plainfield to remove their weapons that day in May of 2006. Sharp-eyed deputy marshals noted the layout of the Browns' home on the property, took photographs, and later sketched out the interior layout of the home. This proved to be pivotal in what ensued in the continuing Brown saga.

The deputies who went there also told Chief DiMartino that they didn't believe Ed Brown had surrendered every weapon in his possession to the U.S. probation officers. The property, they reported, was simply too large and the house and outbuildings had too many places where firearms could be concealed.

Within a few hours of the morning the Browns failed to appear for the continuation of their trial, the news got worse. The USMS learned that heavily armed militia members and supporters of Ed Brown had gathered at the end of their long driveway leading to their hilltop home in Plainfield. Judge Steven McAuliffe issued warrants for the Browns' arrest on failure to appear.

Initially, at the USMS and the prosecution's request, the warrants were sealed. Chief Gary DiMartino counseled that the best course was to call the Browns immediately and convince them to return to court for the remainder of their trial. The marshal and Judge McAuliffe concurred, as Gary had carefully established a rapport with Ed and Elaine while they were detained in the Marshals Service's detention facility at their arraignment in May.

"I had faith in Gary's ability to use his considerable communications skills to convince the Browns that they should return to court to finish the trial," Monier reported. Instead of immediately attempting to arrest the Browns at their home, where Ed's armed followers had gathered, he consented to Gary's suggestion that he try to convince them to return for the remainder of the trial.

Gary DiMartino spent the next three days talking with Ed and Elaine via telephone to do just that. The fact that the Browns took every one of his calls over that weekend was a positive.

At one point, it looked like the chief would be successful and that both Ed and Elaine would return to the court on Tuesday morning. Elaine was more noticeably willing to do that given the chief's convincing arguments that this was a financial crime and that they need not take this to any further level.

Gary argued that it would be hard for them to continue to mount a defense if they weren't in the courtroom to do so. The jury, he said, "will only hear the government's side, and not yours." As it turned out, Chief DiMartino was only partially successful.

Chief DiMartino continued to speak with them directly over the phone throughout the weekend and into the day on Monday, which was a holiday. On Tuesday morning, January 16th, Gary had brokered the return of the Browns for the remainder of their trial. Elaine Brown got into the car to return to the courthouse in Concord. At the last minute, however, Ed demurred and refused to get in the car.

This was a partial victory for the Marshals Service. While it isolated Ed Brown from Elaine, Ed was not alone. He was left with some die-hard armed militia supporters who shared his belief about the "corruption of the federal government." Soon thereafter, others joined the group, including members of the "Free State" movement in New Hampshire who, while not professing violence themselves, joined in the discussion about the "overreach" of the federal government into the lives of ordinary Americans. A select number of the New Hampshire Free Staters, who preached an extreme form of libertarianism, supported the Browns.

In a letter posted on the internet shortly after Ed Brown's public announcement that he would not be returning for the remainder of his trial, New Hampshire native William D. Miller wrote on a blog posting, "I am going to see Judge McAuliffe and U.S. Attorney Colantuono and various other officials hanged for treason for these actions." In response, the U.S. Marshals Service issued a "be on the lookout" (BOLO) to area law enforcement in an attempt to locate Miller.

Miller, a New Hampshire resident who was living in Florida at the time, had a history of local law enforcement contacts. He was also an early disciple of Ed Brown and the Constitution Rangers and had been one of Ed's followers for some time.

When Bill Miller learned of the trial, and Ed's vow to fight any attempt to force him to return to the courtroom, Miller got in his car and drove nonstop from Florida "to protect Brown" at all costs. Miller was armed and ready to take on the role of "chief of staff" to Ed Brown when he arrived in Plainfield, New Hampshire, twenty-four hours later.

With Miller's help initially, Brown made use of the internet, emails, blog postings, and media interviews almost immediately upon deciding that he was going to fight any attempts to arrest him or force him from his property.

"I will defend my property, and I am willing to die before going to jail…" Ed Brown told his followers. Apparently, Ed had concluded that he and Elaine were likely to be convicted at the conclusion of the trial. He was publicly critical of Judge McAuliffe and his rulings and, in interviews with the gathering media, called it a "kangaroo court."

Word was quickly spreading through the militia, U.S. Constitution Rangers, and the sovereign citizen communities that things were heating up in Plainfield. Comments on blogging websites and emails about the federal government unfairly targeting the Browns were spreading hourly. Supporters were calling for all good patriots to stand up for them. One message being spread on anti-government websites was titled, "*Will Plainfield be another Waco?*"

Local and state media also began covering the Ed and Elaine Brown story. The *NH Union Leader*, New Hampshire's only statewide newspaper, the *Concord Monitor*, published in New Hampshire's capital and widely distributed, and the *Valley News* (covering the Hanover, Lebanon, and Plainfield region) all took note. The marshal and chief assigned a deputy, who was particularly adept at high tech, IT, and the internet, to begin monitoring all activities related to the Browns. In a call to HQ, they asked that the Investigative Services Division (ISD) and the Intel Unit do the same.

On January 12, 2007, Margot Sanger-Katz, a reporter for the *Concord Monitor* (a prominent New Hampshire newspaper covering the capital city region) wrote one of her first news stories about the Browns' trial when she reported on the first two days of it. The trial had already gained a local interest amongst the state's papers and the statewide ABC-affiliated TV station, WMUR-TV 9, as supporters of the Browns demonstrated in front of the U.S. district courthouse.

Dave Ridley of Keene, New Hampshire, a member of the "Free State" movement in the state, held a sign reading "Ministry of Torture" in reference to "government-sanctioned torture with taxes." "That's why I support Ed," Ridley told the *Concord Monitor*. "He's standing up to the federal government."

Ironically, Sanger-Katz's article about the trial's proceedings appeared on January 12th, the same day Ed and Elaine Brown both refused to return to the courthouse. The government was close to resting its case against the Browns after the testimony of the lead IRS agent handling the investigation and testimony from several postal service employees about the Browns' habit of purchasing multiple postal money orders just below the $3,000 limit required for notification to the government of the transaction.

According to the government's witnesses, this "structuring" of money orders is a common method to avoid paying income taxes. Over a two-year period, the Browns purchased more than $300,000 in money orders. Ed and Elaine, according to postal service investigators, would wait in line separately and each would purchase a money order for $2,800.

At the close of the court's proceedings on January 11th, both Browns told the court that they would begin their defense in the morning, and both told the judge they planned to testify in their own defense.

Both, however, failed to return to court on Friday, January 12th.

On Tuesday, the 16th of January, 2007, the day that Elaine agreed to Chief DiMartino's entreaties to return to court, she also agreed to have a court-appointed attorney, Bjorn Lange, represent her. Michael Avery, the paralegal, continued in his role and sat in on the plea negotiations between the government prosecutor and Attorney Lange.

Learning of the plea negotiations, Judge McAuliffe agreed to postpone the couple's trial for another day when it appeared that Elaine Brown would be willing to reach a deal with the prosecution. That is, if she pled guilty to the extent of her criminal liability and conduct. As a dentist, Elaine Brown earned most of the couple's income. She also had been charged with failing to collect employment taxes from the staff at her dental office in Lebanon.

The judge continued the trial for another day so that the government could calculate what they expected Dr. Brown would pay in back taxes and penalties and the terms of a prison confinement. Elaine was given until ten o'clock the following morning to make a decision on whether to accept a plea deal. If there was no deal, the judge ruled, the trial would continue with or without Ed Brown in the courtroom.

Because Elaine had failed to appear on Friday, the judge ordered new bail conditions for her. He ordered Dr. Brown to stay with her son in Worcester, Massachusetts, and not to return to her Plainfield, New Hampshire, home. She was only allowed telephonic contact with her husband, and she was ordered to wear an electronic ankle bracelet so that U.S. probation officers could monitor her whereabouts.

The Waco Branch Davidian standoff lasted fifty-one days. When both the Browns failed to appear on January 12, 2007, it set in motion what would become a nearly nine-month standoff, the longest armed standoff in the 234-year history of the U.S. Marshals Service. Would Plainfield, New Hampshire, join the lexicon of American history as another Waco or Ruby Ridge?

District of New Hampshire Chief Gary DiMartino, U.S. Marshal Steve Monier, and USMS Chief Regional Inspector Dave Dimmitt were determined not to let that happen.

CHAPTER 2
THE 2006 IRS INDICTMENTS

S teve Monier had been a law enforcement officer for nearly thirty years when President George W. Bush nominated him as the U.S. Marshal for the District of New Hampshire in early 2002. He had spent his career at the Goffstown, New Hampshire, Police Department.

The Town of Goffstown, incorporated in 1761, was named after the early settler and explorer Colonel John Goffe. It is a college town and community of approximately twenty thousand, which borders Manchester, New Hampshire, the state's largest city. Steve had risen through the ranks and was appointed chief of police of the department on July 1, 1984. He served fifteen years as the chief before retiring in 1999.

During his tenure with the Goffstown Police Department, he oversaw the building of a new police facility, took the agency through the Commission on the Accreditation of Law Enforcement Agencies (CALEA) accreditation process to become a nationally accredited agency, and having been appointed and reappointed by two successive New Hampshire governors served six years on the New Hampshire Police Standards & Training Council. This is the state agency that oversees the training and sets the standards for all certified law enforcement and correctional officers in the state.

A *magna cum laude* graduate of St. Anselm College, located in Goffstown, Monier was a history buff. In 1993, he coauthored a book on the Lindbergh kidnapping case titled *Crime of the Century: The Lindbergh Kidnapping Hoax* with his friend, and sometimes adversary in the courtroom, defense attorney Gregory Ahlgren of Manchester, New Hampshire.

As a history enthusiast, Chief Monier had always been an admirer of the U.S. Marshals Service and their many exploits throughout their long and storied history. When President Bush was elected in 2000, Monier applied for the U.S. Marshals position, one of many chief executive law enforcement officers in New Hampshire who did so.

Three weeks before September 11, 2001, Monier traveled to Washington, D.C., for an interview with senior members of the Department of Justice and the U.S. Marshals Service. He was one of three from New Hampshire brought to D.C. for an interview. Steve Monier also had the backing of U.S. Senator Judd Gregg for the position.

Senator Gregg had served three terms as the governor of New Hampshire before running for the U.S. Senate, and Monier had worked on several law enforcement projects with Governor Gregg and his administration during Steve's tenure as president of the New Hampshire Chiefs of Police Association.

Needless to say, the September 11th attacks on our nation occupied the immediate attention of the Bush Administration and Congress, as the nation prepared to bring to justice those who murdered 2,977 innocent people in New York City, at the Pentagon, and in a field in Shanksville, Pennsylvania. Included in that number were 344 firefighters and 72 law enforcement officers. More than 600 people were injured. They were mothers and fathers, sons and daughters, brothers and sisters, friends and neighbors. They were part of the American family.

The nation's military, national security agencies, and law enforcement went on high alert, as those who swore to uphold and defend the Constitution of the United States vowed to bring to justice those responsible and to protect our country from further attack.

This was the backdrop for Stephen Monier when President Bush nominated him for the post on April 15, 2002, and the U.S. Senate confirmed him on May 7th. On May 13, 2002, he took the oath of office as the fortieth U.S. marshal to serve the District of New Hampshire.

As there were thirteen original states, President George Washington swore in the first thirteen U.S. marshals in September of 1789, including John Parker, the first marshal for the District of New Hampshire.

During his ceremonial swearing in on July 1, 2002, in front of gathered members of the court, dignitaries, friends, and family, Steve provided some history about the U.S. Marshals Service in the District of New Hampshire. He noted that John Parker was born in Portsmouth, New Hampshire, on November 16, 1732.

He added, "When the Declaration of Independence arrived in the State of New Hampshire, it was John Parker who read it from the old state house balcony. And after his appointment as marshal, Parker was selected to be one of the official greeters when President Washington visited Portsmouth in October of 1789."

Monier also said, "Unfortunately, two years later, after a short illness, Marshal Parker died in office." To the chuckles of many in the audience, he added, "It was a feat that I shall try hard not to duplicate."

Monier was very pleased to join the U.S. Marshals Office in New Hampshire with the dedicated federal employees—sworn and non-sworn—who were serving in the office at the time. At his first department-wide meeting, Marshal Monier outlined what he expected of them and what they could expect of him moving forward. "I expect,"

Monier said, "district employees to work hard and to fairly, impartially, and ethically enforce the law."

For his part, he pledged to do the same, and to advance the mission, vision, and values of the agency. Further, he said, "I will work to bring my knowledge of New Hampshire law enforcement, and my network of connections with local and state officials, to bear on the responsibilities federal law enforcement shares with those of state and local agencies."

Monier wanted to expand the New Hampshire Joint Fugitive Task Force to bring the fugitive hunting skills and expertise of deputy U.S. marshals to assist state and local agencies in finding and apprehending New Hampshire's most wanted felons. Taking wanted felons off the streets, who were actively seeking to avoid apprehension, he believed, helped to prevent future crimes and made the state and nation safer.

To members of the district office, he said that if he had an overarching philosophy about enforcing the law it was this: "Firm, but Fair." And when confronted with the great challenges that would inevitably occur in law enforcement, he wanted to "find a better way" to resolve them.

Chief Deputy Gary DiMartino first briefed Steve Monier about Ed and Elaine Brown sometime in January of 2006. One of the senior resident IRS agents from the New Hampshire criminal division had reached out to Gary to give him a heads-up that the U.S. Attorney's Office would likely indict the Browns on a number of charges relating to their failure to pay income taxes in the ten years since 1996.

The agent had worked with Gary on an IRS case in 2001, with another anti-government crew that included several U.S. Constitution Rangers. The case involved defendants with lots of guns, explosives, judicial threats being made requiring protection, and more. After cultivating a source on the inside and hitting the location when everybody was away from the property, the outcome was successful. As a result, the local IRS office was pleased with how the Marshals had assisted the IRS Criminal Division before.

"Given Ed Brown's beliefs about the federal government, and his leadership in the U.S. Constitutional Rangers militia group, we may need your assistance again in this case," the agent told Gary. The chief gave the marshal an overview of what they knew about Ed and Elaine Brown.

Monier had heard the name before, but having been a chief of police in the southern part of New Hampshire, he wasn't as familiar with the Browns as many law enforcement officers in the north of New Hampshire were. So he did a little research on Ed Brown, and the first thing he came across was an interview Brown gave the *New Hampshire Sunday News* on October 9, 1994.[i]

In it, Ed Brown, age fifty-two at the time, was identified as a "spokesman for the Constitution Defense Militia," one of numerous "unorganized" citizen militia groups formed in "response to what they say is a well-orchestrated and far-reaching conspiracy to deprive Americans of their liberty…"

Brown told the *New Hampshire Sunday News* he "likened" the times "we are living in [to] the years in Europe before World War II" and that "he has 18 months' worth of food stored in his basement, and a stockpile of weapons and ammunition."[ii]

Brown warned that "there is a second Revolutionary War approaching." The article then added, "But he [Brown] says this time the citizens have AK-47s." Brown said that "it's easy to dismiss him as a nut" and that he "knows that's how the FBI, the Department of Defense, and other federal agencies he calls regularly have him pegged."

It was a wide-ranging interview with Brown pontificating on a number of subjects and beliefs. He contended, for example, in what may have been a prescient moment, that "there are 130 detention centers set up around the country, including one at the former Pease Air

Force Base [in Newington and Portsmouth, New Hampshire], ready to imprison people like him who resist the government."

While Ed Brown was ultimately imprisoned in federal custody, it wasn't in a detention camp in Portsmouth. In fact, the conversion of the Pease Air Force Base to the Pease Development Authority in New Hampshire became a model for what can be done when the U.S. government closes military bases.

The Pease Development Authority land is now the home of a vibrant business and manufacturing community and is an economic powerhouse on the seacoast employing several thousand people in a variety of businesses. It is also home to the Portsmouth International Airport, a National Passport Center, the New Hampshire Air National Guard, and boasts one of the longest runways on the East Coast. There are no detention centers there.

The *New Hampshire Sunday News* interviewed Ed Brown just six months later for a local militia angle on the April 19, 1995, bombing of the Alfred P. Murrah federal building in Oklahoma City, Oklahoma.[iii] On that terrible day in our nation's history, Timothy McVeigh parked a rented Ryder truck in front of the federal building and set off timed fuses to detonate bombs, while he made his escape in a vehicle parked nearby. At 9:02 a.m., the five thousand pounds of explosives contained in the van detonated, killing 168 people, including nineteen children, and wounded hundreds of others.

McVeigh might have been on the loose for some time but for the alert actions of Oklahoma Highway Patrol Trooper Charlie Hanger, who stopped McVeigh ninety minutes later for a missing front license plate and arrested him for carrying a concealed and loaded handgun. Fortunately, McVeigh was unable to make bail and was held at the county jail awaiting arraignment when the FBI linked McVeigh and Terry Nichols as co-conspirators to the bombing. Both were later convicted in federal court, and McVeigh was sentenced to death. He was executed by lethal injection on June 11, 2001, at the U.S. federal penitentiary in Terre Haute, Indiana.

When the *New Hampshire Sunday News* reporter contacted Ed Brown about this act of domestic terrorism, where the suspects may have had ties to militia groups, Edward L. Brown said that he "knows who is behind the deadly bombing of the federal building."

"It was," Brown said, "an inside operation done by the government itself. We know damn right well that they have orchestrated this whole thing."[iv]

Brown theorized that "officials in the Federal Emergency Management Agency (FEMA) and the federal Bureau of Alcohol, Tobacco, and Firearms (ATF) may have hired people to blow up the building so they could place the blame on the militia." Their next move, Brown warned the reporter, "is to get people against the militia and to start crashing down people's doors and take people's firearms," he said.

Timothy McVeigh, it was widely reported, was "motivated by his dislike for the U.S. federal government and unhappy about its handling of the Ruby Ridge incident in 1992 and the Waco siege in 1993. McVeigh timed his attack to coincide with the second anniversary of the fire that ended the siege at the Branch Davidian compound in Waco, Texas."[v]

McVeigh was a U.S. Army veteran who had trained in combat engineering and the use of explosives and received his basic training at Ft. Leonard Wood, in the Missouri Ozarks, Pulaski County, Missouri. The reader will understand why this is important to recall later in the book.

Edward L. Brown was born on July 22, 1942, and at age seventeen joined the U.S. Navy. Not long after, he received a dishonorable discharge when he assaulted a man in Somerville, Massachusetts, in 1960, while armed with a dangerous weapon and trying to rob him. After a jury trial in Middlesex Superior Court, Brown was found guilty of assault to armed robbery on April 20, 1960, and imprisoned at the Massachusetts Correctional Institute in Concord. He was paroled on January 18, 1965.

According to Massachusetts Governor Council records listing pardons, Edward Brown sought, and received, a full pardon on July 14, 1976, from Governor Michael Dukakis. It was one of 237 pardons Dukakis, then a first-term governor, granted in 1976. Pardons are often requested by those who want to carry weapons.

Following his parole from the Concord, Massachusetts, correctional institution, Brown bounced around in various jobs and was twice married. He was a hairdresser for a time and homeless for another. Circa 1984, Ed Brown became an exterminator. He told several news outlets and others that he developed a unique method for exterminating roaches and was "credited with completely eliminating termites and roaches at the Long Beach Navy Yard."[vi]

Brown was featured in an article in the *Sunday (Worcester, Massachusetts) Telegram* on October 21, 1984, with the heading "Westboro (MA) Man Fights Filth" where he discussed his "Zap Trap" he was marketing and claimed were being used in restaurants, tenement buildings, and at public housing authorities. In the article, and on a twist to a movie popular at the time, Brown said the name of his business was "Roach Busters."[vii]

In 1991, Brown married Elaine Alice Brown, the third marriage for Ed and the second for Elaine. Purportedly, Elaine met Ed Brown when he was hired to do pest control at an apartment building she owned in Massachusetts.

Ed Brown has two children from his prior marriages. Elaine Brown has two children from hers. None of the children supported Ed and Elaine in their armed standoff with the federal government.

Ed Brown had become well enough known for his activities with militias and his thinking on the federal government to earn a mention in the 1994 Anti-Defamation League's state-by-state fact finding report on extremism titled *ARMED & DANGEROUS: MILITIAS TAKE AIM AT THE FEDERAL GOVERNMENT*:

New Hampshire is the home of the Constitution Defense Militia, a well-organized group with at least fifteen members. It is not known if the group engages in paramilitary training or the stockpiling of weapons.

The group has held meetings at the home of Edward L. Brown of Plainfield [New Hampshire]. Brown is outspoken in his support of the concept of militias and devotes much of his time and energy to the causes embraced by them: opposition to gun control, the United Nations and the federal government. He recently lobbied against a bill that would ban guns in school zones, for example.

While much of Brown's activity appeals to mainstream opponents of gun control and big government, his enthusiasm for conspiracy theories and his reliance on extremist propaganda places him on the far reaches of the political spectrum. Brown is a devoted reader of The SpOTlight, the organ of Liberty Lobby, the best-funded and most active anti-Semitic propaganda organization in the United States. In a recent telephone call to ADL, Brown acknowledged that he gets his information on domestic and international affairs from The SpOTlight. He recently wrote letters to his congressman and senators in Washington regarding the alleged build-up of hostile foreign troops inside the United States. Other members of his militia reportedly also embrace conspiracy fantasies involving the Council on Foreign Relations, the Trilateral Commission, and the Rockefeller Foundation. [viii]

While Ed Brown engendered support from a number of like-minded tax-deniers, militia members, and New Hampshire "Free Staters" during their nine-month standoff with the U.S. Marshals, not everyone in the blog-o-sphere was enamored with Ed Brown. None was more evident than in this posting on April 6, 2008, on the Red Crayons Blog account during the trial of the Browns' three co-conspirators:[ix]

WHO IS ED BROWN?

By admin | April 6, 2008

Who is the man that the three defendants (and the people commenting on this blog) support so blindly? Who is this "great man," "hero," "patriot," and "true American" that the supporters all think is such a great guy?

Ed Brown was born in 1942 in Massachusetts. In 1960, he joined the military but was soon convicted of armed robbery and assault with a dangerous weapon and sentenced to five years in prison. Over the next two decades, he was a drifter, a hairdresser, a gun shop owner, and finally settled on a career as a cockroach exterminator. He's been married three times and has two children, neither of whom supported him in his "stand" against the US Marshals.

In the mid-1990s, Ed retired from the cockroach business and was financially supported by his wife Elaine, a successful dentist he had married in the 1980s. Elaine also has two children from a prior marriage, neither of whom supported their stand.

Ed spent his retirement years leading a national militia called the US Constitution Rangers, a group that has since splintered and provided almost no support for Ed's stand.

Interestingly, the only people who lasted more than a couple of weeks supporting Ed in his "you won't take me alive" cause were complete strangers who were attracted to his mad dog rants on the internet. Constitution Ranger Bill Miller was a rare exception—he had known Ed for years prior to the stand, and he took up arms at the Brown residence, but left after a couple of weeks when he found out that part of Ed's plan was to murder Elaine Brown and blame it on the

US Marshals in hopes of inciting a bloody revolution. Mr. Miller currently resides in a mental health facility pending unrelated criminal charges.

Ed and Elaine stopped paying income taxes in 1996, stopped filing returns in 1998, were raided in 2004, were indicted in 2006, and were convicted in January 2007. Ed didn't even bother attending the second half of the criminal trial, leaving Elaine to defend herself (they didn't use attorneys). What a great guy.

Over the next nine months, he made some really violent and ugly threats against Marshals, Judges, a prosecutor, an IRS employee, members of the press, the Plainfield Chief of Police, and numerous others. He bragged about keeping a "hit list" of 50+ people who would be killed if he and Elaine were ever arrested, injured, or killed. What a great guy, eh?

Dr. Elaine Brown, born on February 14th, 1940, is a graduate of the Tufts University School of Dental Medicine in Boston, Massachusetts, one of the most highly rated dental schools in the country. Tufts University, a private research university, is located on the border of Medford and Somerville, Massachusetts, which are suburbs of Boston, and was founded in 1852 as Tufts College.

Following dental school and after obtaining a license to practice dental medicine in New Hampshire, Dr. Elaine Brown first worked with a dentist in Plymouth, New Hampshire, while the Browns took up residence at South Down Shores in Laconia. Ed and Elaine moved to Plainfield in 1990. The couple decided that the New Hampshire Upper Valley was the best location for them. Their home, on 110 acres, is located on a tract of land with a view to the northeast. The house cannot be seen from the street, Center of Town Road.

Dr. Brown opened up her dental practice in West Lebanon, New Hampshire, in a commercial building the Browns ended up owning.

Dr. Brown was the primary income earner for the Browns, and her income and that of the dental practice was the primary focus of the investigation into the couple's joint income during the ten-year period they stopped paying federal taxes.

Elaine became a follower of her husband's belief that the federal government was overreaching into the lives and liberty of ordinary Americans and that the graduated federal income tax laws were unconstitutional. She also stopped paying the required withholdings for her employees.

CHAPTER 3

THE FIRST RUSE: OPERATION JOINT TRUST

May 24, 2006

F ollowing the execution of search warrants at the dental practice in 2004, and further investigation by the IRS Criminal Division, the District of New Hampshire U.S. Attorney's Office (USAO) agreed to present the accumulated evidence against the Browns to a federal grand jury. The grand jury returned a true bill on criminal charges in April of 2006.

It was then that the IRS made the formal request to Marshal Monier and Chief Deputy Gary DiMartino for assistance from the U.S. Marshals–led New Hampshire Joint Fugitive Task Force to serve the warrants for Ed and Elaine Brown's arrests.

These were sealed indictments, and Chief DiMartino and the marshal took a go-slow approach to finding a "better way" to arrest the Browns. They knew Ed Brown's disdain for the federal government. They knew both the Browns were armed wherever they went. They knew that approaching the house, which was heavily fortified and where the Browns had access to high-powered long rifles, was a risk.

Both Marshal Monier and the chief deputy wanted to find the best way to reduce the risk that a law enforcement officer, or the Browns, would be injured or killed while serving the warrants. Accordingly, Gary DiMartino assigned two experienced deputy U.S. marshals to surreptitiously surveil the Browns, track their movements, learn their habits, and help construct a ruse that would lure the Browns away from their fortified hilltop home and successfully take them into custody.

A local New Hampshire police chief, who was also a part-time contract guard for the Marshals Service, had a pilot's license and a plane. He was recruited to do some overflights of the Browns' property to take aerial photographs of the home and surrounding area.

The surveillance and collection of information on the Browns' habits went on for several weeks before possible scenarios—or possible ruses—were discussed that would lure the unsuspecting Browns away from their Plainfield home.

The U.S. Marshals are infamous for conducting ruses to apprehend wanted felons. Perhaps the most famous was conducted on the morning of December 15, 1985, when 101 "guests" arrived at the Washington, D.C., Convention Center wearing Washington Redskins regalia. Little did the "guests" know, the letter they received saying their names had been drawn from a list to receive two free tickets and bus transport to and from the Redskins-Bengals football game scheduled for later that day was really from the U.S. Marshals Service.

In fact, it was a sting conducted by the Marshals to apprehend wanted persons with outstanding federal warrants. There is always risk involved in executing a warrant at a fugitive's home. A ruse to lure an unsuspecting person to a neutral and controlled location reduces that risk.

The NFL was so taken with this ruse to safely take wanted people into custody, they produced a short documentary about the "lure" of attending an NFL game to safely capture wanted persons.

In a sports column in the *Washington Post*, Scott Allen recounted the story about the Marshals' operation on December 18, 2015:

On the morning of Dec. 15, 1985, 101 guests arrived at the Washington Convention Center wearing Redskins regalia and in a festive mood. They had received a letter from a new all-sports television channel—Flagship International Sports TV—indicating that their names had been randomly selected from a clearinghouse list of D.C. residents to receive two free tickets and bus transportation to and from the Redskins-Bengals game later that day.

The invitees were told they could redeem their prize with fellow winners at a pregame party, where they also could enter a drawing for 1986 Redskins season tickets and a one-week, all-expenses-paid trip to Super Bowl XX in New Orleans.

None of the guests made it to RFK Stadium for the Redskins' 27-24 triumph over Cincinnati, much less left the party with tickets to the Super Bowl. The entire event was an elaborate ruse crafted by the U.S. Marshals Service to apprehend federal fugitives and resulted in the arrest of more than 100 criminals with outstanding warrants for 90 felonies and 70 misdemeanors.

Thirty years later, Operation Flagship remains one of the most successful—and creative—stings in law enforcement history.

"It was party time, and they fell for it hook, line and sinker," U.S. Marshal for the District of Columbia Herbert M. Rutherford told the Associated Press in 1985."[i]

The history of the U.S. Marshals to successfully use a ruse to arrest offenders drove the thinking of the chief deputy, the marshal, and the deputies in trying to find a way to lure both the Browns away from their home. Their goal: provide the inducement, and find the means and a space where they could be safely taken into custody.

After surveillance gave the Marshals the information they needed about the Browns' routines and habits, several discussions took place. Knowing that Dr. Brown drove into the dental office in Lebanon each day the practice was open, and knowing that Ed Brown also often drove to the commercial building to conduct his militia business and "activities" in a space above the office, the first thought was to arrange some type of motor vehicle stop on the roads leading from Plainfield into Lebanon.

This was discounted after a bit, however, as there were just too many uncontrollable variables involved. How would all the other traffic be controlled? What if Elaine was apprehended, but Ed chose not to leave the house that day? What if the Browns resisted? What would be the risk to other motorists or homes and businesses? What would happen if Elaine had time to tip Ed off to the stop?

One of the deputies surveilling the Browns, the New Hampshire Joint Fugitive Task Force commander, Jeffrey White, made a suggestion that had strong merit. The dental office was located in West Lebanon, had a good-sized parking lot, and was a standalone building in a relatively uncongested area. What could be done to lure both the Browns to the commercial building before it opened?

Moreover, the Lebanon, New Hampshire, police chief, Jim Alexander, who the marshal and chief had spoken with about the indictments, was very supportive of the Marshals' desire to take the Browns safely into custody.

Chief Jim Alexander, a Vermont native, had begun his law enforcement career with the Windham County, Vermont, sheriff's office after a program at the Brattleboro, Vermont, Voc-Tech piqued his interest in law enforcement. His original plan was to pursue becoming a licensed electrician.

"As part of the Vocational-Technical educational process, however, I was exposed to the law enforcement program, and I pursued it. When I graduated in 1985, I was also a certified part-time law enforcement officer and went to work part time for the sheriff's office at the age of eighteen," he said.

"Of course," Jim said, "being in Brattleboro, and after working for a year at the sheriff's office, I went to work full-time with the Brattleboro Police Department in 1987. I worked there until 1990. As a border community to New Hampshire, we worked closely with the agencies just across the river—the New Hampshire State Police and the Lebanon PD.

"The New Hampshire State Police tried to recruit me," Jim said, "but I was more interested in city policing. I joined the Lebanon PD in 1990, rose through the ranks, and was asked to become the chief of police in March of 2006. I served as the chief until my retirement in March of 2013," he said.

When Marshal Monier asked Jim when he first heard of Ed Brown, the chief said, "I guess everyone in the Upper Valley area knew something about Ed Brown. When the Marshals approached us about helping them conduct a ruse at Elaine's dental office, I remembered a chance encounter that my wife and I had a few years before with Ed and Elaine at a restaurant in Quechee, Vermont.

"My wife and I were out to eat at a restaurant we liked just across the river," Jim said. "I was either a captain or the deputy chief at the time. We were seated at a table, which was separated by latticework from a table behind us.

"In walks Ed and Elaine Brown with another couple, and they're seated at the table behind us. It's only latticework that separates us," Jim said, "so of course we can hear the conversation. Especially since Ed Brown had a distinctive and loud voice. For the next hour, my wife and I listened to Ed try to convince this other couple that they don't have to pay federal income taxes. This was probably in 2004.

"So when you folks called about planning a ruse to arrest the

Browns away from their Plainfield home," Chief Alexander said, "and had developed a plan to do it at the dental office, we looked at our calls for service for that building. There had been a water problem at the office at one point, so when we met with your folks, we suggested that might be something to consider. On top of that, I knew the head of the water department and the director of public works very well. We had a good relationship. I knew that if I asked, they would be on board with loaning us some of their equipment and vehicles. And they were."

The U.S. Marshals "would have the support of the Lebanon Police," he said.

A plan for Operation Joint Trust was coming together.

During the pre-dawn hours on the morning of May 24, 2006, a select team of deputy U.S. marshals and task force officers gathered in Lebanon with several members of the Lebanon Police Department and IRS agents. Several of the deputies were dressed in construction work gear—blue jeans, work boots, work shirts, and orange traffic vests.

The arrest team was led by the District of New Hampshire's Supervisory Deputy U.S. Marshal (SDUSM) Brian Hughes, a no-nonsense deputy and criminal investigator, with years of outstanding work capturing wanted persons.

Today, the operational plan—Operation Joint Trust—that the team had worked out with the chief deputy and Lebanon PD and approved by the marshal was being executed. The team's mission was to safely take Ed and Elaine Brown into custody when they were lured to the commercial building and dental office in Lebanon.

Like any plan, however, the members of the team knew there was risk involved. Both the Browns were armed wherever they went—Ed with a .45 semi-automatic pistol in his waistband and an M1 carbine rifle in his vehicle, and Elaine with a semi-auto pistol in her handbag.

The team knew that even with a well-devised plan, they could control most things, but not everything.

After conferring with members of the police department and checking their concealed firearms, communications gear, and other equipment, the deputies got into the trucks on loan from the Public Works and Water Departments and drove to Elaine's dental office. Lebanon police units would be secreted nearby but out of sight of the commercial building.

There, the "DPW" team used a hose and water from an outside spigot at the dental office to simulate a "water leak" leading from the building out into the parking lot. At approximately six thirty a.m., a signal was sent to the Lebanon chief of police, Jim Alexander, to have their communications center place a call to Ed and Elaine Brown's home in Plainfield.

They did so. Ed Brown answered the phone call.

"Mr. Brown, this is the Lebanon Communications Center. Sir, there is a water leak that's been discovered at your commercial building and the dental office in West Lebanon. We need you to come down as soon as possible to open the building and help Public Works and Water Department people, who are there now, find the source of the problem.

"Could you come down now, please?" the dispatcher added. "I know Dr. Brown's office opens a little later, but the problem could be coming from the dental office. Could Dr. Brown also come to the office?"

Ed Brown agreed to head right down to the office. The Marshals knew that Ed often filled the role of "building superintendent," handling maintenance and other building issues that arose. Ed told the dispatcher that Elaine would be along shortly after.

A few minutes later, a U.S. Marshals fixed-wing aircraft, in the air over the Browns' home in Plainfield, reported to the team that Ed had gotten into his truck and was heading their way. They would monitor the truck's route throughout the drive to the office. This gave the team real-time information on Ed Brown's probable arrival at the commercial building.

Parked at a small strip mall not far from the dental office was a second team of deputies in an unmarked SUV. They were the rapid response team, should the deputies acting as DPW and Water Department workers need immediate backup. Parked a bit further away and out of sight were Lebanon police officers in a marked cruiser. They were also monitoring the communications between the Lebanon PD Communications Center and the Marshals and would be available, if needed, to transport the Browns following their arrest. Or as backup should things go bad.

Chief Deputy Gary DiMartino, Deputy U.S. Marshal Ken Nunes, and the lead IRS agent in charge of the criminal investigation were at the Lebanon PD, which was serving as the command post for the operation. Lebanon Police Chief Jim Alexander joined them. He was key to assisting the USMS with setting up this ruse (and, later, helping with the second).

Marshal Steve Monier and Judicial Security Inspector Brenda Mikelson were monitoring the progress of Operation Joint Trust from the operations room at the Marshals' Office in Concord, New Hampshire.

When Ed Brown pulled into the parking lot of the commercial building, he saw the DPW and water department vehicles, four to five "workers" in and around a manhole cover, and water on the pavement. He didn't pull up right next to the crew but instead parked away from them. When he got out of the truck, instead of going over to talk with the "workers," he walked immediately to the building and went inside.

The team leader, Supervisory Deputy Brian Hughes, saw this: "When I saw Ed go right into the office instead of coming over to us," he said, "I thought, *Oh no, this isn't going to go well.* But within a couple of minutes, Ed came back out of the building and walked toward us.

"I breathed a sigh of relief," Brian reported.

"If he hadn't come out of the building, at some point we would have had to go inside and try and coax him out. I was worried he might have been on to us—our ruse—when he went directly to the building. We didn't know what other weapons Ed might have kept in the office space he used in the building.

"We decided to wait a few minutes before taking any further action," Brian later told the chief and marshal. "When he came back outside, we had a manhole cover partially lifted and we were pretending to look at it."

Brian added, "The plan was for me to go up to Ed and extend my hand to shake his and introduce myself. Steve Mac [a task force deputy] was right behind me. As soon as Ed took my hand, Steve and I took him to the ground to handcuff him.

"That's when things got interesting," Brian reported, "because Ed immediately started resisting and tried to reach for his semi-auto pistol. We told him we were U.S. Marshals and that he was under arrest.

"Ed may have been in his early sixties, but he was in good shape and surprisingly strong for his size," Brian reported. "Steve Mac quickly secured the handgun while the team got Ed under control. We patted him down and then placed him inside the unmarked Marshals SUV we had moved into the parking lot. I stayed with Ed.

"Steve Mac and another deputy then searched his truck, as we knew he kept a loaded M1 carbine in it," Brian said. "Surprisingly, we found other weapons as well."

They secured Brown's loaded firearms and radioed to the command post that Ed Brown was in custody. With Team Leader Brian Hughes sitting next to Ed in the rear seat, and two arrest team members in the front, they transported Ed to the Lebanon Police Department.

With that accomplished, the remaining team members prepared for Dr. Elaine Brown's arrival. How did members of Operation Joint Trust know for certain that Ed would arrive first at the dental office? They didn't.

The Operation Joint Trust plan had accounted for various possible scenarios for the arrival of the Browns: either together or arriving separately, and with either Ed or Elaine arriving first. The optimum scenario was Ed arriving first, so he could be detained and transported away from the office before Elaine arrived. Ed was the most heavily armed and, therefore, the bigger threat. That it happened that way was a boon for the Marshals.

When the Marshals' aircraft reported a few minutes later that Elaine was now en route to the office, she would arrive seeing Ed's vehicle parked there. She would also see the water, the Public Works and Water Department vehicles, and "employees" still inspecting the parking lot area. She wouldn't know that Ed Brown was already in custody and being transported to the Lebanon Police Department.

Unless, of course, someone called her and tipped her off—and that nearly happened.

Shortly after Ed's transport team left for the Lebanon PD, a female member of Elaine's dental staff arrived at the office. When it appeared that she would be going inside the building, one of the DPW "workers" approached her and told her that there were some water issues in the building and that the office would be closed for the day.

The Marshals Service aircraft reported that Elaine was minutes away from arriving at the office. Fortunately, the employee had left the area.

Shortly thereafter, Dr. Brown pulled into the parking lot and parked nearer to the entrance to the building and the work crew. The lead deputy for Elaine's arrest team, Jeff White, approached her car as she was about to get out. Fully in the role of a concerned public works employee, Jeff offered her a hand when getting out of the car.

"Let me help you, ma'am," he said as he offered his hand to her when she opened her car door and was about to stand up.

"Thank you," she said.

As she got out, with Jeff still holding onto her hand, he said, "Dr. Brown, I'm a deputy with the U.S. Marshals; we have a warrant, and

I'm placing you under arrest." She had left her handbag in the vehicle when she stood up, which Jeff White knew was where she kept her handgun.

Jeff turned Elaine Brown around and placed the handcuffs on her. Unlike her husband Ed, Elaine did not try to resist. She was placed into the second USMS vehicle with Jeff White and another deputy and also transported to the Lebanon Police Department.

CHAPTER 4
THE BROWNS' ARRAIGNMENT AND RELEASE

After Ed and Elaine Brown were arrested, they were first transported to the Lebanon Police Department for a further search and processing. As anticipated, an inventory search of Elaine's bag revealed a small, loaded, semi-automatic handgun. At the time, under New Hampshire law, both Ed and Elaine had permits to lawfully carry concealed handguns.

Both of the Browns were then transported to the U.S. district court in Concord and held in the U.S. Marshals Service cell block for an arraignment later that afternoon. Magistrate Judge James Muirhead was scheduled to handle the arraignment.

The decision to indict, arrest, and prosecute people for tax violations does not happen in a vacuum. As one of the lead IRS investigators in the Brown case explained, "There are thresholds that have to be met before our regional HQ will sign off on bringing a criminal case against someone for felony tax violations.

"During the time the Browns were being investigated," he said, "there had to be at least a three-year period of non-payment involved; there had to be a certain level of income and the amount of taxes owed; and there had to be some indication this was an intent not to pay. All of these things were looked at, reviewed, and approved for the case to go forward to the U.S. Attorney's Office for their review and before an indictment was sought."

With the taxes owed and the accrued penalties and interest involved, this was more than a million-dollar tax case over a ten-year period. While Dr. Elaine Brown's dental practice was the majority source of the Browns' income, both Ed and Elaine were involved in the conspiracy to hide income and the failure to pay their federal income taxes.

Whenever possible, prior to arraignment, the U.S. Probation Office conducts a pre-arraignment interview with defendants to provide some basic information to the court. This interview takes place in the USMS cell block within the U.S. courthouse while awaiting the hearing. The U.S. probation officer will want to provide the court with information on the defendants, such as how long the defendants have resided in the district, if they have a prior criminal history, if there are available assets and/or property owned by the defendants, if any threats have been made against potential witnesses, and so forth.

Assistant U.S. Attorney (AUSA) Bill Morse was representing the government and handling the IRS case involving the Browns. He was well prepared for the Browns' arraignment. He had worked with the IRS on the search warrant that was executed at Dr. Brown's dental office in Lebanon, and he presented the case to the grand jury for the indictments.

AUSA Morse was the perfect prosecutor for the job. Bill Morse had grown up in New Hampshire attending Milford High School and graduating from the University of New Hampshire. He attended law school at William and Mary in Virginia and, after graduating, began a job in Washington, D.C., for the U.S. Securities and Exchange Commission (SEC).

Bill had always wanted to return to New Hampshire. Following his time at the SEC in Washington, he took a job in the Boston regional office of the SEC, where he commuted every day from his home in New Hampshire. He did this for several years.

In 2000, he was hired as an AUSA at the U.S. Attorney's Office in Concord, New Hampshire, and was considered a white-collar specialist working in the criminal division. Bill first heard of the Browns when he got an IRS referral for prosecution. By that time, he had handled three or four other what he called "tax deniers" cases for tax evasion.

"In all," Morse said, "the government determined that the Browns had evaded paying approximately $625,000 in taxes on approximately $1.9 million in income over the time alleged in the complaints."

At the arraignment, Bill would ask Magistrate Judge Muirhead to detain Ed Brown pending trial, given Ed's publicly stated beliefs that the federal government had no jurisdiction over them and Ed Brown's professed disdain for the federal court system, federal law enforcement, his conspiratorial rants, and his leadership role in the militia group, the U.S. Constitution Rangers.

An arraignment is the formal reading of the charges the government is bringing against the defendants, in this case, Edward and Elaine Brown. Both the Browns were being charged with conspiring to commit tax fraud, conspiring to disguise large financial transactions, and structuring. The allegations were that the Browns conspired to knowingly divert income from her Half Hollow Dental practice to a trust called the Rock Solid Trust. Elaine Brown, as the primary income earner, was also charged with tax fraud and failing to withhold employee employment taxes in her dental practice.

In addition, the question of bail and/or detention is raised at arraignment. AUSA Bill Morse argued that Ed Brown should be detained pending trial. He pointed out that the Browns—Ed in partic-ular—had publicly stated that there was no law requiring them to pay income taxes, yet they had conspired to conceal their income by various methods for many years. Moreover, Ed Brown made statements during the 2004 search of the dental office for records that he "would never pay his income taxes and that the federal government had no right to search property in New Hampshire."

Further, Brown had said in newspaper interviews that the federal government was conspiring to take guns away from "law-abiding citizens" and that he would defend himself should any federal agent try to take his guns away from him.

"Brown is the head of the U.S. Constitution Rangers," Morse argued, "which is an extremist militia group advocating resistance to the federal government based on conspiracy theories and a belief in the sovereign citizen movement. Both Browns," Morse said, "are armed wherever they go."

Taken in its entirety, the prosecutor argued that Ed Brown should be detained pending trial to ensure his—and Elaine's—appearance at future proceedings of the court and to ensure the safety of the community and federal law enforcement agents tasked with carrying out the court's orders.

Both Browns pled not guilty to the charges. After asking some questions of the Browns and considering the nature of the felony charges—financial crimes—against them, Magistrate Judge James Muirhead ruled that the Browns would be released on conditions, pending their future trial date. Among others, the judge set the following conditions:

- that the Browns agree to turn over all firearms to the U.S. probation officers and deputy U.S. marshals who would accompany them to their Plainfield home upon their release;
- that the Browns agree to show up for all scheduled hearings and their trial in the U.S. district court;
- and that the Browns report regularly to their assigned U.S. probation officers and cooperate fully in any of their requests and reporting requirements.

After the arraignment, Ed and Elaine Brown were returned to the USMS cell block within the federal courthouse. Chief Deputy Gary DiMartino continued to talk to them in the cellblock before they were to be transported back to their Plainfield home. His purpose was to continue to establish a rapport with both Ed and Elaine in the event that he needed to talk with them further during their U.S. Probation pre-trial supervision.

Marshal Monier complemented him on this. "You have an ability, Chief," he told Gary, "to look ahead at the playing field and try and anticipate problems. Great stuff."

Shortly thereafter, a team of U.S. probation officers and deputy U.S. marshals transported both Ed and Elaine to their home. When the team arrived at the Plainfield home, they were amazed by its appearance and construct. Although they had seen aerial photographs of the property prior to going there, the house was unusual, to say the least.

What first caught their attention was the three-story turret, which was a prominent feature of the house. And there appeared to be several levels to the house that seemed to have been built in stages. It looked like a cross between a morbidly shaped castle and a raised ranch, complete with a watchtower.

When they entered the home through the kitchen, it was immediately apparent that there were several sections that seemed disconnected to the rest of the house. Portions of the interior were unfinished. The deputy marshals decided to take photographs of the interior and exterior of the house and surrounding property. They also sketched out the interior layout of the home. Something told the deputies this may be helpful in the future.

It struck the deputies that this was a house designed with a bunker mentality. They also noted the large solar array and the windmill on the property. It was clear the Browns could live off the grid, if necessary.

Armed with the court's bail orders for Ed and Elaine to turn all of their firearms over to the U.S. probation officers, the team conducted a search. Ed and Elaine assisted with this, pointing out where to retrieve the firearms. The firearms were collected and inventoried, a copy of which was provided to the Browns.

On the way back to the district court, both the deputy U.S. marshals and the U.S. probation officers shared their belief that Ed Brown may not have turned over all of the firearms he said he had in his possession. They noted that there were just too many areas on the property where additional firearms and ammunition could be hidden. "I thought that this would become at issue in the future," one of the deputies reported. They were right about that.

In all, the team collected forty-seven firearms to include handguns and long rifles, which were turned over to the custody of a firearms dealer in Hooksett, New Hampshire.

When they got back to the USMS office, Deputy Jeff White had a conversation with the chief about what they found that the property. He relayed his concerns that Ed Brown didn't turn over everything he actually had in its possession. He told the chief that they had taken photographs and done a sketch of the inside of the house and that they would add this to their reports.

Over the next six months, there were several pre-trial motion hearings held in U.S. district court with Judge Steven McAuliffe presiding. Both Ed and Elaine Brown attended those hearings, sometimes accompanied by their paralegal, Michael Avery, of the Outlaw Legal Services of Florida, who had assisted them in preparing most of the motions.

In all, the Browns filed approximately forty pre-trial motions. Judge McAuliffe denied a majority of them. With the Browns showing up for all of the hearings, both Chief Deputy DiMartino and Marshal Monier were encouraged that this might be a good sign for their attendance at the ensuing trial.

There were, however, several indications that Ed Brown was still engaged in a rhetorical campaign against the federal government and the charges the IRS had brought against them. Ed was holding meetings with fellow members of the U.S. Constitution Rangers at his office above Elaine's dental practice. He still railed against the federal government, and he still distrusted any and all attorneys. His rants against the nation's government and courts went back well before the IRS searched Elaine's dental office.

The headline "Jesuit Masonic Zionists targeted by billboard" appeared in the June 5, 2003, issue of the *Connecticut Valley Spectator*, a newspaper for the Hanover, New Hampshire–Thetford, Vermont, area. The author and editor of the paper, Aaron Nobel, reported that the very prominent billboard turning heads on Glen Road claimed that "Jesuit Masonic Zionists… control the nation's government and courts."[i] The billboard "goes on to urge readers to 'Check Computer,' presumably meaning to look up 'Jesuit Masonic Zionists' on the Internet."[ii]

The article continued, "But Ed Brown, owner of the sign and the building in front of which it stands, says the sign is based on his extensive research, which has convinced him of its validity. He believes much of the pain and suffering in the world is caused by high-level Jesuits, Masons and Zionists, and that the world is in crisis and most people are oblivious. But he insists that you shouldn't take his word for it."[iii]

"Don't believe me. I do not want anyone to believe anything that I say. All I am is a guidepost to direct you toward the truth and the facts… My words mean nothing. My opinions mean nothing. Research the truth. Look up these few key words on the Internet."[iv]

Moreover, Ed Brown insisted to the author that "all judges in America are Freemasons. He said the fact that Masonic symbols appear on our currency is an example of them flaunting their power."[v]

At the end of the article for the *Spectator*, Aaron Nobel noted that

"Brown, a retired exterminator, is the state commander for the United States Constitution Rangers, a nationwide paramilitary group sworn to uphold the Constitution. He has also founded an organization called the *UnAmerican Activities Investigations Commission*, based out of his building on Glen Road (Lebanon, NH)."[vi]

CHAPTER 5
THE TAX TRIAL

January 9, 2007

E d Brown once bragged to a reporter that if the feds came to take his guns or property, "I can make one phone call and have thirty armed supporters here in a few minutes." This was the backdrop for the planning that went into making sure the Browns' trial was safe and secure for the court staff, the jury, and people attending the trial.

Chief Deputy Gary DiMartino and the district's Judicial Security Inspector Brenda Mikelson brought in additional staff and developed a plan for this high-risk trial. Intelligence reports indicated that people from the Free State movement were planning to protest at the courthouse during the trial, and blogs from the *Keene Free Press* were urging people to show their support for the Browns by showing up for the trial.

During the pretrial hearings held in front of Judge Steven McAuliffe, the Browns reiterated that they wanted to represent themselves, and they rejected the appointment of an attorney to represent them. Michael Avery from Florida traveled to New Hampshire and sat at the defendants' table during the trial. The judge allowed this and referred to Mr. Avery as the Browns' "paralegal."

The prosecutor, AUSA Bill Morse, thought this was an unusual ruling but understood that the judge was giving the Browns some latitude to ensure they received a fair trial, as they were representing themselves.

Chief DiMartino briefed Marshal Monier about the preparations for the trial at a meeting in his office. "We're good to go, Marshal," Gary informed him. "We briefed the court security officers and the deputies that will be covering the trial. We brought in extra personnel, and we're monitoring some of the online activities of the Browns' supporters to see what they're saying.

"I'm still concerned about his militia supporters, because of the meetings Ed's been having, but I am a bit encouraged that they both showed up for all their pre-trial hearings. So far, they've reported regularly to U.S. Probation and seem like they are cooperating with the court.

"That said, I still have a bad feeling about this case," DiMartino added. "I'm going to assign Jamie Berry, our best internet-savvy deputy, to monitor the internet sites about this trial."

"That's great preparation, Chief. I share your concerns about where this might end up," the marshal replied. "Let's also keep a close eye on any supporters who show up at the courthouse. If you can, have a conversation with them, and try and get some information about who's doing what, what they're saying, and what they may be planning," he added.

Later that day, Monier made a call to U.S. Attorney (USA) Tom Colantuono. Like the U.S. Marshals, the U.S. attorneys in each district are appointed by the president and must be confirmed by the United States Senate. As the top prosecutor and chief federal law enforcement officer in the district, Tom and Marshal Monier spoke frequently on mutual matters of concern. This was certainly true when it came to the court proceedings where inappropriate communications or threats had been made.

Marshal Monier briefed the U.S. attorney on the Marshals' preparations for the trial. "AUSA Bill Morse has done an excellent job in preparing for this case, Tom. As you know, Bill made a strong argument at arraignment as to why Ed Brown should be detained, but Judge Muirhead let both of the Browns out on conditions. We'll keep a close eye on any Brown supporters who show up to attend the trial," Monier said.

The marshal and USA Colantuono agreed to share any intelligence indicating that problems might develop. "I'll have our intelligence analyst, Tim Hanes, keep his ear out on any chatter he hears on the web," Tom told the marshal. "He'll stay in contact with your office."

Over the first couple of days of the trial, Judge Steven McAuliffe gave the Browns some latitude to argue that they believed the tax laws did not apply to them. This was often over the objection of the prosecutor Bill Morse. Morse argued that the court should not allow this line of questioning because it may confuse the jury about what the law actually says. At the beginning of the trial, the judge ruled in favor of the Browns.

On the third day of the trial, however, that leniency came to an end when Ed Brown tried to question the lead IRS agent about excerpts from the federal tax laws and the Constitution, which Ed Brown said proved his theories. The judge shut him down. When the jury left the courtroom, Judge McAuliffe explained to the Browns that "the jury will not be deliberating on whether the tax laws are constitutional. They are. Nor will they be deciding whether the tax laws of the nation are valid. They are."

Later that day of the trial, several U.S. Postal Service agents testified about the Browns' habit of purchasing multiple postal money orders. According to the agents, both Ed and Elaine Brown would wait in line at the post office together and each purchase $2,800 in money orders.

This was just below the threshold of $3,000, which would trigger a form notifying the government about the transaction. A postal inspector testified that over a two-year period, the couple purchased more than $300,000 in money orders this way. One other postal inspector testified that these kinds of structuring offenses commonly are used in an attempt to avoid paying taxes.

The prosecutor, Bill Morse, remarked that "Ed was very affable during the trial. A couple of times he would walk by me in the court-room and pat me on the shoulder. But when he learned that one of the senior IRS agents was being paid as a contractor, Ed became fixated on this and was very upset by it."

The fact was that the senior IRS agent involved in the investigation had turned the mandatory retirement age of fifty-seven during the course of the investigation, and as a result, this required him to retire. Because the case was still going on, the IRS brought the senior agent back on board to help prepare for the trial and could only do so by retaining him as a contractor.

"Ed Brown was very distressed that the taxpayers were paying a retired IRS agent to assist in the preparation of the trial," Morse said. "And apparently, the irony of Ed being distressed about how taxpayer dollars were being spent—since he didn't pay his—was lost on him." Morse chuckled.

A word about the many ways tax deniers claim that the federal income tax laws do not apply to them is in order. "At various times," Bill Morse said, "the Browns made several of the most common arguments, which tax deniers often sum up by saying, 'Show me the law' that says individual Americans have to pay taxes on earned income.

"When you do show them the federal tax code laws," Morse continued, "it becomes a parsing of the statute(s) and often elicits a response that's summed up this way: no, not that law, the other one. It's a losing battle with many tax deniers." So a little history is in order.

In the modern era, Americans are used to paying federal income taxes. But that wasn't always the case. In order for any government to survive, there must be a treasury to pay its bills, and funds to maintain defense and provide services for the common good. In the early days of the Republic, tariffs on imported goods provided revenue to the federal government. The United States briefly imposed income taxes during the Civil War and again in the 1890s, but it was opposed by many.

Because he believed it to be unconstitutional, President Cleveland opposed the income tax, but it became law without his signature in 1893. In 1895, the U.S. Supreme Court ruled five to four against the income tax, saying that its provisions amounted to a direct tax, which was prohibited by the U.S. Constitution. Article I, sections 8 and 9, declare that direct taxes must be apportioned amongst the states according to the census.

The income tax, then, largely disappeared as a significant issue until the first decade of the twentieth century. Theodore Roosevelt, in 1908, endorsed both an income tax and an inheritance tax. He became the first President of the United States to openly propose that the government collect income taxes.

Meanwhile, the United States Congress put together a compromise amendment, and in 1909, President Howard Taft said that, while ratification may be difficult, he had "become convinced that the great majority of the people of this country are in favor of vesting the national government with the power to levy an income tax."[i]

The income tax amendment passed overwhelmingly in Congress and was sent off to the states for ratification. The last state ratified the amendment on February 13, 1913, and adopted the Sixteenth Amendment to the United States Constitution, which reads:

The Congress shall have the power to lay and collect taxes on incomes, from whatever source derived, without apportionment among the several states, and without regard to any census or enumeration.

Of course, the growth of the tax code and the collection of taxes has become increasingly complex since the Sixteenth Amendment was ratified. In April of 1913, Congress passed the first income tax of 1 percent on incomes above $3,000 and applied surcharges between 2 percent and 7 percent on income from $20,000 to $500,000. Congress soon began changing the rates, and during WWII, a pivotal event occurred in 1943, when the government began withholding taxes from payroll on the advice of renowned economist Milton Friedman.[ii]

As many have argued, the federal government had found a fertile method of collecting revenue amongst the working and middle-class taxpayers of America. Many who abhor the complexity of today's income tax laws quote Chief Justice John Marshall when he remarked, "The power to tax involves the power to destroy."

Today's tax code is several thousand pages in length, and an entire industry of tax attorneys, certified public accountants, and online tax preparation software/companies are in the business of helping taxpayers figure out what they owe (and how to use the tax exemptions and loopholes to avoid owing) the federal government at the end of each year.

Nonetheless, most Americans pay their income taxes. Some, like the Browns, believe that they don't have to pay the federal income tax. They cite a number of reasons for this, and many have challenged the law. None of their arguments have prevailed, and the bottom line is, if you meet the criteria for a criminal prosecution in the federal courts and are found guilty, *you will* go to jail.

The IRS maintains a number of publications, now online, that answer the most frequently cited reasons tax deniers claim as to why they do not have to pay their federal income tax. You will find a copy of the most commonly cited claims by tax deniers, and the IRS response to these claims, in an appendix to this book. (See appendix…)

One of the government's last witnesses was on the stand as the court recessed on the third day of the trial. The Browns were set to begin their defense the next day, after the government rested its case. Both Browns told the judge that they planned to testify in their own defense when court resumed on Friday morning, January 12, 2007.

Marshal Monier arrived in the office early that Friday morning. He was working at his desk at about nine thirty a.m. when Chief Deputy DiMartino stuck his head in the doorway and said, "Marshal, the Browns failed to show up for court this morning." He continued, "Before the court issues the bench warrants for failure to appear, I'm going to call Ed and Elaine and see if I can get them to return to the courtroom."

At the chief deputy's request, Judge McAuliffe agreed to hold the bench warrants and give the Marshals Service and the U.S. probation officers the opportunity to convince Ed and Elaine to return for the continuation of their trial.

With the jury already assembled Friday morning, Bill Morse reported that "Judge McAuliffe simply informed the jury that there had been a development that morning, and as Monday was a holiday, that the trial would recess until the following Tuesday morning."

Within hours of the Browns' failure to appear in court, the Marshals Service began receiving reports of some of Ed Brown's followers congregating at the end of their driveway. Many were openly displaying firearms.

Chief Deputy Gary DiMartino got Ed and Elaine on the phone. He asked them why they had not returned to the courtroom. Ed began complaining about it being a kangaroo court and that the judge wouldn't let him introduce evidence in the trial that he thought was necessary for the jury to hear.

The chief did not tell the Browns that the judge had issued a bench warrant for their arrest. Rather, he emphasized that the judge had recessed court until the following Tuesday morning because of the holiday weekend. As a result, Chief DiMartino argued, the Browns were not yet in further legal difficulty, and if they returned to court on Tuesday morning, the trial could continue. He emphasized that this was the right thing to do.

The chief strongly urged the Browns to think about this carefully. He told them that the Marshals Service was not going to go to their house and that the government was near to resting its case. This would then afford Ed and Elaine the opportunity to testify and give their side of the story to the jury. If they didn't return to the courtroom, the jury would only hear the government's case.

The United States Probation Office also reached out to the Browns. They reminded both Ed and Elaine that they had agreed to the conditions of release back at the time of their arraignment in 2006. A failure to follow those conditions would result in further legal jeopardy.

The following day, January 13th, the deputy assigned to monitor internet activities reported that William D. Miller had posted a letter on the internet where he wrote, "I am going to see Judge McAuliffe, and USA Colantuono, and various other officials hanged for treason for their actions." The word was getting out amongst the militia members following the Browns' case that Ed and Elaine had absented themselves from court.

In response, Chief DiMartino, who had also seen the post, ordered an eastern seaboard BOLO (be on the lookout) to locate William D. Miller. Originally from Farmington, New Hampshire, Miller's current location was unknown. As the chief told Marshal Monier over that weekend, "Brenda Mikelson, Jamie Berry, and I all saw it LATE in the evening, maybe even EARLY morning, as we were monitoring the internet from our homes. We connected that night and had a meeting first thing the next morning on how to deal with it... locate Miller, but also make notifications to HQ."

As a result, out of an abundance of caution, the decision was made to start district protection details on the judge, the U.S. attorney, and Assistant U.S. Attorney Bill Morse. The district worked to put together a schedule for 24/7 details on the protectees with the help of neighboring U.S. Marshals Service districts, task force officers, and local police departments, until New Hampshire could get support from HQ.

Chief DiMartino spent the next several days, over the holiday weekend, convincing the Browns that they needed to return to the courtroom on Tuesday morning. By Monday, it appeared that both Ed and Elaine had agreed to do this. However, on Tuesday morning, January 16, 2007, Elaine Brown got into the car for the drive to Concord, but Ed, at the last minute, refused.

As the chief reported later that day, "When Elaine showed back up at the courthouse, I met her outside—as we had worked out and promised. We didn't take her into custody. I thanked her for returning and reinforced that it was the right thing to do. I walked her upstairs to the conference room just outside of our office, and we talked about Ed and trying to get him to come in."

At that point, "she agreed that she will call Ed later and talk to him. I connected her with Defense Attorney Bjorn Lange, and they talked." Shortly thereafter, "we escorted them to the courtroom. After court, and the new conditions of release that the judge imposed, we talked again about her helping us to persuade Ed to come in and she called him."

As Gary later said, "I continued to talk with Elaine and tried to have her convince Ed to return for the completion of the trial. Again, I wanted to have an established relationship with her to try and help us."

Judge Steven McAuliffe assigned U.S. Public Defender Bjorn Lange to represent Elaine. In plea discussions with the prosecutor, Elaine considered pleading guilty to the charges, and Judge Steven McAuliffe agreed to postpone the couple's trial for yet another day to allow prosecutors and the defense attorney the time to calculate how much they expected Dr. Elaine Brown to pay in back taxes and penalties and what the term of imprisonment might be.

Judge McAuliffe also altered the bail conditions for Elaine. He ordered Elaine to stay with her son in Worcester, Massachusetts, and not to return to her Plainfield home. She could talk with her husband by phone but could not go there. She was also ordered to wear an ankle bracelet for the U.S. Probation Office to electronically monitor her.

Plea negotiations with the government broke down that day, and ultimately, Elaine decided to proceed with the trial. Given that, Prosecutor Bill Morse moved to try Ed Brown in absentia. Judge McAuliffe heard testimony from a U.S. probation officer who had spoken with Ed Brown. The probation officer said that Ed was not sick or disabled and that Ed said his absence from the courtroom was voluntary. Given that, the judge granted the motion.

Case law was clear that once a jury had been impaneled and the first witness was sworn, a defendant who voluntarily absented themselves from trial may be tried in absentia. When the jury returned, Judge McAuliffe informed them, "The trial will resume in the morning."

As for Ed Brown, he quoted Patrick Henry to one of his supporters on the phone: "I don't see any point in going down to Concord. This is a Kangaroo Court." He added, "Give me liberty or give me death." This was his explanation for why he refused to join his wife for the remainder of their trial.

Instead, he chose to hunker down at his Plainfield compound, where he quickly surrounded himself with armed supporters and where he gave interviews to members of the media in the kitchen of his Plainfield home.

While his wife was considering a negotiated plea in the U.S. district courthouse in Concord, New Hampshire, Ed talked with reporters. The reporters who made the trek to the compound were greeted by armed supporters and vehicles blocking the entrance to the driveway leading up to the house. One sign read, "Fed Bullies: Leave the Browns Alone." Another on a tree said, "Government Officials and Public Servants – Do Not Trespass."

Ed Brown told press: "If the Marshals come for him—it's going to get really violent." He told reporters that morning that he was expecting more people to show up to support him. He also said that approximately thirty guns were turned over to the U.S. Marshals and U.S. Probation last May, but the semi-auto handgun tucked in his waistband wasn't and was for his protection. The news media took photos of Ed armed with this handgun.

Brown confirmed that he had been speaking with the U.S. Marshals and that he didn't expect them to come for him within the next few days. But if they did, Brown told the Concord, New Hampshire *Monitor*, "You attack my property, it's going to get really violent. I don't care who it is."[iii]

The *Concord Monitor* also reported that one message posted on anti-government websites "urging people to join Brown was titled 'Will Plainfield be another Waco?'"[iv]

Among the supporters at the Browns' Plainfield home were Bill Miller of Farmington, New Hampshire, who wrote the threatening letter saying he would see the U.S. attorney, the judge, and the prosecutor "hanged," his brother John Miller, and their mother Marie.

"If they're coming, we will do what we've got to do," John Miller told the *Associated Press* (AP). Ed Brown also told the AP "… that most Americans would cower and cringe and raise their hands and surrender like a good little slave. I won't. Under no circumstances. I do not tolerate cowardice, oppression, bulliness, and I certainly don't tolerate a

Federal Agency that has absolutely zero jurisdiction in my state, never mind in my county, in my town."[v]

When the trial resumed after the government had rested its case, Elaine Brown took the stand in her own defense. She testified she had tried to work out a payment plan with the Internal Revenue Service in the 1990s after her tax bill significantly exceeded her estimates one year. She said the IRS didn't respond for months, then insisted that she pay her bill in full, plus interest and penalties, even though she had made some payments. Eventually, she told the jury she refused to pay when she later learned of an additional fine for $3,300, and money was seized from her bank account.

On January 18th, following deliberations, the jury returned guilty verdicts on all counts on both Ed and Elaine Brown. Judge McAuliffe continued Elaine Brown's prior conditions of release and warned her again not to go back to Plainfield. Sentencing was scheduled for April 24, 2007.

"I just hope this [verdict] sends a message to those who would rely on frivolous tax theories," prosecutor Bill Morse said afterward.[vi]

According to a report from the AP, "When Ed Brown heard of the verdict in the middle of an interview with a local radio station, he told WNTK-FM in New London, NH: "The verdict is in. I can guarantee you all hell's going to break loose." He later said, "It's all bogus charges. None of these charges are lawful."[vii] The AP article continued:

Ed Brown stayed in his wooded, 110-acre home this week. The large, concrete-walled house features a watchtower that offers 360-degree views of the rural setting. He said the home is capable of generating enough electricity to operate if cut off from the main grid.

Brown and about 25 supporters said they will defend themselves against capture if necessary. Bernie Bastian, a supporter who said he was carrying two guns, said they would stand with their friend.

"He's here at the house, and he's not leaving of his own free will," Bastian said. Some reporters noted that it was unclear how many others were carrying weapons. "We don't like to talk about that. It's cold up here. People up here are wearing their jackets," Bastian said.[viii]

CHAPTER 6
THINGS HEAT UP IN THE COLD HILLS OF PLAINFIELD

February to April 2006

I n the hours after Ed Brown was found guilty of income tax evasion, he held court in his home with his supporters and members of the media. Late that afternoon, while sitting in his home office, he took a phone call from Chief Deputy Gary DiMartino.

"Ed," Chief Deputy DiMartino said, "we don't want to go there, we have no plans to escalate this thing, and I'm not looking for a confrontation with you. But the court has issued a bench warrant for your arrest on the failure to appear, and the bottom line is you have to turn yourself in.

"Right now," DiMartino said, "I have control. But you need to show good faith, ensure that there's no violence, and do the right thing. You know what that is."

Brown talked about the fact that his wife was, for all intents and purposes, in jail. "That's not true, Ed. We worked to keep your wife out of jail," DiMartino said. "Your wife has been released to go live with her son, she's not in jail, and the ankle bracelet is to ensure that she follows the court's conditions of release."

When Ed Brown was asked by reporters that day what he intended to do next, one of his responses was, "I don't know. Continue talking with the U.S. Marshals, I guess." Of course, this was interspersed with ongoing references to Ruby Ridge and Waco. Brown continued to insist that the charges against him were bogus and that the trial had been a "kangaroo court."

When reporters asked U.S. Marshal Steve Monier what the Marshals Service was going to do about Ed Brown, he replied, "We're continuing to talk with Ed Brown. The conversations have been amicable and will continue as such. The U.S. Marshals Service has no intention of creating an armed conflict. We are keeping all lines of communication open and keeping this low key."

But, the media asked, Brown's supporters keep talking about the fact this could be another Ruby Ridge or Waco. What about that? "We're not playing that game," Marshal Monier responded. "Both the Browns have been convicted of financial crimes. We know where Ed is, and Elaine is staying with her son in Massachusetts. We will continue to talk with Ed to encourage him to do the right thing, which is to turn himself in to the U.S. Marshals Service.

"And I would add," Marshal Monier continued, "that anyone who aids and abets Ed Brown in obstructing justice will subject themselves to the possibility of future criminal liability. I strongly encourage anyone going to support Ed Brown to consider this carefully."

The reference to Ruby Ridge was understandable given the U.S. Marshals Service involvement in attempting to execute a bench warrant for Randy Weaver's arrest in 1992. The U.S. District Court in Idaho issued the bench warrant as a result of Weaver's failure to appear at a scheduled hearing on the original ATF indictments on weapons charges. Weaver retreated to his cabin in a remote, mountainous section of Ruby Ridge, Idaho. He threatened to shoot any law enforcement officer who attempted to arrest him.

What happened next, in what turned out to be an eleven-day standoff, is best summarized by the U.S. Department of Justice investigation into allegations that the FBI had badly handled the discipline of the FBI personnel involved in the handling of the standoff:

The underlying events that comprise the Ruby Ridge incident are well known, so we will only briefly summarize them below. Beginning in 1986, Randall Weaver was the subject of an investigation by the Bureau of Alcohol, Tobacco and Firearms. Weaver lived on a mountain in Ruby Ridge, Idaho, and was believed to be associated with a white supremacist group and to traffic in illegal firearms. In June 1990, Weaver was indicted by a federal grand jury on weapons offenses. Weaver was arrested and released pending trial. Due in part to a clerical error notifying him of the trial date, he did not appear for trial and an arrest warrant was issued for him. According to law enforcement sources, Weaver retreated to his cabin and threatened to shoot any law enforcement officers who tried to arrest him.

In August 1992, Weaver's family discovered three deputy U.S. marshals who were surveilling Weaver to prepare for his arrest. Kevin Harris, a Weaver family friend, shot and killed Deputy Marshal William Degan, and Weaver's teenage son Samuel was killed during the gunfire.[i]

During the U.S. Marshals Service's reconnaissance of the Weaver property, three members of the Marshals Special Operations Group (SOG), Art Roderick, William "Billy" Degan, and Larry Cooper, encountered Weaver family friend Kevin Harris, Randy Weaver's fourteen-year-old son Sammy, and the family dog Striker in the woods near the road leading to the family cabin. A shootout took place. Harris shot Deputy U.S. Marshal Billy Degan, and then Sammy Weaver and the dog, Striker, died in an exchange of gunfire.

In the subsequent FBI-led siege that resulted, Randy Weaver's wife Vicki was shot and killed by an FBI sniper while holding her baby daughter. Kevin Harris was wounded. All the casualties happened in the first two days of this confrontation. Ultimately, the standoff was resolved with the aid of civilian negotiators. Kevin Harris surrendered and was arrested on August 30, 1992. Randy Weaver and his three daughters surrendered the next day.

Both Randy Weaver and Kevin Harris were subsequently charged with a variety of federal crimes, including first-degree murder for the death of U.S. Deputy Marshal Billy Degan. During the trial, which was held in Idaho, Weaver's famed defense attorney, Gerry Spence, made accusations of wrongdoing against all of the federal agencies involved in the standoff, including the FBI, the U.S. Marshals Service, and the ATF. Neither Harris nor Weaver took the stand in their own defense.

When the jury returned its verdicts on July 8, 1993, Kevin Harris was acquitted of all charges. Weaver was acquitted of all charges except the original bail conditions violation for missing his original court date on the firearms charges. He was fined $10,000 and sentenced to eighteen months in federal prison. With time served, he was released after sixteen months.

On the thirty-year mark following the tragedy of Ruby Ridge, Art Roderick, now the retired associate director for operations for the Marshals Service, and retired deputy and SOG member Larry Cooper appeared on Christopher Godsick's podcast *Chasing Evil*. Both Roderick and Cooper agreed that "… Gerry Spence was a master at public relations before and during this trial, and he did it well. What the Marshals Service did that day, and our… involvement in the case, was conflated with what the ATF and in particular, what the FBI did, following the shooting of Billy Degan."[ii]

"The whole narrative evolved that this showed the great 'overreach' of the federal government," Cooper said. "Randy Weaver became a folk hero to the militia groups and to the sympathetic anti-government types."[iii]

This podcast in August of 2022 was the first time in those intervening years—other than at the Weaver and Harris' trial—that Roderick and Cooper had given public statements or an interview about what happened at Ruby Ridge.

"At the time of the incident and up through the trial and after, the U.S. Department of Justice (DOJ) read us the riot act not to say a thing to anyone about the case. The same message went to the U.S. Attorney's Office in Idaho. So the only story being told was that being told by Harris and Weaver," Roderick said. "During that time, Harris changed his story several times about what happened."

Both the Weaver family and Kevin Harris subsequently brought civil suits against the federal government over the gun battle and siege. Interestingly, after Kevin Harris was finally deposed under oath in these cases for the first time, the Department of Justice was able to have the U.S. Marshals Service and both Roderick and Cooper, who had also been named individually in the suit, removed as defendants from the lawsuit.

"The Weavers won a combined out of court settlement in August 1995, of $3.1 million. After numerous appeals, Harris was awarded a settlement of $380,000 in September of 2000."[iv]

In the 2022 podcast, both Art Roderick and Larry Cooper reported that the settlement that was reached awarded most of the monies to the children of Randy and Vicki Weaver for the FBI's "accidental" death of the mother during a law enforcement operation. Randy Weaver got $100,000. Each of the children received $1 million.

This event, along with that of the incident near Waco, Texas, approximately six months later, are often cited by militia, sovereign citizen groups, and sympathetic commentators as a catalyst for the Oklahoma City bombing that Timothy McVeigh and Terry Nichols carried out on the second anniversary of the Waco incident.

This is the reason that when the standoff in the hills of Plainfield, New Hampshire, began to heat up, following the conviction of Ed and Elaine Brown for tax evasion and other financial crimes, there were frequent references to Ruby Ridge and Waco. Ed Brown made them repeatedly, and so did many of his online supporters.

It's also the reason that U.S. Marshal Steve Monier adopted a media strategy of downplaying those references and insisting that the Marshals Service efforts to bring Ed Brown to justice were to keep an open line of communication, while also insisting that the Marshals had no desire to create an armed conflict.

Marshal Monier also spoke with U.S Attorney Tom Colantuono shortly after the jury returned a verdict. "Tom," Marshal Monier said, "I know Assistant U.S. Attorney Bill Morse gave some statements to the press at the conclusion of the trial. That's appropriate, as he did a great job prosecuting that case. But, going forward, here's what I propose. Since some potentially violent nut cases have congregated around Ed Brown, and there have been some specific death threats directed toward the judge, you, and Bill Morse, I would like to have an agreement that you allow me to be the point person on any media statements going forward.

"The reason for this is simple," Monier continued. "The internet and blog postings are exploding with references to Ruby Ridge and Waco. The question is being asked, 'Is Plainfield the next Waco?'"

Monier continued, "Local supporters of the Browns who are going to the compound in Plainfield are making those same references. The Marshals Service strategy is that we want to tamp down such talk, wherever and whenever possible.

"I think I should take the lead on this," Monier said. "It's the Marshals Service's job to protect members of the court family. That includes you, the judge, and Bill Morse. By making the Marshals Service the sole focus of contact with the media, it takes attention away from the court family members and puts it on law enforcement.

"Besides," the marshal added, "we carry guns 24/7. You don't."

Monier shared a prepared statement, the gist of which was going to be his statement anytime a media inquiry was requested about a potential "confrontation" at the Browns' compound in Plainfield:

> The United States Marshals Service has no intention of creating an armed, violent confrontation with the Browns, and continues its careful effort to resolve this situation peacefully. We are proceeding in a purposeful, methodical, and deliberate manner, and lines of communication remain open.[v]

USA Tom Colantuono was fine with this. "I understand, Steve," Tom said, "and I greatly appreciate the fact that the Marshals Service has stood up 24/7 protective details on myself, Judge McAuliffe, and Bill Morse. Please stay in touch about developments as they occur."

Marshal Monier assured the U.S. attorney that he would. Up until the end of January 2007, District of New Hampshire personnel in the Marshals Service were scrambling to provide coverage for the protective details, and everything else that had to be addressed, when Ed and Elaine Brown first failed to appear for the continuation of their trial.

Once Chief DiMartino reached out to HQ to request additional support from both the Judicial Security Division (JSD) and the Investigative Operations Division (IOD), it took time for JSD to assign deputies from other districts around the nation to travel to New Hampshire to assist. Chief DiMartino assigned New Hampshire's Judicial Security Inspector (JSI), Brenda Mikelson, the task of coordinating the protective details on the three protectees.

Brenda Mikelson grew up in Massachusetts, just outside of Boston. She served in the Air National Guard for six years to help pay for college and worked for four years as a civilian law enforcement officer on the National Guard base. She attended Westfield State College and graduated in 1988 with a Bachelor of Science in Criminal Justice.

She started her career in the USMS in 1992. Her interview took place in the Southern District of New York, but by a "stroke of luck," she reported that she was offered a position in the District of New Hampshire. In the early part of her career, she traveled often on special assignment to other districts in the nation for high-threat trials and protection details, and she loved the diversity of assignment that the USMS had to offer.

This experience served her well, and she was promoted to judicial security inspector in 2005. The position specialized in protecting the judiciary, employees of the U.S. courts, and the courthouse from threats, intimidation, and physical harm. Little did she know when it started, but the Edward and Elaine Brown case, and that of their supporters, would consume her life for several years.

While the Marshals Service was working on ramping up additional support for the District of New Hampshire USMS office, Ed Brown, of course, continued to make threats toward the court and the prosecutors. On February 2, 2007, on the DezertOwl radio show, Ed said the following:

This is the beginning of one very huge movement. I'm not quite sure you understand the ramifications of what's going on right now. This is massive. This is international. We are fed up with the Zionist Illuminati. That's what this is all about. Loud and clear. Zionist Illuminati. Lawyers, whatever they are, okay, it's going to stop. And if the judge is a member of that, I know that McAuliffe is, I know that US Attorney Colantuono is, they'd better stop. This is a warning. You can do whatever you want to me. My job is to get the message out, and I'm getting the message out, and I'm warning you guys—not you guys [referring to the show hosts], them—to cease and desist their unlawful activity in this country and every other country because once this thing starts, we're going to seek 'em out and hunt them down. And we're going to bring them to justice. So anybody wishes to join them, you go right ahead and join them. But I promise you, long after I'm gone, they're going to seek out every one of you and your bloodline.

Chief Inspector David Dimmitt was born in Los Angeles, California, in the mid-1950s but was raised in the great state of Iowa. He graduated high school from the Red Oak, Iowa, Community High School, and began his college studies at Dana College in Blair, Nebraska.

Chief Dimmitt said that he left Dana College at the end of his freshman year to enlist in the United States Marine Corps (USMC). As he reported, "I was out of money, only had C's for grades for my mandatory courses, and I needed to grow up."

Dave served in the USMC from 1975 to 1979. He worked first in the training section of a Marine correctional facility in Camp Lejeune, North Carolina. In 1977, he volunteered for Marine embassy duty with the United States Department of State and spent fifteen months in the American Embassy in Kuwait and fifteen months at the American Embassy in Ottawa, Canada. He was honorably discharged from the U.S. Marine Corps in 1979 at the rank of sergeant.

Following his discharge from the Marine Corps, Dave Dimmitt started college again in Buffalo, New York, where he went on to earn a Bachelor of Science degree in Criminal Justice in three years, while working as a security supervisor at a local Buffalo hospital. He graduated in 1982.

After working for a short time as a welder for a manufacturing company in Red Oak, Iowa, Dimmitt was offered a job in November of 1983 as a deputy U.S. marshal in the District of Nebraska. "From 1983 to 1985," Dave said, "I continued my work as a deputy in the District of Nebraska and also became a member of the Marshals Service Special Operations Group (SOG). This is the Marshals Service elite team of volunteer deputy U.S. marshals who would go out on special assignments to handle difficult situations.

"In 1985, I laterally transferred from the U.S. Department of Justice to the U.S. Department of State. I had had an application on file with them from 1982," Chief Dimmitt said. "There had been a series of terrorist incidents against the U.S. overseas, and the Department of State was hiring to address this issue. After six months of assignment in the States for training, I was assigned to overseas operations and spent time in Liberia, the Sudan, El Salvador, and Columbia.

"In 1987," Dave continued, "I was assigned to the U.S. Embassy in New Delhi, India, and for two years served as the assistant regional security officer at the American Embassy in New Delhi."

Dave Dimmitt made a lateral transfer back to the U.S. Department of Justice in 1989 and rejoined the U.S. Marshals Service as a deputy in the District of Nebraska. "There," Dave noted, "I did everything from chasing fugitives, to courtroom assignments, to whatever was ordered by the court. I was promoted to a supervisory deputy position in the District of Nebraska in 1998."

In the ensuing years with the USMS, Dave Dimmitt was promoted to Chief Deputy U.S. Marshal for the District of Northern New York (1998-2006) and from 2006 to 2009 served as a regional chief inspector for the U.S. Marshals in the Northeast Regional Investigative Operations Division (IOD).

This was the background in January of 2007, when Chief Dimmitt got the call from Mike Earp, assistant director of the Investigative Operations Division (IOD) at HQ, to put a New York/New Jersey Regional Fugitive Task Force team together to assist the District of New Hampshire with an arrest of a barricaded fugitive.

"The fugitive, Ed Brown," Assistant Director Earp told Chief Dimmitt, "was associated with militias, sovereign citizens, and other anti-government radical groups."

"Shortly after I got the first call, Mike Earp called back and said it's a no-go. He called a third time and said it is a go," Dave said. "When I arrived in district, after speaking with Chief Deputy Gary DiMartino and Marshal Monier, I found out there were no plans for an immediate arrest.

"I had to explain to the team that there would not be an immediate arrest," Dave said. "I kept a couple of team members in district and sent the rest back home to their families in New York and New Jersey."

Gary DiMartino and Dave Dimmitt had known each other from their first days in the U.S. Marshals Service when they trained or were stationed at the academy at the same time. During that time, they both served in the USMS Special Operations Group (SOG) and had gone out on various assignments together.

More than that, as Chief DiMartino said, "Billy Degan, who we lost in the line of duty at Ruby Ridge, was our team leader during several of our out-of-district assignments in the late 1980s and in '90-'91.

"There was a lot of trust between Gary and I because we knew each other," Dimmitt added.

Billy Degan's August 1, 1992, end of watch was a huge blow to the U.S. Marshals Service, and especially to those who knew him. He was a highly decorated deputy U.S. marshal, a very respected member of SOG, and a lieutenant colonel in the U.S Marine Corps Reserves. USMS members who served with Degan have kept in touch with his wife and two sons. Both of the sons are now public servants themselves.

Chief Inspector Dimmitt explained that "members from the Regional Fugitive Task Forces (RFTFs) on the West Coast, the Great Lakes, the Southeast, and New York and New Jersey continued their support during the covert and eventually overt endeavors to enforce the District of New Hampshire's court orders and to arrest Ed and Elaine Brown. These were a cadre of experienced criminal investigators we brought in who were willing to work 24/7 if assigned to a case.

"I came to respect the leadership of the USMS district managers in

New Hampshire during the extended time I spent there," Chief Inspector Dimmitt said. "I told the marshal that the service had brought in the best for these special assignments. There were no pretenders. They were all proven in the field in real time.

"At the same time," Dave said, "I knew that the team was blessed to work with active, involved, and intelligent district managers who were willing to listen and respond accordingly. I also came to respect and support the go-slow approach that Chief Gary DiMartino and Marshal Steve Monier had adopted in order to resolve this protracted standoff peacefully. That continued, even when pressure rose from both some in HQ, and people in the Plainfield, New Hampshire, areas to 'end the standoff quickly' [and] reached a fevered pitch."

For a month following the jury's guilty verdicts in Ed and Elaine's tax trial, Elaine Brown followed the court's order to stay with her son in Worcester, Massachusetts. That changed on February 20, 2007.

In defiance of the court-imposed conditions of release, Elaine called a friend and asked for a ride back to Plainfield, New Hampshire. She did this while her son was at work. When she arrived at her Plainfield home, Ed Brown cut off the electronic ankle bracelet.

Within minutes of her arrival in Plainfield, the internet sites about the Browns started to blow up. Many postings indicated that Elaine was back home with Ed! Chief DiMartino quickly learned of this while at work at the U.S. Marshals Office in Concord. The chief went into Marshal Monier's office and said, "Marshal, it looks like Elaine is back at the house with Ed." They both groaned.

Chief DiMartino walked next door to the U.S. Probation Office and connected with U.S. Probation Officer Dan Gildea. Gildea confirmed that there was, according to the monitoring unit, a breach noted on Elaine's ankle bracelet. Gildea reported this development to the court and asked for a bench warrant for violation of the terms of her release.

The marshal and the chief agreed that Gary should reach out and try to get Elaine on the phone. "As I recall," Chief DiMartino said later, "at some point that day, I'm able to get Elaine on the phone. I talked to her for quite some time. I don't remember exactly how long, but our conversation was lengthy.

"Our conversation was very cordial, and she was very calm and soft spoken. I mostly tried to reason with her about the potential consequences she was facing and that if she would leave the property we would not charge her with a probation violation."

DiMartino continued, "I asked her how she got to the property, but she quickly indicated that she did not want to get anyone in trouble, so she would not tell me.

"I tried to negotiate her return and gave her several options, such as: stay there for the day with Ed and that I would come and pick her up and drive her back to Massachusetts. I also told her I'd talk to the judge and see if the conditions could be amended to allow for visits.

"We went back and forth," DiMartino reported, "but I did most of the talking and selling.

"I also told her that I was really concerned for her safety and that I wasn't comfortable with her being there with all of the crazies they didn't know that were migrating to the property with arms. It's just not safe there," DiMartino said.

"I also assured her that we would not be 'raiding' the property, so she didn't have to worry about Ed's safety, at least from us. But again, Ed could also be in danger from some rogue characters. So help me get him out, too," was how Gary explained it to the marshal. "We went around and around, and she mostly listened and would interject with an occasional comment."

When she did talk, it was about how she missed Ed and their home and that Valentine's Day had passed and that made her really sad being away from Ed.

"Elaine told me," the chief said, "that she had given this decision much thought and consideration. That she appreciated my concern for her, and my willingness to try and help her with the courts, *but* she belonged with her husband and that was her final decision.

"At that point, I decided to end the conversation but wanted to leave the door open to reconsideration, so I asked her if she would talk to me again tomorrow. She agreed, so the conversation ended."

When Gary DiMartino was able to talk with her again and tried to bring up the topic of leaving the property, she politely, but assertively, told Chief DiMartino that "she wasn't going to discuss that topic again."

Elaine returning to the property was the first of several turning points in the standoff. Any hope of resolving the situation with Ed quickly died with this news. Elaine's return would mean that she was once again supporting her husband's defiance of the court process and the law.

Chiefs DiMartino and Dimmitt and Marshal Monier met to discuss possible next steps. DiMartino shared that it was his gut feeling that once "she settled back in with Ed and company, she would most likely be in it for the long haul.

"My only hope," he said, "was that if there was too much chaos in and around the house that she might reconsider."

That did turn out to be an issue with her, but instead of leaving, she and Ed restricted many of the supporters from actually accessing the main house, so it would be a bit more "homey" for them.

As to next steps, the marshal and the two chiefs discussed stepping up the covert surveillance of the Browns, introducing the Marshals team members to local area law enforcement, and continuing to monitor blog sites and internet postings. During that discussion, Chief

DiMartino asked the marshal, "What's the one thing we've noticed so far about people going to the Browns' house?"

The marshal replied, "People just drive up the driveway. It seems that Ed and his supporters are prepared for the tactical team coming through the woods, but they've let most anybody just drive up the driveway."

"Exactly," Gary said, "it's their Achilles heel. We need to find a way to exploit that."

Chief Inspector Dave Dimmitt teamed up with District Deputy U.S. Marshal Ken Nunes, and the task force members kept in district, to work out a schedule for their travel to Plainfield, their covert surveillance, and an introduction and briefing of the team to local law enforcement. This would include meeting with the chief and members of the Plainfield PD, the Sullivan and Grafton County Sheriff's Offices, Lebanon PD, and New Hampshire State Police working the Plainfield/Lebanon area.

Deputy Jamie Berry continued to monitor the internet. This included keeping track of who was coming and going at the Browns' compound. The cast of characters—a mix of some militia/Constitution Rangers members, some from the New Hampshire Free State movement, some tax deniers, and some who were just plain nutty—cycled in and out of the hilltop compound.

This followed a closed briefing the marshal and chief deputy held at the U.S. district court's large meeting room for the CEOs of those agencies. They were briefed on the developments to date, provided an "overview" of the compound with aerial photographs, and told what the USMS's overarching strategy was: *to use every means possible to end this peacefully without a shot being fired... and with no one getting hurt.* In other words, *to find a better way...*

CHAPTER 7
NEW HAMPSHIRE FREE STATERS... AND OTHERS GET INVOLVED

After Elaine returned to the Plainfield home, both she and Ed made it clear they were not going to leave or turn themselves in. Both Marshal Monier and HQ Assistant Director Art Roderick encouraged Chief DiMartino to continue communicating regularly with them.

DiMartino expressed some concern, however, that he was not *per se* a "trained negotiator." In fact, it was unlikely that the Marshals Service had anyone specifically trained as a negotiator.

"Just keep talking with them, Gary," Roderick said. "You've established a rapport with them, and they're taking your calls."

The marshal was even more unambiguous in his belief that Gary had the needed skillset for this task. He had watched Gary demonstrate his considerable people, interpersonal, and leadership skills for five years.

"People who meet Gary like and respect him almost immediately," Monier said. "He's engaging. He listens. He's funny. And besides, he's from a community of Italian immigrants from Rhode Island and tells great stories.

"I had complete confidence in Gary's ability to keep an open channel of communication with the Browns. If this was a hostage situation, it would be different. There are people specifically trained in that, but that wasn't the case here," Monier said.

"We had a volatile situation on our hands, but what we needed was to continue to keep the lines of communication with Ed and Elaine open. Without question, Gary was the best person to do that," Monier reported.

"The Browns already see you as a person, as someone from federal law enforcement that they know, Gary," Monier told the chief, "not just another 'federal agent,' and that's important."

As some of the more militant characters showed up at the compound, and as Chief Inspector Dimmitt's and Deputy Ken Nunes' team began more covert surveillance of the comings and goings in Plainfield, a communication "window" into the Browns' hilltop home became even more important.

Chiefs Dimmitt and DiMartino, Deputy Ken Nunes, and the marshal met to hold a conference call with Assistant Director Art Roderick and others from HQ. The district leadership team gave a situation report (sitrep) on where things stood with the Browns and what steps were being taken to monitor who was coming and going in Plainfield. This included Chief Dimmitt and Ken Nunes' team of out-of-district deputies sent to assist the district with the armed standoff.

When a team of deputies was working in Plainfield, and when Chief Inspector Dimmitt was not on site, Ken Nunes served as the team leader. Nunes was an experienced and respected member of the District of New Hampshire's roster.

Nunes grew up in the Indian Orchard section of Springfield, Massachusetts. He attended Western New England College, graduating with a Bachelor of Science degree in 1993. Prior to joining the USMS, Nunes worked for the Hampden County Sheriff's Office in Massachusetts for three years.

He had also taken the exam to become a deputy U.S. marshal. He got the call from the Marshals Service in May of 1997. After graduating from the academy at the Federal Law Enforcement Training Center, in Glynco, Georgia, he was assigned to the District of Columbia Superior Court.

Nunes said, "The deputies in the D.C. Superior Court were outstanding and helped each other out. Many times, there were two hundred to three hundred people in the cell block. It was quite the experience."

In May of 2003, Nunes was approved for a transfer to the District of New Hampshire. In the district office, in addition to the normal duties and investigative responsibilities of a deputy U.S. marshal, his specialties included firearms, training, and CPR. He also served as the communications officer. As Deputy Nunes said, "When I got the transfer to New Hampshire, my wife and I were quite pleased. We were back in New England and very happy that our kids would get to enjoy the great quality of life here."[i]

Chief DiMartino and Marshal Monier had also both spoken with the local FBI office, the IRS, and the ATF. The bureau indicated they may have some confidential sources who could visit with Ed Brown at the compound, provide information on who was there, what the environment was, and what Ed was thinking. The same was true of the ATF. One of the FBI agents was made the point person on this and stayed in regular contact with Chief DiMartino. This was an important development as this agent cultivated confidential sources to visit the Browns' compound at key junctures.

Bill Miller, who had traveled from Florida at the beginning of the standoff, and whose brother and mother also went to visit Ed during the first several days in January, stayed with Ed at the house. He was armed. And he handled many of the internet postings while there.

In those postings, he described himself as Ed's "Chief of Staff." By mid-to-late-February, that relationship soon turned sour, however, when Ed believed Miller was becoming more erratic, and Miller thought the same of Ed.

Miller was also clashing with "Anthony," who had traveled from Binghamton, New York, by bus to stay with Ed at the house. Until his arrival at the compound, Anthony was unknown to Ed. Anthony took over management of Ed's Myspace page and internet and blog postings.

According to a report in the *Concord Monitor* on February 10th, "Brown does not maintain the Myspace page himself, but the friend who manages it is living with Brown and says he is creating content at Brown's request. The webmaster, who has identified himself only as Anthony, took a 16-hour bus ride from Binghamton, N.Y., to New Hampshire about two weeks ago and has been at Brown's side ever since."[ii]

Anthony turned out to be forty-one-year-old Anthony Sciarrone, a convicted felon from Binghamton, New York, who decided to become a supporter of Ed Brown after reading media, blog, and internet postings about the case. He traveled to Plainfield, drove up the driveway, and introduced himself to Ed Brown.

When asked by the press how Ed determined who got to stay at the house and help him, Miller said, "… he's not sure how Brown decides which visitors to trust, but he said he's less inclined to put his trust in strangers like Anthony than Brown seems to be. In matters such as this one, one always has to sort of wonder who is who and who was sent by who and how they got involved…"

Miller continued, "There's only X number of people that I have been dealing with for a number of years who I trust to a high degree. There's been indication that there's been some efforts at infiltration and psychological operations against us in this matter."[iii]

One of these supporters, who appeared at the Browns' home after deciding he was going to be an Ed Brown supporter, was apparently frightened by something that happened at the compound late at night.

At approximately 11:33 p.m. on Thursday, January 25th,

Raimundas "Ray" Kirkus, age forty-seven, from New Buffalo, Michigan, abruptly left the property, ran down Center of Town Road with a gun, and banged on a neighbor's house. They called the Plainfield PD to report a man wearing little more than an overcoat, and who they believed might be carrying a gun, in the middle of the road shouting "something" about Ed Brown.

Chief Gordon Gillens, the long-time police chief of Plainfield, New Hampshire, responded from his home to the disturbance. There, at approximately twelve fifteen a.m., he confronted Kirkus, quickly discovered a concealed handgun, disarmed him, and took him into custody. The New Hampshire State Police responded as backup.

In a subsequent interview, Kirkus said that on Thursday evening, he believed Miller was going to "kill him," so he grabbed a handgun off the counter as he fled from the house. He ran down the driveway and ended up going to the door of one of the Browns' neighbors.

Kirkus was charged with carrying a concealed 9mm handgun and held on a $10,000 bond to await arraignment in the Claremont District Court. Once again, Chief Gordon Gillens had responded to the area of the Browns' property and expertly took control of a situation that had the neighbors quite alarmed.

Chief Gordon Gillens, the long-time Plainfield police chief, grew up in Canaan, New Hampshire, and joined the U.S. Marine Corps after graduating from the then-new Mascoma High School. A combat veteran, he had served four years in the USMC, including a year at Khe Sanh, during the Vietnam War. He saw heavy action in Vietnam.

Gordon began his law enforcement career with the Windsor, Vermont, Police Department after graduating from the police academy, and served as a patrolman there for the next fourteen years. He established a very good reputation throughout the Upper Valley law enforcement community and was hired as Plainfield PD's chief in 1985.

Marshal Monier and Chiefs DiMartino and Dimmitt kept in close contact with Chief Gillens throughout the standoff with the Browns.

Gordon knew both Ed and Elaine Brown, and he had valuable insights and multiple contacts with the Browns during the nine-month ordeal. He supported the Marshals in their quest to end this without violence and was a strong voice of reason in the community.

In 2007, Plainfield PD consisted of Chief Gillens, two full-time officers, and a few part-time officers. The chief had established excellent relationships with the New Hampshire State Police troopers working their area, as well as the Sullivan County Sheriff's Office.

As to Ed Brown, he continued to give interviews to members of the media. In the January 25, 2007, edition of the *Connecticut Valley Spectator* (New Hampshire), he was quoted as saying, "I'm a citizen of the soil. This is a due-process case, not an IRS case. They have no jurisdiction here."[iv]

Brown called out New Hampshire Gov John Lynch, saying that as a lawyer, Lynch understood jurisdiction and was among the state and local officials who had broken the law by allowing federal agents to arrest the Browns.

The article continued, "Worldwide, Brown is among the many who have identified the Illuminati, [which they believe is] a secret society of high-powered politicians, bankers and businesspeople, as the sinister force behind the plot to create a global government known as the 'New World Order.' He believes the Illuminati 'targeted him as an enemy,' and that his current predicament is a result of that."[v]

Ed Brown continued to make frequent references to the "Zionist Illuminati" during his many media and internet radio interviews.

Elaine Brown was also interviewed for the article while still at her son's home in Worcester and still wearing an ankle bracelet. She and Ed talked by phone several times a day during this period before she finally decided to rejoin Ed at their hilltop compound.

"[Elaine] Brown said her uncertain future is frightening, and sleep hasn't come easily over the past few weeks. She's scared for her husband,

Ed Brown, who has been holed up in the couple's Plainfield home since he refused to appear in court for the final days of their trial."[vi]

"I'm not having any regrets," Dr. Brown said. "We still maintain our position that we are correct."[vii]

Miller, ironically, wasn't wrong about people driving up the driveway that Ed didn't know. By the second week in February, others had traveled to support Brown after reading about the case or visiting the anti-government websites and blogs that were tracking the Browns' "standoff" with the feds.

Again, during the initial stages of the Browns hunkering down at their fortress-like home, it was clear that Ed Brown was letting people he really didn't know anything about just drive up the driveway.

In the summer of 2003, the Free State Project (FSP), a nascent movement founded in 2001 by Jason Sorens, took a vote to identify the best small state to which 20,000 liberty-minded and freedom-loving people could migrate. Sorens was a libertarian activist and political science graduate student at Yale who had written a widely circulated essay advocating a mass migration to a small state in the aftermath of the 2000 election.

An earlier essay touted the need for a secessionist movement, but Sorens altered his thinking on this and hit on the premise that a mass migration would better serve his view of a libertarian—many would say the more extreme libertarian—movement.

By 2003, the FSP had collected 5,000 signatures and held a vote among those committed to the goals of the project. The vote would determine to which state committed FSP members would pledge to relocate.

The newly formed nonprofit organization "used an outside firm to count and certify the ballots."[viii] There were ten states on the ballot.

After tabulation, New Hampshire, the "Live Free or Die" state, was the clear winner.

The goal was to find a small state where a concentrated mass migration of more than 20,000 people, the "Free Staters," as they soon came to be called in New Hampshire, could maximize their impact as "activists, entrepreneurs, community builders, and thought leaders."[ix] New Hampshire's natural beauty, excellent quality of life, low crime rate, large state legislature, and a tradition of local community involvement provided "great opportunities for activism and political involvement."[x]

The Free State Project's target of 20,000 people pledging to move to New Hampshire within five years of reaching its targeted 20,000 signatures was intended to function as an "assurance" that those pledging to move to New Hampshire would do so.

In June 2003, the FSP got a boost when then–New Hampshire Governor Craig Benson met with, and officially welcomed, about twenty members and leaders of the FSP to New Hampshire.

By 2007, approximately 2,500 "Free Staters" had already moved into the state. As of 2023, according to the FSP website, more than 6,000 are now there.

It's fair to say twenty years later that not everyone in New Hampshire has "welcomed" the FSP the way Gov Benson did in 2003. Part of the Free State Project's attraction is their belief in activism to promote their concepts of freedom, liberty, and constitutional federalism.

Today, there are frequent letters to the editors in New Hampshire's newspapers expressing the belief that many "Free Staters" practice an unwelcome and extreme form of libertarianism and that the activists' tactics are offensive and counterproductive. Many express resentment that "the outsiders—the free staters" move here intending to impose their "disruptive views" on New Hampshire's time-worn local and state political processes.

Indeed, in 2022, in a more organized effort to oust Free Staters and other closely aligned "Liberty" activists elected to the state legislature from Belknap County, members of both the Democrat and Republican parties, along with a good number of Independent voters, formed a political action committee (PAC) called Citizens for Belknap. Its purpose: defeat the liberty activists who were "wreaking havoc" in the legislature as part of the county's delegation.

Four of those elected representatives targeted for defeat at the polls had voted to support a bill for New Hampshire to secede from the Union. The PAC notes, "We are fed up with runaway extremism in our County Delegation!"

Citizens for Belknap had little trouble raising money and getting broad support and attention to their cause. Governor Chris Sununu, a popular Republican governor who was just elected to a fourth term as Governor of New Hampshire, was quoted as saying, "The[se] Libertarians are not Republicans. Okay? I know a lot of them like to sign up as Republicans and pass themselves off as Republicans. But they're not. Not even remotely."

It seems the Free State Project's activism generated pushback among many New Hampshire voters. The FSP website's statement on *effective activism* notes:

> The state has an active jury outreach movement, and *civil disobedience* is practiced by peaceful communities that *challenge authority*. Groups regularly gather to publicly smoke marijuana, conduct open-carry litter pickups, film police encounters, and detour traffic prior to police checkpoints.

As the Browns' tax trial attracted the attention of the local, state, and national media and lit up the internet and blog sites, some of the "very active" of the Free State activists already in state in 2007 got involved in supporting Ed and Elaine's resistance to federal law, federal law enforcement, and the judicial system.

For those, the Browns' refusal to surrender became the "cause célèbre" of the day. The Marshals Service had contact with several during their effort to take Ed Brown into custody.

The first—and continuing—hotbed of Free Stater activity arose in the Keene, New Hampshire area, and several of the Free Staters that had settled there got involved early on in the Browns' case. This included David Ridley, a self-described journalist whose mantra is "Don't get mad. Get video!"

On his *RidleyReport* website, David Ridley posts video segments he has filmed from around New Hampshire on issues of concern to him and supposedly to others in the Free State movement. The videos purport to show how Ridley is "exposing" the tyranny of government. Ridley is especially fond of saying that he is working to bring "transparency" to New Hampshire government, law enforcement, and the judiciary.

Ironically, New Hampshire has a very strong open government and transparency law, New Hampshire Revised Statute Annotated (RSA) 91-A, known as the "Right to Know" law. It's odd that the Free Staters vote to move to New Hampshire because it's known for its limited government, low taxes, and a "Live Free or Die" philosophy, yet when they get here, the Free Staters seek to expose a "lack of transparency" and conduct "ambush interviews of politicians" in that government.[xi]

Ridley was one of the first to be seen in the opening days of the Browns' tax trial in Concord, New Hampshire, holding a sign in front of the U.S. District Court that read "Ministry of Torture" in reference to the IRS. After the Browns failed to return for the continuation of their tax trial, Ridley visited Ed Brown while he was holed up at the compound.

Ridley describes his activism as taking "… you to the front lines of the peaceful but pistol-packin' struggle for more freedom in America's Least Authoritarian State, with ambush interviews of politicians and anti-aggressionist commentary. This is Live Free or Die country, where a hidden history unfolds before your eyes."[xii]

Apparently, spotting yet another twist of irony is not Dave Ridley's forte.

Lauren Canario was another Free State gadfly from the Keene area, who also inserted herself early on into the Browns' defiance of federal law enforcement and the federal judiciary. By the time the U.S. Marshals Service would successfully resolve the standoff with Ed and Elaine, Lauren Canario would be twice arrested for her planned acts of civil disobedience. Canario defied court orders and/or lawful directions from deputy U.S. marshals on both occasions she was taken into custody.

She, too, visited Ed and Elaine frequently, brought them supplies, and posted videos and statements supportive of the Browns' criminal obstruction of the government during the standoff.

Joseph "Joe" Haas was another well-known New Hampshire personality who decided that Ed and Elaine Brown were wrongfully being prosecuted, and they needed his help. Joe Haas followed the news and kept up on postings on the internet involving "injustices" when people's "legal rights" were violated, and he was determined to help.

Born in Pennsylvania in January of 1953, Joseph Haas was raised in Wellesley, Massachusetts. His father was an account executive for an advertising firm. Joe's mother raised Joe and his two brothers and was active in community organizations.

Joe Haas, like many who entered the Browns' orbit, was also well known to New Hampshire law enforcement, members of the state legislature, and the clerks of courts in both state and federal courts in Concord and other jurisdictions within New Hampshire. At one point, Haas could frequently be found walking his dog on the state house grounds in the evening or stalking the halls of the state house during the day.

Many people who have met Joe Haas will avoid him. He can be off-putting and makes some people nervous when he talks about the government and governmental or public officials.

He will often carry with him well-earmarked photocopied pages of state law, a court filing, the state or federal constitution, or sometimes all of the above. When he speaks, it's often with a sense of urgency.

Joe Haas didn't know Ed and Elaine Brown well before taking up their case. But the Browns' case involved taxes, and in Joe's view, the federal government lacked the legal authority—and the jurisdiction—to collect taxes from Ed and Elaine.

Marshal Steve Monier first heard that Joe Haas was visiting with Ed Brown shortly after Ed refused to return to Concord for the continuation of their tax trial. "Not long after we received that information," Monier reported, "Joe appeared in the lobby of the Marshals Service Office in the U.S. courthouse. He wanted to talk to me.

"I went out into the lobby to talk with Joe, first to introduce myself, and second to hear what Joe had to say about going to visit Ed Brown," Monier continued. "I knew Joe liked to talk, and it was my goal to give him some prompts and find out some information about what he saw, who he talked to, and what Ed was saying during the time that Joe was up in Plainfield.

"Joe didn't disappoint," Monier said. "I learned some valuable information about who was at the property and what they were discussing. But I also had to listen to Joe's thesis on why the federal government, in particular the U.S. district court, had no jurisdiction over the Browns.

"According to Joe Haas," Monier said, "New Hampshire had adopted a state law which required the federal government to make a filing with the New Hampshire Secretary of State's office before they could be recognized as having jurisdiction in New Hampshire. And Joe told me that he had researched all the records of the secretary of state's office germane to this filing, and the federal government had not filed the appropriate paperwork.

"Therefore," Monier said, "Joe Haas concluded that the federal government was operating illegally in New Hampshire and the court's orders in the case of Ed and Elaine were null and void.

"Joe Haas told me that the U.S. Marshals Service could not enforce illegal court orders and that I was violating my oath of office in attempting to arrest Ed Brown," Monier said.

The marshal added, "I told Joe that I was pretty sure that was not how things worked and that maybe he should do a little more research on the supremacy clause of the U.S. Constitution. That doing so might help him better understand what the situation was.

"But that in any event," Monier said to Joe, "*if* you go back to see Ed again, you should try to let Ed know that we [the Marshals] want there to be a continuing dialogue. You should convey that message to him. Moreover," Monier explained to Joe, "*if* you go back to visit Ed, please let me know, because this will be helpful in understanding how best we can come to an accommodation with Ed to end this peacefully."

Before he left, Haas assured the marshal that he *would* be going back to see Ed and that he would be back in their office. Haas said he would also do some more research.

This became a pattern over the next several weeks into February. And for a time, even after Elaine returned to rejoin Ed at the compound, Joe Haas would periodically stop by the Marshals Service offices and talk with either the marshal or Chief DiMartino. He wanted to talk more about their "illegal actions in attempting to serve arrest warrants."

"We in turn," the marshal said, "would steer the conversation to other things going on at the compound—who was there, what was being discussed, what Ed was doing and thinking at the time—and any other tidbits we could get.

"The downside, however, was that we had to listen to Joe Haas repeat his legal interpretations of federal and state law. Sometimes, he would become agitated and start yelling. In turn, Gary or I would tell him that we'd remove him from the courthouse if he continued in that manner," Monier added.

"He would often bring highlighted pages from state statutes, case law, and other literature he had read. He continued to insist the federal government had no jurisdiction in New Hampshire," Monier said. "It wasn't that he didn't do a lot of research. He did. It was that he didn't connect all the dots in the correct way. Most of his conclusions about what he read were simply wrong."

Sometime toward the summer of 2007, Haas sued both Marshal Monier and Chief DiMartino in federal court. All of the judges in the District of New Hampshire listed a conflict in hearing the case, and the lawsuit was assigned to a judge from the District of Rhode Island. Monier couldn't remember what Haas was alleging in the complaint.

"We were so busy during that time period that I don't even recall what Joe Haas was saying the cause of action was," Monier said later. "At one point, Haas asked to see a copy of the oath of office that marshals take. So one contention might have been that Gary and I had violated our oath of office in working to secure Ed and Elaine's arrest. In any event, within a short period of time, the judge from Rhode Island dismissed Joe's lawsuit."

In mid-March, a few weeks after Elaine rejoined Ed at the Plainfield compound, Joe Haas had an argument or disagreement of some kind with Ed Brown during one of his visits. Ed threw him off the property and told him not to return. Apparently, Ed and Elaine had grown tired of his presence at the property.

That effectively ended Joe Haas's direct involvement with Ed and Elaine, but it didn't end Haas's involvement with the case.

. . .

In order to try to stem any day-to-day conflicts, and in order to keep things calm at the Plainfield hilltop, Chief Gary DiMartino kept the lines of communication with Ed and Elaine open. This was to temper any potentially volatile situations, to verify information we heard or picked up while monitoring the internet, discover who else might be at the compound and, of course, try to negotiate a peaceful resolution.

Chief DiMartino described his conversations with, and message to, the Browns this way: "I would tell Ed Brown that the Marshals are not coming to the property to arrest him, so chill!

"What I said to the Browns was, 'We need to be able to talk this out. Right now, I have control, but if it gets too dangerous or something goes sideways, that will escalate things, and we will have to secure the situation for public safety. We don't want anyone to get hurt. No one has to die!'

"Most of my conversations were cordial, but Ed would often rant and get upset easily," DiMartino said.

"Whenever an incident occurred, like when the supporter ran from the property in the middle of the night with a gun and was arrested by Chief Gillens, I would bring this up the next day with Ed. I would emphasize that such things could trigger an incident where people could get hurt. I told Ed and Elaine they needed to control this stuff.

"Oftentimes," DiMartino continued, "I would ask about the day, the weather, or engage in other small talk to continue to develop rapport. Sometimes the conversations bordered on the comical.

"At one point, when I was talking to Ed," DiMartino said, "he noticed I had a cold. He started telling me what I should do to get rid of it and gave me some natural peppermint remedies. He called back to Elaine for more details, as she was an herbalist and into holistic remedies. Elaine started to provide some useful tips on how to get over my cold.

"Then," DiMartino said, "it was like a lightbulb turned on. And suddenly, I could hear Elaine in the background saying to Ed, 'Hey, why are you so worried about Gary and helping him…. He's trying to arrest us!'

"Almost always during our conversations, Ed Brown would obsess about his conspiracy theories like the Illuminati, the New World Order, and other anti-government bombast," DiMartino said. "Ed would talk about the coming revolution and emphasize that if he or Elaine were hurt or arrested, *everyone* was going down.

"Ed would tell me," the chief reported, "that '*everyone*' included people related to the case or those trying to do him bad. Ed said that there are people out there who know what they have to do, and who is involved, and implied there was a 'list.' 'It's big, it's global,' Ed would say, 'and once it starts, it can't be stopped!'

"Whenever Ed would talk about the case and say the judge would not let him present evidence, he would get into the court not having jurisdiction, and other sovereign citizen stuff," DiMartino said.

"In turn," he said, "I would always remind him that the legal process is complicated and that he and Elaine should get a good attorney to help them navigate the system. Ed would always say that he didn't trust attorneys, that they are all part of the conspiracy!

"When I talked to Ed and Elaine, I always brought up our concern about all of the armed supporters coming to the property. I explained this added potential danger to everyone, including them. One wrong move, at the property or in town, or with law enforcement, could spark a tragic outcome," DiMartino said. "I told them that their neighbors are upset about the situation, and they don't like what's going on. You need to fix this for them."

Most times, Chief DiMartino used his cell phone to call the house number, so he would have a record of the call, the dates, times, and duration. Strategically, he tried to call at the end of the day, after dinner. He usually called from inside his vehicle on his way home and sometimes would pull over in a parking lot while executing some counter-surveillance tactics to ensure he wasn't being followed.

On average, Chief DiMartino would call the Browns three to four times a week. "After the June 2007 attempt to take Ed into custody at his mailbox," the chief said, "I tried calling several times, but Ed wouldn't talk to me. After that, I started using Bernie Bastian, a New Hampshire Constitution Ranger and friend of Ed, to get messages to the Browns."

During the first several months of the standoff, Ed Brown made several statements to the media about his conversations with Chief DiMartino. Ed Brown said that "DiMartino, a negotiator for the U.S. Marshals, has been a gentleman," and that neither he [Brown] or his supporters "have been abused or threatened."

"DiMartino has been honorable and is a good negotiator," Brown added. "He's just rather confused after twenty-five years of brainwashing," he said in referring to the legality of the income tax.

"I told him [DiMartino] you've got to do your job…" Brown said at one point. And he added, "I have been around police all my life. They're my brothers."

Earlier, Ed Brown was quoted by the *Associated Press* as saying "he expected federal agents to swarm his property soon. 'Live free or die,' he said, quoting New Hampshire's Revolutionary War Hero General John Stark and the state's motto. 'What else can I say?'"

Brown also said, that "he feels sorry for DiMartino because the marshal is being forced to uphold unconstitutional laws. He's caught in the middle. He's got a job to do, and I've got mine. Mine is to save the nation. His job is to help the other side destroy it… Frankly, I'd like to see this go away so we could go fishing or maybe play some golf."

At the beginning of February, Ed Brown had posted blog messages calling for more supporters to come to the compound to assist and said that he was also looking for a ham radio operator. By mid-February, Brown and his supporters made a strategic decision to move away from mainstream print and electronic media to use the internet, internet radio, and YouTube sites to post written, audio, and video blogs about the Browns' case and to promote their messages about the "corrupt government and the corrupt judicial system."

The initial call to arms to support Ed Brown was dubbed "Operation Alamo," then it changed to the "Freedom University." Over the course of the Browns being holed up at their compound, the adopted names for Ed's crusade would change, as would his many conspiracy theories on the "Zionist Illuminati's" attempts to create a new world order.

Chief DiMartino and Marshal Monier set up an "Ops and Intel Center" at the U.S. Marshals Service District Office in what had been the conference room for the district. Aerial photos of the Browns' compound were displayed, along with a growing list (with photos and summary information) of Brown supporters deemed to be of concern to the Marshals. A secured link to the district's server was created for the collection of intelligence so that the investigators and principals involved in the case both in the district and at HQ could access information about the supporters and other information about the Browns.

There were frequent telephone conference calls between district management, Chief Inspector Dimmitt, and the various HQ divisions involved in supporting the district's operations concerning the Browns. Because of the protective details on the judge, the U.S. Attorney (USA) and Assistant USA, this included the Judicial Security Division, as well as Investigative Operations and the Special Operations Group.

Marshal Monier provided regular written reports to the director and HQ staff summarizing what the current situation was and what steps the district was taking to serve the arrest warrants on the Browns. This included developing joint tactical plans between the USMS Special Operations Group and the New Hampshire State Police tactical team, should that be needed.

Marshal Monier, Chief DiMartino, and Chief Inspector Dimmitt also stayed in regular contact with their federal, state, and local law enforcement partners about the Browns. The marshal and the chiefs emphasized that the goal was to find the best way, the best method, and the best opportunity to take the Browns into custody without anyone getting hurt. This could include Ed Brown making a mistake by traveling off the property or developing another ruse to successfully take them into custody on the property.

Most of the people who just showed up at the Browns' from out-of-state were those who paid attention to the blog sites and internet radio interviews that Ed Brown was participating in. Anthony Sciarrone, who had arrived from New York, ended up at the compound that way and was posting on the internet on Ed's behalf.

Chief Inspector Dave Dimmitt, working with District Deputy Ken Nunes, continued their effort to conduct loose surveillance on the Browns and the people coming and going from the compound.

As Dimmitt noted, "Being the tip of the spear meant trying to get close enough to the Browns' property while taking care not to be seen. I found out quickly that this was an extremely rural area where it snowed a lot between October and April. The woods surrounding the compound on the hill were barren in January of 2007, and that the most effective time to conduct surveillance on the property would be from April to October."

Dimmitt continued, noting that during the April to October time period, "the woods would be full of cover, and we wouldn't have to battle a foot or two of snow to move through the woods, not to mention a dead-end dirt road where the compound was located. If an op to arrest were to be planned, it probably had to be inside the April to October window.

"The compound," Chief Dimmitt noted, "was the next to last house on Center Town Road, a dead-end dirt road. It was about an hour and twenty minutes away from the U.S. Marshals Office in Concord, New Hampshire—a long way for backup.

"So," he continued, "Ken and I decided that among our first goal was to introduce ourselves to local law enforcement: the sheriff, the chief of police in Plainfield, the chief of police in neighboring Lebanon where the dental office was located, and the New Hampshire State Police assigned to this area of New Hampshire. We also quietly attended community select board and council meetings to get a feel for the community's point of view.... The community wanted this over yesterday. Me, too! But I knew that wasn't going to happen," Dimmitt said.

He added, "I knew this was going to take some time."

CHAPTER 8
MORE CHARACTERS GET INVOLVED

n another bizarre turn of events in mid-March, the district learned the Browns decided to have a fellow Constitution Ranger from Vermont, who was dying of cancer, moved into their home from a hospital so that he could receive "holistic" medical support and treatment and he could take advantage of the "hyperbaric oxygen chamber" that the Browns had in their home.

When Chief DiMartino reported this to the marshal, Steve asked Gary, "They have a hyperbaric oxygen chamber at their house?"

Gary deadpanned, "Well, doesn't everyone?"

The marshal paused for a moment. "You know, Chief, if this were a movie about this case, and a script writer suggested that they write this into the storyline, they'd probably fire the scriptwriter. No one could possibly make this stuff up."

So "Joe" was moved into the house, hospital bed and all. Ed and Elaine were going to "treat" him, after he left the Mount Ascutney Hospital in Windsor, Vermont. As one might imagine with a person who had a terminal disease and was at the end stage of life, that didn't go well.

At approximately four p.m., on March 20, 2007, a 911 call was made from the Browns' home requesting emergency medical support for a "friend" they were caring for at the compound.

Plainfield PD Sergeant Larry Dore was the first to respond. The police department was often first to arrive on medical calls, as Plainfield relied on volunteer rescue and ambulance squads for their EMS. The Plainfield PD knew of the federal warrants for Ed and Elaine's arrest and of the Browns' threats toward law enforcement, but Chief Gillens and Sgt. Dore handled this call with expert discretion and professionalism.

The next day, when the *Concord Monitor* asked Chief Gillens about the EMS call to the Browns' compound, the chief said, "Our contact with Mr. Brown was by phone, and the officer has known Mr. Brown for a long time and just got permission to come to the property and assist the man that needed medical attention."[i]

While Sgt. Dore went to the house with the ambulance, Chief Gillens and the New Hampshire State Police waited at the end of the driveway as backup. "Joe" was transported from the home, and Sgt. Dore left shortly after without any issues.

According to the same *Concord Monitor* article on March 22nd, "in internet radio interviews this week, the Browns described how they have been caring for their friend since he left Mount Ascutney Hospital for their home."[ii] "'We have become a hospital,' Ed Brown said on Tuesday, a few hours before the 911 call. Brown said that one of his best friends was being killed in the hospital. He has cancer, Brown said, and doctors were giving him sugar."

Elaine Brown added that "they'd put the patient on a natural protocol since his arrival and that he was looking better and sitting up."[iii]

That was, until the Browns had to call 911 and have him transported back to a hospital, once again demonstrating that in Ed and Elaine Brown's world, paying taxes to support government isn't useful to citizens... until it is.

Marshal Monier spoke with Chief Gillens the morning after the ambulance call to the house. He complimented the chief and the department on their expert handling of the call. Sgt. Dore reported that there were a number of people at the home when he arrived. The chief told the marshal that Sgt. Dore did not see any weapons openly displayed, and no one attempted to interfere with getting "Joe" the appropriate attention and transport from the house.

As Monier told the *Concord Monitor* when he was asked about the EMS call, he said the PD "handled it, and they did a terrific job. They're aware there's a federal warrant, but it's up to a law enforcement officer on the scene to make an assessment of the facts and circumstances on the ground.... The officers were not obligated to act on them [the federal warrants]."[iv]

With Deputy U.S. Marshal Jamie Berry continuing to monitor the internet postings, blog sites, and other radio interviews the Browns were giving, he captured a web video Elaine recorded in late March. In it, Elaine says, "We don't know how this will end. But there are only two ways we are coming out of here: either as a free man and as a free woman, or in body bags."

The web-captured video would prove to be one of several key pieces of evidence in subsequent trials related to this prolonged standoff.

Elaine's statement may have been influenced by the arrival of a man named "Sonny," who reportedly had flown to New Hampshire from Hawaii to visit with Ed and Elaine Brown in late March. During his approximate week-long stay, Sonny shared his religious and legal teachings with them, and the Browns converted to a non-denominational form of Christianity that Sonny espoused.

According to accounts from the Browns' friends and visitors during this time, Sonny wore a long white beard, all-white attire, and sandals. Elaine Brown is quoted to have said during this time "that the only law book we now recognize is the Bible," and in documents and letters would refer to themselves in the third person, as "Edward Lewis and Elaine Alice of the family Brown, bodies of the Lord."

When the local property tax bills were mailed out to Plainfield town residents on June 1st with return envelopes, a town employee opened the return envelope from the Browns. There was no check in the envelope for their property taxes. Instead, there was a note that read:

> Nay! Nay! The land… at 401 Center of Town Road, Plainfield, New Hampshire, and all that is in and upon it, including the Lords [sic] bodies, are in the kingdom of heaven, belonging to the Lord, have been claimed by him, and thus can be claimed by no man, nor can any man have beneficial interest in it.… Stand down and away from the Lords [sic] land and the bodies of the Lord. So it is written. So it is done.

When the Marshals Service learned of the day Sonny was leaving the compound and flying out of the Manchester-Boston Regional Airport to return home, they alerted the Londonderry, New Hampshire, Police Department's Airport Unit of his planned departure. The Airport Unit officers were able to speak with Sonny and took several photographs of him as he waited in the departure area for his flight out. He was wearing an all-white, short-sleeved shirt, white shorts, and sandals and carried a small white carry-on shoulder bag.

Nearly a year later, in June of 2008, and seven months after the U.S. Marshals Service had finally taken Ed and Elaine Brown into custody, Sonny would make another appearance at the Brown compound. On that day, he left the compound in handcuffs. Or was it Sonny? And if not, who was he?

~

As March 2007 turned into April, the district continued to monitor activities at the compound. Chief DiMartino was still speaking regularly with both Ed and Elaine, while the U.S. Marshals Service efforts to collect intelligence intensified.

The Technical Operations Group (TOG) from the Marshals Service HQ was also working with Chief Dimmitt's and Ken Nunes' team on the means to electronically surveil the Browns and their property. This would serve as an adjunct to the ongoing covert surveillance of the property.

On April 11, 2007, the district learned that Cirino "Reno" Gonzalez from Alice, Texas, was en route to the Browns' compound to support them. While the Browns didn't know Gonzalez, it's probable that he connected via internet and email with Anthony Sciarrone, the convicted felon from New York that was staying at the Browns' through the end of March and who had taken over posting some of Ed's musings on Ed's Myspace page.

By April 13th, Reno Gonzalez had arrived at the Browns' home and had set up a blog page. Shortly before that, the Marshals learned that Anthony left the Browns' property on March 28th to attend a "Freedom" conference in Washington, D.C. In a few short days, Reno had become the new resident "internet" and "security" person.

The Marshals learned that Reno Gonzalez, age thirty, was a former enlisted member of the U.S. Navy, a divorced father of four, who supported the Browns' anti-government views and Ed's refusal to surrender to the marshals. Following his navy enlistment, Reno also did a tour in Iraq as a contractor, servicing weapons.

Reno Gonzalez had a lot of what Ed Brown needed: the ability to use the internet effectively, a license and a car, and willingness to run errands for them.

More concerningly, the Marshals learned that Reno purchased a .50-caliber rifle and brought it to the Browns' compound. For those unfamiliar with a .50-caliber, semi-automatic rifle, consider this description from *The Small Arms Review*:

> The fifty caliber's ability to be deployed by one individual and give that person the capability of discretely engaging a target at ranges of over one mile away are definitely alluring from a tactical standpoint. While the .50 Cal sometimes seems to be exaggerated, it is hard to imagine a round that at ranges of over a mile and a half away, has more kinetic energy than a .44 Magnum, and has unbeatable penetration as well.

Because of its large caliber and kinetic energy, military snipers will often use their .50 BMG weapons to detonate unexploded ordinance from a safe distance and disable unarmored and lightly armored vehicles. It provides a greater mass and an extended range beyond that which a typical .308 sniper round can achieve.

With Ed and Elaine's sentencing scheduled for April 24, 2007, in the U.S. district court, the Marshals were beginning to focus their efforts on those individuals who were most proactively supporting or conspiring to support the Browns in their continuing obstruction of justice. This included, in particular, those bringing any weapons, ammunition, or other supplies that would aid in the Browns' active resistance to any attempt to serve the arrest warrants.

In addition to the people traveling from out of state to help the Browns, this included some of his long-time supporters and fellow members of the U.S. Constitution Rangers, including Bernie Bastion from Dunbarton, New Hampshire; Bill Miller, from Farmington, New Hampshire; and Robert Wolffe from Vermont.

While Miller had left the compound and was no longer visiting, it was clear that Bernie Bastion and Robert Wolffe were regularly visiting. Moreover, the district was getting information that Wolffe was serving as the conduit for the collection of "supplies" Ed Brown was requesting via internet postings. This included but was not limited to bullet-resistant vests, helmets, flares, smoke grenades, and other materials. Brown had also requested a ham radio operator.

As the sentencing date approached, media interest in the case once again ramped up. In addition to saying that the Marshals Service was continuing to communicate regularly with the Browns in an effort to persuade the Browns to surrender, U.S. Marshal Steve Monier also issued a specific warning to those who might be aiding and abetting the Browns that they were subjecting themselves to legal jeopardy in doing so.

On April 24, 2007, Assistant U.S. Attorney Bill Morse entered the courtroom prepared to recommend that Judge Steve McAuliffe sentence Ed and Elaine Brown to serve time in a U.S. Bureau of Prisons (BOP) facility beyond the range outlined in the sentencing guidelines.

In each case before sentencing, the U.S. Probation Office also prepares a sentencing report for the judge, which gives the court the background on the offender(s), whether there is a prior criminal history, the nature of the offense, and a statement about the guidelines and the range of sentencing for the convictions before the court.

Not surprisingly, both the Browns failed to appear for the hearing and voluntarily absented themselves from the courtroom. The judge ruled that they would be sentenced in absentia.

Prosecutor Bill Morse noted their absence and more in his sentencing recommendation to the court. "The defendants," he said, "are thumbing their noses at the rule of law every step of the way."

Bill argued that "both the Browns' sentences could be increased under federal sentencing guidelines because they had disrupted government functions and committed further crimes as fugitives."

Morse mentioned the destruction of Elaine's electronic monitoring bracelet and made references to threats made against the court and other public officials and their continuing refusal to surrender to the U.S. Marshals Service, knowing that warrants had been issued for their arrests.

Judge McAuliffe listened carefully to the government's recommendations but decided not to increase Ed and Elaine Brown's sentences outside of the range recommended by the U.S. probation officers. The sentences handed down for each of them were nearly the same. They were both to serve sixty-three months in the custody of the U.S. Bureau of Prisons (BOP), followed by three years of supervised release, with the condition(s) that they file accurate tax returns for the years of their income tax crimes and that they comply with any payment plan the IRS required.

The court also finalized an order requiring the forfeiture of their interest in their home and office building found to be related to the crimes for which they were convicted. Judge McAuliffe noted that the defendants had ten days to appeal their convictions and remanded them to the custody of the United States Marshals.

Security for the sentencing hearing was heightened given the attention that the Browns' case had garnered throughout the nation. Approximately fifteen to twenty of their supporters either attended the hearing in the courtroom and/or demonstrated in front of the courthouse before and during the proceeding.

Free Staters Lauren Canario and Kat Kanning from the Keene area held a sign that read, "Fed Bullies, Leave the Browns Alone." Another read, "Taxation is Slavery." Another demonstrator identified by the New Hampshire *Union Leader* newspaper as Kira Dillon, also from Keene, held a "Don't Tread on Me" flag and a sign that read, "Honk if you hate Taxes."

Bernie Bastion was also in attendance in front of the U.S. courthouse. He was quoted in the *Concord Monitor* as saying about the sentence the court imposed on the Browns, "The whole thing was unfair, so it's still unfair. I expected them to do wrong, and they met my expectation."[v]

Never shy about talking with the media, the same article quoted Ed Brown when he was asked about his sentencing. "I've been convicted of crimes?" he asked.[vi]

When New Hampshire *Union Leader* correspondent Kristen Senz contacted Ed Brown about his sentencing, Ed told her, "I don't react to these people. They don't exist to me."[vii]

In that same article, Reno Gonzalez, who was now staying at the compound, made one of his first media appearances since joining Ed and Elaine. He met two "reporters who were walking down the driveway toward Edward and Elaine Brown's secluded Plainfield home. A resident of Alice, Texas, the man sent the reporters away after a brief conversation during which he gave the online address for his blog on Myspace.com."[viii]

"It's all there," said the man, identified as "Reno" on his blog, which features photographs of him aiming various firearms and wearing a gas mask. "Ed Brown and Elaine Brown KNOW their rights.... They are not crazy. The line in history is on their land. This is where the corruption will end. This is where the government will hand power back to the people or it will be taken back," Reno said.[ix]

Bernie Bastion also spoke with the *Associated Press*. "Show me the law," Bernie said. "They can't, because there is no law."[x]

In the press following the sentencing, and in response to numerous requests to answer questions on what the Marshals Service planned to do to serve the arrest warrants, Marshal Steve Monier reiterated that the U.S. Marshals Service had no plans to engage in a violent confrontation with Ed and Elaine Brown and their supporters.

When pressed about the outstanding arrest warrants from the court, and the threats being made by Brown and some of his supporters that this could be another Waco involving violence, Monier said, "We're not playing that game. In this case, we believe patience is a virtue. The Browns have said all along that 'we're not leaving!' We believe them. We know where they are. We're keeping track of them, and we have kept an open line of communication with them to encourage them to do the right thing. And the right thing to do is to surrender to the U.S. Marshals Service."

Monier released a letter to the media that day, which he had sent to Edward and Elaine Brown. It read:

April 24, 2007
Edward and Elaine Brown
401 Center of Town Road
Plainfield, NH 03781

Dear Mr. and Mrs. Brown:

Proceedings in the U.S. District Court have now concluded. You have been convicted of felony offenses against the United States, and have now been sentenced to a period of confinement in the United States Bureau of Prisons. This is now a matter for the U.S. Marshals Service and their law enforcement partners.

As you both know, there are outstanding warrants for your arrests. To date, you have made statements threatening law enforcement if attempts are made to serve those warrants. This creates a public safety concern for the community and subjects both you, and anyone who may be assisting you with this obstruction of justice, to further prosecution.

Until they are served, these warrants are not going away, and neither is law enforcement. The United States Marshals Service has maintained an open line of communication with both of you. We have, and will continue to take, all reasonable steps to resolve this peacefully. But, in order to remedy the situation you have placed yourselves in, without subjecting yourselves to further liability, here is what you need to do:

1. Contact us to make arrangements, and
2. Surrender peacefully to the United States Marshals
   Service.

You have my assurance that you will be treated professionally, with courtesy and respect. This is the right thing for you to do, and I encourage you to do it.

Sincerely,
Stephen R. Monier
United States Marshal

Monier reiterated the point that the warrants were not going away, and neither was law enforcement. "The U.S. Marshals Service is the oldest federal law enforcement agency in the nation, with more than 217 years of storied service to the United States. We're not going anywhere, and it is our duty to enforce the orders from the U.S. courts," he said.

Monier then issued a stern warning to Browns' followers and any would-be supporters. "For those who are aiding and abetting the Browns in their obstruction of justice, and for anyone considering doing so, you are subjecting yourself to arrest and prosecution for felony offenses. Any such action will be thoroughly investigated."

A few days later, Deputy Berry reported to the marshal that he knew the Browns had received his letter, because they were talking about it in their internet postings. Jamie's work on keeping internet tabs on the Browns had been exemplary. Deputy Jamie Berry, a New Hampshire native, joined the U.S. Army following high school. He worked for ten years as a military police officer and investigator while attaining the rank of sergeant. He was honorably discharged in 2003 and joined the U.S. Marshals Service that same year. Marshal Monier brought Jamie home to the District of New Hampshire after he was hired. His contributions in developing essential tools and templates for the agency to use during the Brown case were invaluable.

"Marshal, we know that the U.S. Postal Service delivered it to their mailbox and that Ed Brown has received and read your letter. He's talking about it online. His response has been similar to all our other entreaties for them to peacefully surrender to us—his usual rants about not recognizing the court, its jurisdiction, or any of their orders," Jamie informed the marshal.

"I expected as much, Jamie, but it's one more thing to show—in addition to the chief talking with them regularly—that they should end this now and turn themselves in," the marshal responded. "This time it's from me personally to them, and it's in writing. I also released the letter to the media."

Not everyone thought that the Marshals Service patient approach to dealing with the Browns, by allowing them access to the internet—especially their almost daily internet radio broadcasts—was the wisest choice in how to proceed.

In an editorial in New Hampshire's *Concord Monitor* titled "Nabbing tax protesters not worth loss of life," published on April 29, 2007 —five days after their sentencing in absentia, the *Monitor* editorial said, "This month marks the 14th anniversary of the assault by federal agents in Waco, TX, on a religious cult known as the Branch Davidians that left some 76 people dead. As we write, millionaire tax protesters Ed and Elaine Brown are holed up in their fortified Plainfield home."[xi]

The editorial continued, "U.S. Marshal Stephen Monier is gambling that, with patience, the Browns can be brought to justice without risking their lives or those of anyone else.... Since so far they haven't assaulted anyone allowing them to remain effectively under house arrest is preferable to a shootout."[xii]

However, the editorial continued, "The authorities probably made the wrong call when, so as not to escalate the situation, they decided to allow the Browns to communicate with the outside world and even host an internet radio show."[xiii]

Back at his office when Monier read this, he couldn't help but smile. *Because they talk every day, particularly Ed*, Monier thought, *we get excellent information about what's going on at the compound, what they're thinking… and we're capturing every statement.*

But Monier also understood the frustration expressed in the article. Not only was it the month of the 14th anniversary of the Waco siege, it was also the month millions of Americans dutifully filed their annual income taxes with the federal government. These facts were not lost on him.

On Monday, April 30, 2007, following the extensive press coverage of the Browns' sentencing in the U.S. district court and their continuing efforts to resist arrest, Marshal Monier received an important phone call. It was from Bethany Hatch, Elaine Brown's adult daughter from her first marriage. Like her brother, whom Elaine had been ordered to stay with pending the sentencing, Bethany lived in Massachusetts.

They had a pleasant conversation, and the marshal generally told Bethany what he had been telling the media. "We have no intention of creating a violent confrontation with Ed and your mother," he told her. "We want this to end in the best possible way, which is for them to peacefully be taken into custody with no one being injured. We are working very hard to have that be the outcome, despite the statements from Ed and their supporters that they will violently resist arrest."

Bethany told the marshal several things of importance. First, she appreciated the Marshals Service's approach to this, and second, that Bethany strongly believed that "if the Marshals could somehow get Ed out of the picture, my mom will come out of there."

Bethany didn't pull any punches about her feelings toward Ed. "Ed's an a..hole, and my mother is under his thumb."

Bethany gave the marshal her cell phone number, and the marshal gave Bethany his. He encouraged her to reach out at any point and urged her to continue to talk with her mother about surrendering to the Marshals Service. He assured Bethany that if Elaine did so, the USMS would make the appropriate arrangements and ensure that she was treated with respect and dignity. The marshal ended the conversation by saying, "I'm sure we will be talking again, Bethany."

On May 1st, the marshal, Chiefs DiMartino and Dimmitt, and Judicial Security Inspector Brenda Mikelson held a conference call with the deputy director of the Marshals Service. They discussed the protective details the Marshals were running on the judge, the U.S. attorney, and Assistant U.S. Attorney Bill Morse. The district also updated the deputy director on their current plans and the activities involved in getting more information on the Browns, including the Technical Operations Group's (TOG) efforts to enhance the electronic surveillance of the compound. The deputy director said that he would send "all available resources to TOG."

On May 2nd, Dave Dimmitt reported to the marshal and Chief DiMartino that there was now a two-year-old female German Shepherd on the property, which they soon learned was named Zoe. The marshal told the team that, in his view, this was not good news.

As the marshal later reported, "I was chief of police in Goffstown, New Hampshire, for fifteen years and worked for the PD for thirty," he said. "Goffstown PD was the first agency in the state to form a K-9 police corps in 1963. The department started with three German Shepherds and trained with the Boston, Massachusetts, Police Department. I was never a handler, but I often helped in the training of these working dogs for their patrol work and tracking ability. I love dogs and have owned them all my life. German Shepherds are working dogs. Highly intelligent, loyal, alert, easy to train, and they have a tracking and scenting ability that is probably only second to the bloodhound. They are widely used to find lost children, track suspects, detect narcotics or explosive devices, and were originally the predominant working breed to work as guide dogs for the visually impaired."

Even an untrained young female Shepherd will be alert to anything out of the ordinary within her space. This certainly proved to be the case when Zoe played a role in the first attempt to take Ed Brown into custody.

On May 9, 2007, the Marshals Service received information from another governmental agencies' confidential source that Daniel Riley, an electrician from Cohoes, New York, traveled across state lines to the Brown compound. Having learned of the Browns' stand against the federal court system and their refusal to surrender to the U.S. Marshals, Riley decided to support the Browns.

He did it in a very direct and concerning way, when the source told law enforcement that he brought with him an SKS semi-automatic rifle and five hundred rounds of ammunition and magazines. The SKS was designed by Soviet small-arms designer Sergei Gavrilovich Simonov in 1945. First produced in the Soviet Union, it has since been widely exported and manufactured by various nations. The rifle is chambered for the 7.62 x 39mm round, which is well known as being the caliber of choice for the AK-47 and SKS rifles.

In a rather short period of time, Daniel Riley would prove to be one of the significant people in the Browns' orbit who provided Ed and Elaine with the support needed to defy court orders and significantly aid and abet them in their obstruction of justice. District marshals began to focus their investigative efforts on his comings and goings at the compound.

CHAPTER 9
JUNE 2007: A FIRST OPPORTUNITY PRESENTS ITSELF... AND ED BROWN NEARLY DIES

Not long after investigators had provided the means to electronically surveil the Browns, Chief Dimmitt's team succeeded in surreptitiously setting up a well-concealed camera and video-recording device at the base of their long driveway. After some fits and starts with their first efforts to accomplish this, and their work on the camera and recording device, the recordings showed an interesting pattern.

When the recordings were pulled from the camera, Dimmitt's team noticed that Ed was going down to retrieve his mail from the bottom of the driveway. The postal service generally delivered their mail between nine fifteen a.m. and noon each day.

Knowing this, Ed Brown would get on an ATV or his tractor and drive to the end of their driveway. He would dismount the ATV, retrieve their mail, then get back on the ATV to return to the hilltop compound. This pattern was the only time the Marshals had determined Ed or Elaine Brown left the security of their house and the immediate grounds of their compound.

When alone at the bottom of the driveway, Ed was exposed. Though the exposure was relatively brief, it was nevertheless an opportunity that might possibly present itself for an arrest. The Marshals continued to monitor the video recordings the surveillance camera had captured. On one or two occasions, Reno Gonzalez was seen retrieving the mail, but it seemed Ed liked to make the trek to the mailbox.

In the interim, as spring arrived in the upper valley of New Hampshire, Chief DiMartino worked on the planning for another possible ruse to successfully take both Ed and Elaine into custody. As DiMartino later explained it, "It became apparent early on that Ed, and then later Ed and Elaine, weren't going to leave their fortified property willingly," he said.

"What did become apparent," the chief said, "was that many like-minded supporters of the Browns and others that were just curious, plus the media (both mainstream and alternative media) would simply just show up at the property. Just drive up unannounced and be welcomed, and in some cases stay and become embedded into the situation.

"Ed stated on numerous occasions that he was expecting and preparing for the 'raid.' He acquired guns, ammunition, bomb-making materials, booby traps, etc. Yet all kinds of people that they had no clue who they were just showed up. The marshal, Dave Dimmitt, and I all took note of this," he said.

Chief DiMartino added, "This is the perfect scenario for the Trojan Horse operation. The success of this type of operation is in the 'set up,' the illusion, what does the target, the mark, need, want, value? We did this once already at the dental office," he said, "and I believe with the right circumstances, we can do it again."

For those not familiar with the expression "Trojan Horse," a little history—and perhaps fable—is in order.

The Trojan War was a "legendary conflict between the early Greeks and the people of Troy in western Anatolia, dated by later Greek authors to the 12th or 13th century, B.C. The war stirred the imagination of the Ancient Greeks more than any other event in their history and was celebrated in *The Iliad* and *The Odyssey* of Homer, as well as a number of other early works now lost, and frequently provided material for the great dramatists of the Classical Age. It also figures in the literature of the Romans (e.g., Virgil's *Aeneid*) and of later peoples down to modern times."[i]

There is some dissension as to whether the Trojan War was real. "There has been much debate over historical evidence of the Trojan War. Archaeological finds in Turkey suggest that the city of Troy did exist but that a conflict on the immense scale of a ten-year siege may not have actually occurred. There is also contention over whether the ruins in Turkey represent the same Troy as the one Homer and others described in Greek mythology."[ii]

Nevertheless, the Trojan Horse strategy that the Greeks used to gain entrance into the heavily fortified city of Troy is the stuff of legends. Whenever a ruse is employed to successfully infiltrate an unsuspecting adversary, it's often referred to as Marshal Monier did in his press conference following the eventual—and successful—arrests of Ed and Elaine Brown. What the Marshals Service employed to take them into custody was "the oldest trick in the book—the Trojan Horse strategy," he said.

Why the Trojan Horse? According to Greek mythology, the "Trojan horse [was a] huge hollow wooden horse constructed by the Greeks to gain entrance into Troy during the Trojan War." According to the mythology, "the horse was built by Epeius, a master carpenter and pugilist. The Greeks, pretending to desert the war, sailed to the nearby island of Tenedos, leaving behind Sinon, who persuaded the Trojans that the horse was an offering to Athena [goddess of war] that would make Troy impregnable. Despite the warnings of Laocoön and Cassandra, the horse was taken inside the city gates. That night Greek warriors emerged from it and opened the gates to let in the returned Greek army. The story is told at length in Book II of the *Aeneid* and is touched upon in the *Odyssey*. The term Trojan horse has come to refer to subversion introduced from the outside."[iii]

As Chief DiMartino later explained, "This was the premise for the two ruse plans that developed. The first was thought out and planned; the second emerged organically. Both had merit and a good chance of success, if 'set up' correctly, and the conditions were right. There were a couple of others, but they were never developed significantly."

As DiMartino related, "The first plan, which wasn't executed as first envisioned, was based on a ruse around the media. Many different media outlets, both mainstream and alternative types, showed up and camped on the property. We knew," he said, "that Ed was a classic narcissist. Definition: thinking very highly of oneself, needing admiration, believing others are inferior and lacking empathy for others. Bingo, that was Ed!"

In explaining the thought process that went into planning what Ed wanted, the Marshals knew that he needed to get his message out, as twisted as it was. As Gary noted, "He craves attention and gives countless interviews and statements to the media."

What was the set-up for the ruse? As the chief explained to the marshal in May, "We set a good backdrop, do our 'homework,' and assemble a media 'crew out of Canada' to do a documentary on the situation, and of course, Ed will be the STAR of the show."

The "pitch" to him was that, "It's going to go INTERNATIONAL... Ed loves this. He can't help himself. We'll tell him that he'll have total control over editing and the final product/message that goes out," the chief said.

"To make the pitch, we will use another governmental agencies' confidential source that Ed is comfortable with, to make the introduction and be the 'convincer.' This person," he said, "will rope Ed in."

The chief explained that to carry this out, he had researched renting a mobile media/video production truck. (Some companies offered this.) The truck would be able to secrete gear/weapons, in addition to the necessary video and sound equipment the "Canadian media crew" would need.

Then, a "crew" of five or six deputy U.S. marshals would get trained up in the basics of the cameras and editing-type stuff in the unit, probably a couple of weeks of training on the equipment and the operation. Chief DiMartino told the marshal that there was a Florida deputy who had been a newscaster and had worked in TV before joining the Marshals Service. He could lead the team.

"After the intro from the source," the chief said, "the team travels to the compound, meets with Ed, and does what film crews do, takes a tour of the property, films the interviews, talks with both Ed and Elaine. They play the situation out and play the 'role.'"

As the chief proposed this plan, he said, "When the timing and situation is right, the team lures Ed, and hopefully Elaine, too, into the truck where the editing equipment is, so they can have full control over the product and message. When they're going over the video and distracted, Ed and Elaine are taken by surprise, controlled, and locked down in the rear of the truck as it rolls off the property with our packages.

"Of course," DiMartino said, "we'll give them a copy of the documentary after it is completed. And the beauty is we will have collected tons of evidentiary video, as well!"

As DiMartino explained later, "I actually put a significant amount of effort into this and had targeted a few operators for the mission and had several other good 'crew' members in mind, as well."

During this planning, however, an opportunity in late May of 2007 arose that was too good to pass up.

When the video was pulled on May 18th from the bottom of the

Browns' driveway, Dave Dimmitt and their team noticed something immediately over the course of several days. Ed was traveling on his ATV to the mailbox on Center Town Road, dismounting from the ATV, retrieving the mail, and then traveling back up the driveway to the hilltop.

This was the only confirmed time that Ed and/or Elaine had left the confines of the cleared property line surrounding the house and outbuildings on the compound. The Marshals had received one or two reports that Ed had been seen in a vehicle traveling into town or nearby Lebanon, but none of those could be confirmed, and Dave Dimmitt's and Ken Nunes' team had never observed this.

Ed was smart enough to know that the property was likely being surveilled in some manner, and he knew that leaving the property in a vehicle exposed him to the risk of being subjected to a felony traffic stop, where he would be arrested. Reno had said on his blog that they assumed they "were being watched."

Because it was a remote rural area, there were both technical and communications issues for the team working in that area. Cell phone coverage was sparse and intermittent. The recording unit was attached to the camera surveillance unit, and the recordings had to be pulled manually. A live feed to a remote monitoring site would be much more beneficial, but it needed a power source to accomplish that.

The USMS Technical Operations Group worked on a solution for both issues. It took several fits and starts, but ultimately, a live feed became operational. By May 24th, with both an additional temporary cell "tower" and the power source enabled, a live video feed was sent to a remote command post site in nearby Lebanon, New Hampshire. Chief Dimmitt reported that Ed was seen retrieving his mail at 10:55 a.m. on his ATV. The color and resolution were good, and a DVR to record the live feed was set up.

Noting this new opportunity to take Ed into custody, planning and discussion shifted from the "international news team" to a Special

Operations Group effort to take Ed Brown into custody when he was alone at the driveway entrance to pick up his mail. The district staff involved in the investigation met to discuss this possibility. There were a number of questions, some of which would have to be answered by HQ and the commander of SOG, David K. Robertson. Among the questions,

- What would a SOG team need for support for such an operation, if it's deemed an operation with a strong likelihood of success?
- What warrants or writs from the court would be needed?
- Would the USMS have the support of the State of New Hampshire for a joint operation with the New Hampshire State Police Tactical Team, and for support from the New Hampshire National Guard?
- Will the Marshals or other federal law enforcement agencies provide the needed intelligence and support?

The marshal and Chief DiMartino were concerned about all of these issues, which they would need to explore with Chief Dimmitt and his team, and with HQ. The marshal's conversation with Bethany Hatch stuck in his mind, especially the confidence with which she said that "if Ed is out of the picture, I can get my mother out of there."

On May 29th, Monier and DiMartino met with Assistant U.S. Attorneys Bob Kinsella and Arnie Huftalen. Bob Kinsella was the chief of the Criminal Division in the U.S. Attorney's Office (USAO), and Arnie was a member of that division. Both were very experienced prosecutors with the District of New Hampshire's USA's Office. Monier and the chief outlined that there was a possibility that the USMS could take Ed into custody in the near future, should everything align.

The discussion centered around what would be needed to control the utilities, the internet, and phones to the Browns' compound and what would be the prospect of charging those who had been most complicit in aiding and abetting the Browns' conspiracy to obstruct justice. They spoke principally about Reno Gonzalez's efforts. The prosecutors advised that the question would center around whether there was enough admissible evidence to prove that Reno's intent was to help the Browns avoid arrest.

The marshal noted this and thought more about the need to continue to gather evidence toward the successful prosecution of those most involved in being an accessory after the fact 18 USC §3, or §372 conspiracy to impede or injure an officer, and/or § 924(c) possession and use of a firearm in relation to a crime of violence and other possible violations of the U.S. Criminal Code.

Tracking such evidence, collecting it, and preserving it for review by the U.S. Attorney's Office involved significant work and would need more resources from HQ. With only eleven full-time sworn U.S. Marshals Service personnel—including the marshal and chief deputy—the District of New Hampshire office of the USMS was already stretched very thin. The marshal made a note to discuss this more with Chiefs DiMartino and Dimmitt.

As to the authorities needed to shut off electricity to the compound and control the internet and phones, both Bob and Arnie said that could be done under the All Writs Act, with an order from the court. The District of New Hampshire office of the U.S. Attorney's Office could work with the Marshals Service and their Office of General Counsel (OGC) on that, and as to any possible charges against Reno could probably participate in that.

There was a question, however, whether the District of New Hampshire U.S. Attorney's Office (USAO) could proceed with the indictments of the Browns and any other supporters for any new allegations pertaining to their threats and continuing obstruction of justice. Given that both U.S. Attorney Tom Colantuono and AUSA Bill Morse had been threatened and were under the protection of the USMS, that could constitute a conflict. The USAO's office in New Hampshire had been in discussion with the District of Massachusetts USAO, Kinsella and Huftalen said, should the need arise for assistance in that regard.

With all this information in place, a tentative target date for an arrest of Ed Brown at the mailbox was set for June 6th. On May 30, 2007, Chief DiMartino, Chief Dimmitt, and the marshal had a conference call with SOG Commander David Robertson. The current conditions and the draft operations plan developed for an arrest at the mailbox were thoroughly discussed.

It was David Robertson's opinion that, given Ed was getting the mail on his ATV on a nearly daily basis, now was the time to move forward. Robertson started to filter SOG team members into the district to coordinate with District Deputy U.S. Marshal Steve Bartlett, a long-time SOG member, and with Dave Dimmitt and Ken Nunes' team.

A third-generation law enforcement officer, David K. Robertson was born and raised in Baton Rouge, Louisiana. David began his career in 1977, working at two small local police departments before becoming a Louisiana State Trooper in 1979, the youngest trooper hired by Louisiana as of that year. He worked as a uniform trooper, narcotics agent, field training officer, and a criminal interdiction trooper.

In 1987, David was hired by the U.S. Marshals Service as a deputy U.S. marshal, where he worked in the Districts of Arizona and Eastern and Middle Louisiana. He was a member of the Special Operations Group from 1990 through 1996. In 2000, he became the chief of the Tactical Communications Program for the agency and in 2006 became the Commander of the Special Operations Group (SOG), where he served until his retirement at the end of 2012.[iv]

Ken Nunes and the Regional Fugitive Task Force members who were on a temporary duty assignment (TDY) to the district also played an important role in getting SOG safely into and out of the woods.

Coordinates for feasible entry and extraction points were established before SOG arrived to assist.

SOG Commander David Robertson was set to brief the HQ senior staff, the deputy director, and the chief of staff on the operations plan. The marshal forwarded a summary update and some talking points for that purpose to the chief of staff.

On May 31st, the marshal spoke with Chris Dudley, the chief of staff. At approximately 3:05 p.m., he was told that Director Clark had greenlit the operation. "We were good to move forward with the operation to arrest Ed," the marshal reported, "and then communicate with Elaine for her surrender."

The Operations Plan included a reliance on backup support from the New Hampshire State Police tactical unit, as well as the use of the National Guard armory in Lebanon as the command post. Because there was some intelligence that had also developed that Ed was stockpiling some unknown chemicals, it was felt that the New Hampshire National Guard's Civil Support Team (CST) should also be on standby to assess any hazards on the property post-arrest. The initial sweep would be conducted by SOG team members.

The New Hampshire National Guard's Civil Support Team was specially trained in the recognition and handling of weapons of mass destruction (WMDs), chemical, and biological materials.

Accordingly, Marshal Monier got on the phone to seek the assistance of the respective heads of those agencies. He made calls to the colonel of the New Hampshire State Police, the commissioner of safety, to whom the colonel reported, and to the adjutant general of the New Hampshire National Guard.

He emphasized that he would like the agency heads to keep the planning for this operation close to the vest for operational security. He knew that, particularly in the case of the New Hampshire National Guard, the adjutant general would need the governor to authorize the mobilization of the Civil Support Team and any other National Guard assets needed at the Lebanon Armory. He also spoke with U.S. Attorney Tom Colantuono.

On June 1, 2007, the marshal received a phone call from New Hampshire's attorney general, Kelly Ayotte. She was at the New Hampshire Department of Justice with the commissioner of safety, the state director of homeland security, and the adjutant general of New Hampshire's National Guard. They had all just met with Governor Lynch about the Marshals Service's request to support the operation to arrest Ed Brown. General Ayotte asked if Marshal Monier had the time to meet with all of them for a briefing on the case to ensure that they were able to answer any further questions Governor Lynch may have.

The marshal said of course and that he'd be happy to walk over to the New Hampshire DOJ office and meet with all of them. General Ayotte said, "No, we know you must be busy. We'll come to your office at the U.S. district court. It's a short walk, Marshal," she said.

When everyone arrived at the Marshals Office, they sat down with Monier and Chief Deputy DiMartino. Marshal Monier provided a briefing and overview of the Browns' case from its origin through the current situation. After the briefing, he and DiMartino answered any questions they had about the proposed operation to take Ed into custody when he picked up his mail. At the end of the meeting, the agency heads assured Monier and DiMartino that the backup support from the state police and the National Guard would be provided.

Attorney General Ayotte mentioned that she and the governor had been getting calls from some "legislators and other well-placed people in the Plainfield area asking what was taking the Marshals Service so long to arrest 'two elderly people' in Plainfield." As the attorney general for New Hampshire, she was the chief law enforcement officer in the state. She knew of the risks involved in confronting armed members of a fringe militia group. She also said that she supported the Marshals' patient approach to finding a "better way" to avoid a violent confrontation.

With that, planning continued. But there were some reservations that caused both the chief and the marshal some concerns about the operation. When asked about this later, DiMartino gave this summary of some of the concerns: "Once it was decided to go with the mailbox op, and then leading up to the op, we gave David Robertson as much info as we could and the 'lay of the land' and area of operation. SOG trained for the mission and got the green light from HQ."

The chief continued, "I hooked Dave Robertson up with the New Hampshire State Police (NHSP) SWAT team leader. We had several meetings in my office, and the NHSP SWAT team leader agreed to have his team assist with the op once approval was obtained from his bosses. David Robertson, our SOG commander, asked for a Bearcat [light armored personnel carrier for law enforcement use]. The NHSP didn't have any, so the NHSP team leader reached out to his counterpart at the Mass State Police, and MASP agreed to provide the carriers and additional Tac support."

This expansion on the number of people and agencies involved in the operation was concerning from an operational security standpoint. To be effective, it was very important that word not get back to the Browns in some fashion, or one of their supporters, that the Marshals were about to try to arrest him.

The other issue was the number of people at the Browns' compound when the attempt to arrest Ed occurred. As Gary DiMartino explained, "The premise was to have limited supporters and activity at the property at op time. In the interim, more problematic supporters [Reno and Riley] and others were in and out and started to show up at the Browns' during the lead-up to the operation.... And the Browns had gotten Zoe the dog."

Another governmental agency's confidential source had gone into the house the day before the operation was to start. The source confirmed that Reno was there and that a couple of other people had been in and out, as well. The chief discussed this with SOG

Commander David Robertson, but the assets were in place, and the operation was still a go for the target date of June 6th.

By June 5th, Ed had been seen on video or the live feed coming down to the mailbox on six consecutive occasions. On Monday, June 4th, Ed spent over a minute at the mailbox while off of his ATV. He was alone. All of the USMS Special Operations Group (SOG) team members were in the district and ready to go.

Very early on the morning of June 6, 2007, SOG members, with backup from the New Hampshire State Police tactical team, successfully concealed themselves at the end of the driveway and inside the wood line of the compound. The marshal, Chiefs DiMartino and Dimmitt, the SOG commander, a major from the New Hampshire State Police, the chief of police from Lebanon, and members of the New Hampshire National Guard and other support personnel from a sister federal law enforcement agency were gathered in the command post at the Lebanon, New Hampshire, armory.

Marshal Monier had called Chief Gillens from the Plainfield Police Department late in the afternoon on June 5th to let him know of the operation in the morning. He asked him to keep the information close to the vest and for the department to conduct business as usual for June 6th. Monier let Chief Gillens know that he would keep him informed on what happened the next day.

June 6th is an important date in history, of course. It's the day the Allies launched the largest amphibious invasion in history when they successfully landed Allied troops on the beaches of Normandy during WWII. The foothold was successful, and the invasion into northern France marked a turning point in the war, but it was not without cost. Involving more than 156,000 Allied soldiers, it is estimated that more than 10,000 American, British, and Canadian troops were killed or wounded on June 6, 1944, during the landing. An amateur history buff, Marshal Monier knew there were risks involved in any planned operation. Even a well-planned one.

While the Marshals SOG team and its state police backup were successfully inserted, there were several people at the house with Ed and Elaine. At one point in the morning, some people left the Browns' in a silver vehicle. While the mail was delivered during the expected time-frame, Ed Brown did not go down to retrieve it. Instead, at approximately 12:10 p.m., the silver vehicle returned, and the driver picked up the mail from the mailbox and drove back up to the house.

Upon seeing this at the command post, and after a brief discussion among the leadership team, the decision was made to stand down and to try again the following morning on Thursday, June 7, 2007. The appropriate situation report was made to HQ about this, and both the SOG and the New Hampshire State Police tactical teams successfully exfiltrated from the property. The marshal informed Chief Gillens of Plainfield that they would try again in the morning.

Once again, very early on the morning of June 7th, the SOG and NHSP teams successfully inserted into their positions. The same people and assets gathered at the Lebanon National Guard Armory to watch the live feed from the end of the driveway and receive reports from the field.

At approximately eight a.m., Marshal Monier and others were watching the feed and noticed a figure coming into focus and walking down the driveway toward Center Town Road. Moments later, one of the SOG members reported that it was Daniel Riley, and he was carrying a cup of coffee. As the figure drew closer to the camera's view, Monier noticed a shape following along. Seconds later, the marshal said, "That's the dog, Zoe the German Shepard, following Riley. She'll alert on our folks in the woods!"

Riley appeared to be unarmed, carrying only his coffee cup. But, sure enough, Zoe crossed the road in front of Riley and went to the opposite side of Center Town Road, where a SOG team member was secreted in a full ghillie suit in the woods. (A ghillie suit is a type of camouflage clothing that is designed to break up the human form and help the wearer blend into their surroundings.)[v]

Zoe sniffed around. Riley followed her across the road, noticing that she had gone to investigate something. He peered into the woods where Zoe had looked for several moments and then seemed to recognize that there was a person wearing camouflage there.

The SOG member later reported that Riley asked, "Hey, are you hunting turkeys?"

The SOG member didn't reply directly, although a relevant response might have been, "Sort of…" Instead, he rose up from his prone position while cradling a long gun, which was when a lightbulb apparently went on for Daniel Riley. Seeing the deputy U.S. marshal, Riley dropped his coffee cup, turned, and started running back up the driveway toward the compound. The deputy shouted, "Stop, U.S. Marshals!"

Riley didn't stop but continued up the driveway and began yelling, presumably to alert the Browns that law enforcement was here. All of this was seen live at the command post. Nearly simultaneously, the marshal and chiefs all said, "Damn." They all knew that this operation was compromised and wouldn't end with Ed Brown in custody.

Because the Special Operations Group (SOG) team had radio contact with one another, the member alerted other SOG members that were posted on the sides of the driveway from the compound, but closer to the Center Town Road juncture, that Riley had "made them" and had been ordered to stop. They knew he wasn't stopping. The team members converged along the sides of the driveway, and those closest to him again told him, "Stop! U.S. Marshals."

When he didn't, one of the deputies, armed with a modified shotgun, fired non-lethal bean bag rounds at him in an attempt to stop him from fleeing up the driveway and alerting the Browns. Riley later claimed in online posts, and during his subsequent court proceedings, that the Marshals had "fired live rounds at him" as he could "hear the rounds pass by him in the woods."

No lethal rounds were ever fired at Daniel "the Dog Walker" Riley.

He was finally stopped by the deployment of a taser and a USMS SOG member putting hands on him a bit further up the driveway. He was cuffed, taken into custody, and loaded into an armored response SUV that had been secreted further down the road from the Browns' driveway.

Riley was transported to the Lebanon Police Department for processing and a debrief with deputy U.S. marshals and agents from a sister law enforcement agency. The lead agent from this agency had been coordinating closely with the Marshals on this case, and it was his confidential informants going in and out of the Browns' compound.

Zoe the dog—much faster than Riley or any deputy—ran unharmed, uninjured, and unimpeded back to the home she knew, the Browns' hilltop house. The Browns knew something was wrong when Zoe ran back to the house without Riley. They were there with Reno Gonzalez.

Subsequently, the USMS overflight team circling high overhead with long-range scopes observed Reno walking around the house with a long rifle and saw Ed move several vehicles to block the driveway at the wood line. Ed also carried a long rifle.

What the overflight team didn't see before Ed moved vehicles, however, was that Ed Brown came very close to dying. Deputy U.S. Marshal (DUSM) Edward Recor, a sniper member of the SOG team, had deployed in camouflage in the wood line around the Browns' home that day. From his position, he had a clear view of the three-story watchtower. As he would later testify at Ed and Elaine's July 2009 trial, Recor saw Ed Brown appear in the "tower" that morning holding a .50-caliber rifle.

Recor had heard, but not seen, the commotion at the end of the driveway when Riley was taken into custody. He heard the communications from other SOG members, heard the deployment of the non-lethal rounds, and Recor knew something was happening down the driveway. When Recor saw Brown appear in the tower and then place ammunition next to the rifle, he worried that Brown might be able to see the SOG members down the driveway. Recor knew that a .50-caliber rifle was capable of hitting targets with high accuracy at long distances.

Recor then aimed his sniper rifle at Brown's left temple. He took the safety off, placed his finger on the trigger, and took the slack off the trigger. Had Brown raised the gun to his face to create a "cheek weld," Recor said, "I would have shot."

Fortunately, Ed Brown did not raise the rifle to his face, and left the tower to move vehicles and join Reno in patrolling the grounds of the compound while armed.

Meanwhile, at the command post, Marshal Monier gathered the chiefs and Commander David Robertson in a secured area to make a phone call to HQ. The director, deputy director, and senior staff were waiting for a situation report (sitrep). The marshal was connected via speakerphone to the HQ leadership team. He gave a brief summary of what had occurred and where things stood.

The crucial decision before the Marshals was the next step, now that the planned arrest of Ed Brown would not take place. There was discussion about shutting the driveway down completely; cutting the electric, phone, and internet services to the compound; and keeping personnel in place to conduct a 24/7 cordoned perimeter on the Browns to negotiate their surrender.

Or they could pull everyone back, while cutting the power, phone, and internet to the compound; see if Riley could be "flipped" and sent back in as an informant; then regroup for another day.

The team went back and forth with the director on next steps. After getting all the available information from the marshal and the command post team, Director John Clark said, "Pull everyone out, fall back, cut the power and phones to the house, and we'll regroup with another plan."

The marshal, Chiefs DiMartino and Dimmitt, and the SOG commander went to work to implement the director's orders. There was a lot to accomplish, and word would quickly spread that the Marshals Service had amassed a huge law enforcement presence in and around Plainfield. Questions would follow.

The IRS Criminal Division and Marshals Service had a standing order from the court to seize the dental office in neighboring West Lebanon, New Hampshire. The plan was to execute that seizure order the next day, after the arrest of Ed Brown, and Elaine's surrender.

Chief DiMartino then had a quick meeting with the lead IRS criminal investigator at the command post and said, "The deputies have been made, obviously, and the plan to arrest Ed today has failed, but we'll need to respond to all the inquiries that are going to be made about what we're doing here. So, can you pull some more of your IRS CID agents in and meet us at the dental office to execute the seizure order this afternoon?"

The lead agent said, "Yes, we can make that happen." In response, Chiefs DiMartino and Dimmitt and Commander Robertson shifted some assets from the Plainfield Center Town Road area and sent them to the commercial building/dental office in West Lebanon. Chief DiMartino went there to help oversee that seizure with his IRS counterpart.

The marshal quickly informed Lebanon Police Chief Jim Alexander and the state police major of the current situation and explained what they were going to do. He made a brief call to Chief Gillens and promised to talk with him more in a later phone call.

Meanwhile, a problem was already about to develop in the skies over Plainfield. Specifically, the Browns' compound off Center Town Road. The command post received word that there were news helicopters on the way to Plainfield. Apparently, people in the area had noticed the sudden heavy traffic of armored vehicles, New Hampshire State Police, and other law enforcement vehicles on roads leading into Plainfield and had alerted one or more news organizations that a "big operation" was underway.

While it was inevitable that the media would get wind of the activity in Plainfield, what the Marshals didn't need was one or two (or more) news helicopters circling the Browns' property transmitting live aerial shots of that activity. To that point, Ed and Elaine (and Reno) knew something was going on, but they didn't know exactly what. The Marshals wanted to keep it that way for as long as possible. Riley was being debriefed, and teams were heading to Lebanon to seize the dental office and commercial building. More importantly, news helicopters would interfere with the CBP plane doing an overflight to keep an eye on the Browns' property.

At the command post, one or more people told the marshal that the FAA needed to be contacted ASAP to ask them to shut down the airspace over Plainfield. The call was made. The word came back that they would do that, but it would be about an hour before the authorization got to the tower at the Lebanon Airport to broadcast that message to all pilots in the area.

That would be too late. By then, the choppers would be in the area.

Overhearing this, Chief Jim Alexander said, "I can get the airspace cleared immediately, if you want."

The folks in the command post said, "You can do that?"

"Yes," Jim said, "I know the person working in the tower at the airport. If you can guarantee to me that he'll get the authorization soon from the FAA, I'll call him and ask him to do it now."

"Do it, Chief," the leadership team said. "Make the call. We talked to the FAA, and they will authorize it. It just takes some time for him to get the word."

Chief Jim Alexander was immediately helpful with this issue

because of his extensive personal relationships with so many people in Lebanon. Like Chief Gillens, people who knew Jim Alexander trusted him. In this regard, both Chiefs Gordon Gillens and Jim Alexander proved to be invaluable during the armed standoff with the Browns.

The chief had the number of his friend in the tower and made the call from his cell phone. His friend—the supervisor—asked Jim if he was sure the tower would eventually get the authorization from the FAA to shut down the airspace. Jim said, "You'll get the call."

"Okay, Chief, that's good enough for me. We'll send out the message to all aircraft nearing that area that the airspace must be cleared," the chief's friend said.

All of which demonstrated the level of trust and cooperation that had developed amongst the USMS and other federal, state, and local agencies that day in the command post. The skies above Plainfield that morning *were* kept clear, and the CBP plane was able to continue to provide overflight surveillance for a good part of the day.

However, this would not prevent the media from driving to Center Town Road in Plainfield, and it would be only a matter of time before that happened.

Meanwhile, as Chief DiMartino later reported, "As the operation went south, and as we moved additional tactical support into the area of operation, we lost contact with the New Hampshire State Police tactical team. The state police major at the command post was very concerned about this and wanted his team out of the area ASAP. The major and SOG Commander Robertson hooked up, and communication with the state police team was finally restored, but it was a tense moment. Fortunately, the state police team successfully exfiltrated from the area."

Additionally, Gary DiMartino noted, "At some point, the NHSP had Ed on the phone line and asked if I wanted to talk to him. I said no (I wasn't sure at that point how I was going to navigate the situation with him) but to put him on speaker so I could hear him. Ed was ranting and raving about the situation, and the NHSP talked to him and did a good job trying to de-escalate the current set of circumstances. They told Ed they would try and find out what was going on."

Shortly after that, the news media started making calls to the Marshals Service, the state police, and the Plainfield and Lebanon PDs. Marshal Monier gathered at the command post with a public affairs person from HQ that had traveled to assist, along with the leadership team.

It was agreed that since reporters were already heading toward the Browns' compound, the marshal would hold a press briefing that afternoon in a field on Center Town Road, about two miles from the Browns' driveway. The press would be stopped there until the marshal and his team could arrive to make a statement about the large presence of USMS and other law enforcement in the area.

By the time the marshal, the public affairs officer from HQ, and a deputy drove to Center Town Road, there were both television and print reporters waiting for them. The marshal made a brief statement that the USMS, supported by state and local law enforcement, were in the area to do surveillance on Brown and his supporters. They were doing this while the IRS criminal division, supported by the USMS, were executing a seizure order on the dental office in West Lebanon, New Hampshire.

"The order," Monier said, "allowed the Treasury Department to seize the building that housed Elaine Brown's dental practice. During the seizure of the commercial building, it was important that we conduct surveillance on the Browns so that we would know where Brown was and where his supporters were during the operation."

"During this surveillance, a deputy U.S. marshal encountered one of Brown's supporters walking a dog, and we detained him for questioning," the marshal said.

As Monier expected, one of the first questions from a reporter was, "But what happened to the dog?"

"The dog was unharmed and ran back up the driveway to the Browns' home," Monier replied. The marshal took only a few questions that day and emphasized that the heavy law enforcement presence was to ensure "officer and community safety."

Everything the marshal carefully told the media that day was true—the USMS and its partners *were* conducting surveillance in and around the property, they *were* discovered by a Brown supporter walking Zoe the dog, and there *was* a seizure warrant for the commercial property in Lebanon.

What he didn't tell them, of course, was that the Marshals *were* also trying to arrest Ed Brown that day.

As one could predict with the discovery of a large police presence in Plainfield, the internet and the web—which had quieted down from when the standoff first began in January—was again ablaze with "news" and chatter about what was going down in Plainfield. Most of it was speculative and wrong. One report was that the Browns' home was under siege. Another even reported that the house was on fire. There were many calls to flock to the Browns' compound and show solidarity with the Browns.

After the press briefing—which allowed all the law enforcement personnel to quietly withdraw from the area—the reporters made a dash up Center Town Road to the Browns' compound. Always willing to give more interviews to the press, Ed spoke to the gathered cameras and reporters from an open second-story window at the house.

According to the *Concord Monitor*, Ed said, "I guess we've got a lot of paranoia among our Freemason police. Big boys with bigger toys. That's all that amounts to," in reference to the large law enforcement presence near the compound.[vi]

Ed Brown also explained to the reporters that the dog walker "had been a plumber, and the dog, a young shepherd named 'Zoe,'" belonged to the Browns. About an hour after they had left for a walk,

Brown told the gathering media that his dog had come running home.[vii]

It was either a slip of the tongue, or Ed was once again only focused on himself. Daniel Riley was an electrician, not a plumber.

Within hours of his release and his return to the Browns' compound, Daniel Riley went online and identified himself as the person who had been walking Zoe down the driveway. Forever after, to the media, to bloggers, and even to the Marshals Service, Daniel Riley became known as "Riley, the Dog Walker."

Commenting about the seizure of the commercial property and the detention of one of his supporters, Ed Brown also told the press that the phone lines and internet connection at the house had been cut. Brown reiterated that he wasn't concerned about that as they had both solar and wind generators and "could live off the grid."

In a rather bizarre turn of events, according to the same *Concord Monitor* article of June 8th, "Brown also has a cell phone now, thanks to a journalist who tossed it to him through the window on request. Aaron Noble, an editor at the local *Connecticut Valley Spectator*, agreed to loan Brown his phone for the night."[viii]

"'Do you have a charger for that?' Noble asked Brown following the handoff."[ix]

And of course, Ed Brown issued yet another threat to any law enforcement that attempted to arrest him. "I would say to the marshal, and all of those people responsible for any unlawful action, to be very apprehensive and very nervous about conducting any criminal activity against our land or ourselves. We are a very reciprocal people. You do us good, we do you good. You do us bad, we're gonna do you bad. It's that simple," Brown said.[x]

Disappointed with the day's outcome, Marshal Monier returned to the district USMS office in Concord and immediately made phone calls to the heads of the other law enforcement agencies to debrief them on the outcome of the day's operation. They had all received reports from their people in the field, but it was important to also thank them directly for the support they'd given the Marshals Service. Most understood that when it came to a law enforcement operation, sometimes everything went according to the plan, and sometimes it didn't.

The Plainfield police chief, Gordon Gillens, was not at all happy with the day's outcome when he spoke with the marshal. "From my perspective, this puts my officers at greater risk than they were before. Now more people will show up to support the Browns, when it was starting to quiet down," he told the marshal. "What are you going to do next to end this?"

"I completely understand your position, Chief, and we will continue to support your department with our presence in the area and do everything we can to help you keep your community safe," Monier told him. "Look, I was a local police chief also for fifteen years. I know that having a federal investigation going on in my community could be difficult. Sometimes, I didn't even learn about them until after an arrest went down, but the Marshals Service hasn't done that. We've kept you informed.

"So I'll tell you what we won't be doing to end this standoff. We won't be going there and engaging in a violent confrontation with Ed and Elaine Brown and any supporters who might be there. We are going to find a better way, so that no one gets hurt. That's what we're going to do," Monier said.

At the end of the day, one thing the Marshals Service was grateful for was that, once again, no one was hurt. As to the debriefing of Daniel Riley while detained at the Lebanon Police Department, he gave useful information on the number of weapons at the compound and the names of the people who had been supporting the Browns. Since the Marshals Service and its sister agency already knew most of what Riley provided them, they knew that Riley was being candid about what he did, saw, and heard while in Plainfield at the Browns.

He also said that he would cooperate in providing information to the lead agent questioning him, but on that (and as expected), he was not at all candid. In consultation with the U.S. Attorney's Office, all agreed that there was not enough evidence yet to charge the "dog walker" with an offense. So, with Riley's "promise" to cooperate with the feds going forward, he was released and returned to the Browns' compound late that afternoon.

The dog walker's promise lasted until he was out of sight of the federal agents while walking back up the driveway to the Browns'. He later blogged about his "arrest" by the U.S. Marshals Service, said that the Marshals shot at him with live rounds while he was running away to try and warn Ed and Elaine they were coming to arrest them. He wrote that he was "more committed than ever" to help protect the Browns.

Of course, he said nothing about giving information to the Marshals about the people helping the Browns or of the weapons and other supplies that people were bringing to the compound. And he said nothing about promising to cooperate with the feds.

The "dog walker" was back online.

CHAPTER 10
THINGS GET WEIRDER

June 17, 2007

The fallout from the failed attempt to arrest Ed Brown at his mailbox was swift. The internet was alive with all sorts of theories and wild speculation on what was happening at the Browns' compound in Plainfield.

Late in the day of the attempted arrest, June 7th, Alex Jones and his coauthor wrote on his website *InfoWars* that "Ed Brown's power and phone line has been cut—the Browns are still under siege! New Hampshire police erected a mile around [the] seclusion zone, set up armed roadblocks, closed airspace, cut the Browns' power and phone lines before descending with a heavily armed SWAT team and APC vehicles."[i]

They continued with, "Neighbors a mile around were also evacuated from their homes," and postulated that, "The fact that authorities had sent a surveillance drone over the Browns' property the night before also clearly indicates that they were conducting reconnaissance to prepare for a confrontation."[ii]

There was no "mile around seclusion zone" nor were "neighbors a mile around… evacuated from their homes," Marshal Monier said to himself when he read the posting. But the postings on the internet would only increase in the next few days.

Ed Brown had been chatting with Alex Jones and the people from *InfoWars* almost from the beginning of the standoff. They did regular interviews on Jones' internet radio show, the *Alex Jones Show*, and were quoted in the same article on June 7th. The Browns also had regular internet radio broadcasts on the Republic Broadcasting Network (RBP), with hosts John Stadtmiller and Michael Herzog.

Alex Jones, of course, is the same Alex Jones who, on October 12, 2022, had a jury in Connecticut say that Jones should pay almost $1B in damages "to the 15 plaintiffs who suffered from his lies about the Sandy Hook school massacre."[iii] Jones was also sued for spreading conspiracy theories about the Parkland, Florida, school shooting, which took place on February 14, 2018.

Within five days of the attempt to arrest Ed at the mailbox, and in yet another pro-Brown website, a mass email reported that another raid was taking place. The manager of the website *MaketheStand*, Shaun Kranish from Illinois, sent an alert saying, "It's happening again! Neighbors have evacuated the area again. There are many men in the woods in ghillie suits and other camouflage." This was one of the many websites and radio interviews the USMS were monitoring on a daily basis.

Over the course of the nine-month standoff in Plainfield, Kranish would make several trips from Illinois to Plainfield to meet with the Browns to further support their refusal to surrender to federal law enforcement.

In the week following the June 7th operation, the U.S. Marshals Office in Concord received dozens—if not hundreds—of calls from local, regional, and national print and electronic media for comments.

The marshal spoke with New Hampshire media, and the office took messages from the national media.

People from around the state, but particularly from the Plainfield area, called to express their impatience with how long this whole saga was going on. Most said, "Arrest the Browns, this is taking too long! Make the whole thing end, now!"

The marshal told Gary he agreed with that sentiment. He wanted it over, too. But he wanted it over the right way.

The other calls to the office were from around the country. Those calls were either from the Browns' supporters, who said, "Leave them alone, there is no law!" or those who wanted to express their strong opinion that Ed and Elaine Brown were thumbing their nose at the courts and law enforcement.

"So, Gary," the marshal said to Chief DiMartino, "we basically have two camps of opinion here—it's either, 'Leave the Browns alone, they've done nothing wrong,' or 'Why aren't you driving a tank through their living room?'"

According to New Hampshire's *Concord Monitor* in an article published on June 26, 2007, a presidential candidate even got in on the act. "[Ron] Paul, a Texas congressman who had campaigned on promises to lower taxes and rein in the Federal Reserve, said 'the Browns' civil disobedience should be commended. People who point this out and fight the tax code and fight the monetary code are heroic,' he said in a video that's been linked to several pro-Brown websites."[iv]

The article continued: "I compare them to people like Gandhi," he said, "who was willing to speak out and try to bring about change in a careful manner. Martin Luther King fought laws that were unfair and unjust, and he suffered, too."[v]

Many readers of the *Concord Monitor* were outraged by Paul's statement. They correctly pointed out that Paul overlooked the most salient fact that differentiated Gandhi and Dr. King from the Browns. That is, of course, that Dr. King and Gandhi were opposed to the use of violence in challenging unfair or unjust laws, and they peacefully submitted to arrest when law enforcement took them into custody. They engaged in peaceful demonstrations and civil disobedience to bring about change. They would never approve of the Browns' calls for violence against a judge, a prosecutor, or a law enforcement officer.

Nor would they approve of the threat of bringing another Waco to the peaceful community of Plainfield, New Hampshire.

In fairness to Representative Paul, these statements were taken from an interview he gave to Lee Rogers, who was running the website *RogueGovernment.com*. Marshal Steve Monier was later told that it was unclear whether Ron Paul had been given the "big picture" of what was going on with the Browns. Monier later read that Ron Paul subsequently walked back his statements of support for Ed and Elaine.

On June 15th, Steve Monier sent a second letter to Ed and Elaine Brown. It read:

Dear Mr. and Mrs. Brown:

You are both well aware that there are outstanding warrants for your arrest. You have been tried, convicted, and sentenced in a court of law to a term of imprisonment in the United States Bureau of Prisons. Last week, we executed a seizure order on the commercial property in W. Lebanon, and we have shut off utilities at the property in Plainfield.

It has been five months since your trial, and despite our repeated requests encouraging you to do the honorable thing and surrender to the U.S. Marshals Service, you continue to make threatening statements if attempts are made to serve the arrest warrants. Please understand that threatening violence towards law enforcement does nothing to resolve your legal difficulties; it only adds to them. Moreover, your actions endanger the community.

You also continue to encourage others to assist you in your ongoing obstruction of justice, which subjects you and anyone who aids you to further prosecution.

Until they are served, these warrants are not going away. The United States Marshals Service is committed to resolving this peacefully. Once again, I am asking you to surrender to us. You can do that simply by calling us to make arrangements to turn yourselves in. Both of you will be treated courteously. You have the choice to do the right thing, and I encourage you to do it.

Sincerely,

Stephen R. Monier

United States Marshal

That was the second letter from the Marshals Service to the Browns. Shortly thereafter, the marshal received a letter from Plainfield, but it wasn't from Ed and Elaine Brown.

On June 6th, the Plainfield Selectboard mailed a letter to U.S. Marshal Steve Monier demanding a swift resolution to the Browns' armed standoff. They sent copies to the Plainfield Police Department; Michael J. Guarricino, a marshal with the U.S. Supreme Court Police; U.S. Senators Judd Gregg and John E. Sununu; and to the Attorney General of the United States.

The letter read:

Dear Marshal Monier:

The Plainfield Selectboard, through this letter, is adding its voice to those that are expecting the Federal Government to use the necessary means to take into custody convicted felons Edward and Elaine Brown. The Federal Government is charged with this work and has significantly more resources at their disposal than our local police department. While we understand

and support efforts to achieve a quiet resolution to this matter, the longer the Browns remain at large the better the chance, in our view, that our local police force will be involved in an incident with them or their group of supporters. In short, we believe that it is time that definitive action be taken.

The Selectboard is available (in public or private session) to discuss this matter further. Thank you for your consideration of our comments.

The Plainfield Board of Selectmen

Mark H. Wilder, Chairman

Robert W. Taylor

Patience was wearing thin in Plainfield, and the community wanted the situation to end soon. The board released the letter to the media.

Monier read the letter. He couldn't disagree with the sentiment expressed. He wanted the situation to end soon, too. A New Hampshire lawmaker from Plainfield said he was upset that *local* authorities were not informed of the U.S. Marshals' plans to surround the Browns' compound a week ago.

Oh great, Monier facetiously thought after reading this, *I guess we should have just released a statement to the press saying we planned to try and arrest Ed Brown at his mailbox on June 6th. That certainly would have helped! Patience, while never my strong point, is needed here,* he said to himself.

Monier was not immune to the thinking that motivates most law enforcement officers. They're given a mission—serve a warrant from the court—and they go serve the warrant. But there is an overriding responsibility. Protect life. No one should die.

Monier was frustrated. But the idea of driving up the driveway, of having someone on the inside, never strayed far from his or the leadership team's thoughts.

As it turned out, there were several leaks after the first day's attempt to arrest Ed Brown (June 6th). That night, the Marshals learned that the security staff at the local hospital were asking if "Ed Brown had been arrested when he picked up his mail."

In hindsight, the operation set for June 6th had gotten too large, and there were too many moving parts. Even inadvertently, the chance that a slip of the tongue would get back to a Brown sympathizer grew proportionately as the size of the operation grew.

Then, to add to the burning embers, on or about June 15th, the Marshals Service also got word that Randy Weaver was going to travel to Plainfield to meet with the Browns. Randy Weaver was the target in a 1992 eleven-day armed standoff of his own making with the USMS and FBI at Ruby Ridge, Idaho. During this tragic operation, both Weaver's wife and son, and Deputy U.S. Marshal Billy Degan, were killed.

In an internet radio interview, Weaver said that he was going to Plainfield, New Hampshire, to "advise" the Browns on how to manage their conflict with the Marshals Service and to help Ed and Elaine negotiate with the Marshals to "reduce the likelihood of bloodshed."

Ed Brown confirmed to local media outlets that Weaver had called him and was coming to Plainfield. Brown said that they would hold a two p.m. press conference at their property on Monday the 18th of June, with Randy Weaver.

Not wanting to undergo a security screening, Weaver refused to fly to New Hampshire. So he got in a car and drove to New Hampshire with RBN radio show hosts Stadtmiller and Herzog. They arrived in Plainfield on June 17, 2007. Chief Gordon Gillens from Plainfield PD confirmed this with Marshal Monier when he called him early the next morning, June 18th.

"Good morning, Marshal," he said, "this is Gordon Gillens. I wanted to let you know I met Randy Weaver last night. He and two companions, in a vehicle with Texas plates, made it to town early last evening and were looking for directions to the Browns' home."

The marshal asked the chief how the interaction went with them.

"Randy Weaver was in the vehicle with the two other men. The driver was well dressed and very polite. All of them were, in fact," Gordon told Monier. "Weaver was sitting in the rear seat. He has a full white beard. They all said they were going to visit the Browns last night but are staying off the property in the Upper Valley area."

"Did they say anything about the press conference that was supposed to occur today at two p.m., Chief?" Monier asked him.

Gillens replied, "They said it may not happen today [Monday], but may be rescheduled for tomorrow or the next day."

Chief Gillens and the marshal talked about the press conference and their preparation for it. They agreed that the press conference should just go on and that law enforcement would monitor activities at the compound. The marshal told Chief Gillens that Deputy Ken Nunes and his team of two to three deputies would be up in the area conducting surveillance but not attempting to infiltrate the property.

"This surveillance, Chief, will be more like patrols in unmarked government SUVs to keep an eye on who was coming and going and to support your officers," Monier told Gillens. "The Marshals Service is going to be a bit more visible in the area and to the community.

"We anticipate, Chief," Monier told Gillens, "that the press conference will be held today at two p.m. I got a call from WMUR TV-9 from Manchester, New Hampshire [the statewide ABC affiliate station]. They said they are sending a film crew and reporter to the Browns' today and wanted us aware of it. And they told me other news outlets are doing the same. In fact, WMUR said they were going to broadcast it live on WMURTV9.com.

"Brown is going to talk, and we want to hear what he, Elaine, and Randy Weaver are going to say, so in addition to watching it live, we'll capture the video," Monier said.

Back at the USMS office in Concord, the marshal met with his leadership team and Chief Dimmitt and had several conference calls with the Washington HQ senior staff. The protection details were stepped up on the three protectees, with counter-surveillance to ensure that no new efforts were being made to follow the judge, the prosecutor, or the U.S. attorney.

The marshal had a discussion with the resident supervisory agent in charge of the New Hampshire FBI field office on whether Weaver would be a useful ally in trying to get the Browns to surrender. Both were skeptical that Weaver would help, but they agreed to see what Weaver said at the press conference and then revisit that question.

Deputy Jamie Berry continued working with the intel analysts from HQ and the U.S. Attorney's Office to flag any new threats and to monitor any statements from the Browns or their close supporters. All of the statements that Ed and Elaine—and others—made online were potentially testimonial evidence against them for the conspiracy to obstruct justice.

At 1:09 p.m., Deputy Ken Nunes reported that there was a film crew at the dental office in West Lebanon filming the dental office/commercial building but otherwise that it was all quiet there. In Plainfield, they noted that there was a good amount of traffic and a couple of film trucks going up Center Town Road and then driving up the Browns' driveway.

At two p.m., with TV film crews from New Hampshire, Massachusetts, CNN, and both local and national print media collected in the front of the compound, the Browns, Randy Weaver, and his associates from the Texas-based RBN radio network stepped out on to the front porch of the Browns' house and held their "press conference." District leadership watched the broadcast live on the WMUR website.

A number of microphones from the news organizations present were set up on a podium on the porch. It's unclear where the podium came from. The day was partially sunny but warm. Zoe, the German Shepherd, made an appearance.

Ed and Elaine Brown kicked off the event. "It's pretty clear... they [the Marshals] intended to come in that day," Ed Brown told the gathered press crowd. "Two weeks ago, a dozen guys in ghillie suits rose up and shot two rounds that day at Danny Riley. If he hadn't been zigzagging back and forth as he ran, they would have killed him. They then grabbed him and threw him on the ground, and then they tasered him," Ed said.

"They were coming to kill him, and then kill us," Brown asserted. "We're just sitting here minding our own business. If they want to break the law and come on to this land... it's not their land, it's not even our land... it's God's land," Ed said.

Elaine then leaned into the microphones and said, "If they are not stopped at our door, next they'll come in through your door."

Ed added, "We're doing this for you, the people."

When Randy Weaver was introduced, he stepped to the microphones and thanked everyone for coming today. "Really, though," he added, "you should all be at the IRS Commissioner's Office to ask him why you have to pay your income tax. There is no law."

Weaver continued, "Ask him why all this is going on, when you have a gunman [USMS] enforcing a non-law. My grandpappy, Harvey Weaver, used to say, 'Government is just like a garden; it has to be weeded every now and then.' You want to know why he said that?" Weaver then held up a picture of his wife of twenty years holding his oldest daughter as a toddler. "She was a great wife and a wonderful mother. She homeschooled my kids... and the FBI shot her."

Weaver then gave a long and emotional story of his version of Ruby Ridge and why it happened. He concluded by saying, "This is one reason we need to weed out the government now and then. This is one reason people make the decision to stand up to the government.... Armed agents with guns ordered to enforce non-laws."

"This is why I'm here," Weaver said. "I'd rather die on my feet than submit to this de facto government that will lie to you and steal from you."

Weaver then took some questions from the media. One reporter asked, "What advice have you given the Browns?"

"These people have been convicted of a non-law," Weaver responded. "They were in court, but they were railroaded. The Browns here are smart enough themselves to figure this out... I'm not going to give them any other advice. I'm hoping the American people can see how they [the Browns] are being buffaloed... The U.S. Marshals are told, 'Go get these guys.' They don't care [about the Marshals], the IRS will just find someone to replace them... if one of them is killed."

Weaver continued when asked if he was afraid or afraid for the Browns, "It's strictly self-defense from this side of it. I'm not afraid. I don't pay my tithes to the church, 'cause I don't believe in Jesus. And I don't pay my tithes to the government, either.... The government and religion, they go hand in hand."

"But what about mediation? Is there mediation going on with the government?" another reporter asked.

Weaver replied, "The mediation part is just to educate people... I don't take orders."

"How long will you be here?" was another question.

"I don't know. I may decide to leave in ten, fifteen, twenty years." (Laughter) "I'm hoping the U.S. Marshals go home and get another job or something. I ain't afraid to die anymore. I'm kind of curious about the next life, and I'm an atheist."

Then Weaver asked the reporters, "Who are the original tax protesters?"

Someone shouted back, "The Founding Fathers."

"That's right," Weaver said. "The Founding Fathers, and they were upset about three percent. Look at the mess we have now."

Weaver concluded by saying, "I'm hoping you go down to the IRS and tell them that filing your taxes is voluntary. They have ruined the lives of lots of nice folks."

The questions then shifted back to Ed and Elaine. Someone asked, "What about an appeal of your convictions?"

"We don't appeal to a criminal organization," Ed Brown said.

Elaine added, "We have not appealed."

Ed said, "When you study this…. It's Freemasonry. Whether you like it or not, they're everywhere."

When Ed said that—talking about "Freemasonry"—Elaine could be seen leaning in toward the microphone and could be heard saying quietly to Ed, "Okay… okay… okay," when he made that statement. It was clear that she didn't want Ed continuing on about "Freemasonry."

However, Elaine then repeated the statement she had previously made in one of their daily radio shows. "If they come in," Elaine said, "we're dead. That's it. We will not be arrested. We will not volunteer to go in to prison for a non-crime. We have committed no crime. *We either come out of here free or we die.*"

The press conference at the Browns' lasted one hour and seven minutes.

After watching the press conference held at the Browns' compound, Steve Monier and Gary DiMartino talked about it in the conference room at the Marshals Office. "It's pretty clear, Chief," Monier said, "that Randy Weaver isn't going to be much use as someone who can negotiate Ed and Elaine's surrender. He's invested again in this belief that the federal government is bad and that Ed and Elaine haven't gotten a fair shake."

"Weaver's older," the marshal said, "and he seems a bit dejected, resigned to a script that isn't really his to write. When he was asked the question about giving the Browns advice or being a mediator, he struggled for answers. He really didn't have any."

DiMartino had similar thoughts. He didn't think Weaver would stick around long in Plainfield. "It's not really his battle, Marshal, and the people from the radio station and the Browns' supporters had a big hand in getting him to travel to Plainfield. Without prompting from both, and getting bank rolled, and the ride here from two radio people, I don't think Weaver would have come," Gary said.

Monier followed up with the supervisory resident agent in charge of the New Hampshire FBI office. They both agreed that Weaver wouldn't be of any help in negotiating the Browns' surrender.

In the days following the "press conference" with Randy Weaver, Ed and Elaine continued to give interviews to selected members of the media, while supporters came and went. Randy Weaver and his Texas associates stayed at the compound during the day. Reno Gonzalez continued posting to the Browns' Myspace page while others brought food and supplies. A member of the Free Staters from Keene gave them a cell phone to use.

In an interview with the *Boston Globe* published on June 22, 2007, Ed told the reporter, "They think they [federal agents] can intimidate us. They can't. Not everyone in the world is a coward. We're men."[vi]

Ever the narcissist, apparently to Ed Brown, his wife Elaine's efforts didn't count. Only the "men" did.

The *Globe*'s article pointed out what the Marshals knew from the beginning, that this standoff, unlike Ruby Ridge and Waco, "carries a new dimension: Brown's antigovernment crusade has rocketed through cyberspace, transforming the once-anonymous couple into a cause célèbre among fringe groups around the world and leaving federal agents wary of turning them into martyrs."[vii]

"'It's too late to stop [me],' Brown, 64, said. 'Too many people are aware.'"[viii] The reporter noted that, "Ed Brown's beliefs are well outside the mainstream."

Certainly, this was an understatement. In the article, Ed Brown expressed his admiration for President Mahmoud Ahmadinejad of Iran and said President George W. Bush "ordered the killing of thousands on Sept. 11 to justify a takeover of the Islamic world on behalf of Freemasons."[ix]

Ed said that he "and his allies around the world are compiling a list of Freemasons for future reference. For years now, we've been identifying them… in each town, each city, each state, each nation," Brown said. "We know who they are."[x]

The *Globe* contacted Robert Trestan, a lawyer with the Anti-Defamation League (ADL) for a statement about the Browns' situation. He told the *Globe* that with their use of the internet, the Browns were "able to tell someone a thousand miles away what's happening right now in [their] house."

In that manner, "a lot of extremist media are covering him around the world… and this multiplies the effect of Brown's message," Trestan said.[xi]

Monier and the leadership team at the District of New Hampshire office recognized this immediately. The marshal knew that the internet had given Ed Brown a twenty-first century stage from which he could spout his anti-government beliefs and conspiracy theories.

But it was that same internet that gave the Marshals Service a window into the Browns' compound every day without having to step foot onto the property. The local media and some people in the Plainfield, New Hampshire, area thought that allowing the Browns to have this platform was a mistake.

But the Marshals wanted to keep that door open. Principally, for two reasons. One, people who the Browns didn't know were being introduced to the Browns through that door. And two, the more Ed and Elaine talked, the more evidence the Marshals collected.

That duty had been assigned to Deputy U.S. Marshal Jamie Berry, who had the IT knowledge and expertise to track the various blog sites, group chats, Myspace pages, and internet radio shows on which Ed and Elaine were making statements every day.

It became clear to Monier and Chiefs DiMartino and Dimmitt, however, that the accumulating evidence would need to be catalogued, analyzed, and checked to determine if there was probable cause that a felony had been or was being committed. Beyond the planning on how to take the Browns into custody without harming them, the team needed someone to oversee the investigation into the ongoing obstruction of justice. They needed some more help.

When the request was made to HQ and the Investigative Services Division for assistance, the word came back that Chief Inspector Andre LaBier would be assigned to the district. LaBier, working with the district's leadership team and assigned deputies, would oversee the ongoing criminal investigation and work with the U.S. Attorney's Office to pursue subpoenas, search warrants, and indictments where and when warranted.

This marked a turning point in the armed standoff with the Browns and the USMS. Chief Inspector Andre LaBier, a Vermont resident, was a highly respected member of the USMS and an experienced and decorated supervisor who had risen through the ranks of the Marshals Service. He had held leadership assignments as the commander of the New York–New Jersey Regional Fugitive Task Force, as the chief of the Organized Crime Drug Enforcement Task Force at USMS HQ, and as a chief inspector with the Investigative Services Division (ISD).

"I got the call from Assistant Director Mike Earp at HQ, I believe, to go help the District of New Hampshire with the Ed and Elaine Brown case," LaBier said. "I traveled to New Hampshire on a temporary duty assignment (TDY). I met with Marshal Monier and Chiefs DiMartino and Dimmitt and their team and got briefed on where they were at in the planning to arrest the Browns.

"This was a big case," Chief LaBier said. "It was already a six-month-long armed standoff with the Browns, which involved some key players from all over the country. People were bringing them weapons, ammunition, and other supplies. The Browns, and some of their supporters, were repeatedly threatening that Plainfield would become another Waco. Randy Weaver had traveled to New Hampshire. Elaine was vowing to either come out as a free woman or in a body bag. And all of this, ultimately, was an effort to prevent federal law enforcement officers from carrying out their duties," he explained.

"The potential for violence to erupt at any time was very real," Chief LaBier said. "I was impressed with the fact that despite the enormous pressure the marshal and the chiefs were under to end the standoff NOW that they were equally determined to find a way to end it the right way—without violence.

"I set up shop in the Marshals' conference room—later nicknamed the 'war room'—and basically spent the next two-plus years leading a complex multi-agency investigation into a conspiracy to thwart law enforcement, threaten members of the courts and the prosecution, and obstruct justice. I worked with some remarkable people in the Marshals Service's District of New Hampshire office and with dedicated and determined prosecutors from the U.S. Attorney's Office for the District of New Hampshire."

Given the nature and length of this assignment, and the subsequent prosecutions involved, Chief LaBier spent a lot of time in the District of New Hampshire. Fortunately, Vermont is a bordering state, and LaBier was able to get home to his family on occasion.

"It was an intense period of investigation," LaBier noted. "It involved hundreds of hours of reviewing statements from the Browns and key supporters, dozens of interviews, the collection and analysis of intelligence and source material from other governmental agencies, and seemingly endless discussions with HQ, with Attorney Cedric Bullock from the USMS Office of General Counsel, the U.S. Attorney's Office, and local and state agencies."

As Marshal Monier said, "I often wondered if Andre got any sleep while he was here in the district. We'd get phone calls or notes from him at all hours. He was relentless in his pursuit of evidence, and he was a great resource to Chiefs DiMartino and Dimmitt on the operational side and to the dedicated assistant U.S. attorneys assigned to this case on the prosecutorial side. Andre's addition to the team had an immediate impact. I involved him in our conference calls with HQ senior staff and in the planning for another ruse to safely arrest the Browns."

"Chief LaBier has good instincts and good insights," the marshal reported to the deputy director in a phone call to HQ. "After Andre studied all the information that Deputy Jamie Berry had collected, and reviewed the supporters' postings, blogs, and related social media sites, this was quite evident."

More importantly, he connected well with Assistant U.S. Attorneys Bill Morse, Bob Kinsella, Arnie Huftalen, and Terry Ollila. He also spoke often with Tim Hanes, the intel analyst from the U.S. Attorney's Office who was sharing notes and research with DUSM Jamie Berry.

The files being gathered in the "war room" were expanding. The Marshals Office in the U.S. District Court in Concord lost its conference room but was gaining a nerve center with the information flow needed to end an armed standoff in Plainfield.

On June 20th, Chief DiMartino reported to the marshal that Rob Jacobs of Allenstown, New Hampshire, another armed Free Stater who had inserted himself into the Browns' standoff, was "urging people to attend the Plainfield Board of Selectmen's meeting tonight." He did this through a posting on the New Hampshire Tea Party's website.

To assist the Plainfield PD and in preparation for the meeting, Chief DiMartino said that we would have four of our people in and around the meeting. The state police would also support Plainfield PD with a uniformed presence. Plainfield PD Chief Gillens was informed of this. To further add to the evening's drama, the Lebanon, New Hampshire, PD had obtained an arrest warrant for Joe Haas for criminal threatening in their community, and they planned to arrest him if he showed up at the meeting.

On that same day, June 20, 2007, Marshal Monier received a phone call from the governor's office asking if he would meet with the governor, New Hampshire's Attorney General Kelly Ayotte, and the commissioner of safety the next morning. The governor wanted to be updated on the Marshal Services' plans with respect to Ed and Elaine Brown.

At eleven a.m., June 21st, Marshal Monier met with Governor John Lynch, Commissioner of Safety John Barthelmes, and Deputy Attorney General "Bud" Fitch at the Governor's Office in the State House in Concord. The governor said that, understandably, he had been getting calls from a number of people in Plainfield and the surrounding area who were concerned about the developments at the Browns' compound.

Marshal Monier gave an overview of the Brown matter and reiterated the USMS strategy to move forward to resolve this in the right way. Commissioner Barthelmes told the governor that he supported the approach that the USMS had adopted in this case and that the communication between federal, state, county, and local law enforcement had been quite good.

Governor Lynch listened, asked a few questions, but didn't try to suggest that the Marshals Service adopt a different strategy. Nor did he attempt, as some had been doing, to pressure the marshal to end the armed standoff quickly. The marshal thanked the governor for authorizing assistance from the New Hampshire State Police and the New Hampshire National Guard. They briefly discussed the Plainfield Board of Selectman meeting the night before and noted that Lebanon PD did arrest Joe Haas when he showed up for it. Otherwise, the selectboard meeting was attended by a good number of people but was peaceful.

Monier also explained why some sort of roadblock or checkpoint system to prevent people from going to the Browns would be counterproductive at this point. Without getting into details, the marshal said that it was still helpful that people were being allowed to drive up the driveway. The USMS, Monier said, "was getting some very good real-time intelligence, as a result." Commissioner Barthelmes again supported this view.

At the end of the meeting, Governor Lynch asked the marshal,

"What else can we do to help?" Monier said that the state police had been very supportive and were continuing to support the Plainfield PD and the sheriff's office in that area with stepped-up patrols. Monier assured the governor that the USMS would reach out for more specific forms of assistance when needed.

"I have no doubt," he said, "that time would come." In the interim, he stressed that a slow, methodical, and patient approach was the best way forward.

CHAPTER 11
THE BROWNS HOST A PICNIC/CONCERT

J une 23, 2007

At about the same time the U.S. marshal was meeting with the governor, the Marshals got word that there was going to be a "sponsored *Power Hour*" jamboree/picnic at the Browns' on Saturday, June 23, 2007. Flyers were placed in the Browns' neighbors' mailboxes inviting them to come to the picnic, and twelve signs were placed around the Plainfield area.

A confidential source to another governmental agency (OGA) reported that Randy Weaver was still present at the Browns' when the source was there late on Tuesday evening. The Browns, supporters, and Weaver were discussing the BBQ and "picnic" that was being planned for the weekend. On the Friday night before the event, Chief Gillens reported that fireworks were set off at the Browns' compound.

The invitational flyers and signs announced a "*Power Hour*" concert hosted by Dave VonKleist, who was a co-host of what VonKleist billed as "the increasingly popular radio talk show *The Power Hour*."[i]

A Maine-published *Fort Fairfield Journal* article from that day identified Dave VonKleist as the "concert promoter/entertainer" for the event, which was billed as "the Freedom Concert."[ii] According to the article's author, who also attended the Freedom Concert, VonKleist performed many of his "original politically-oriented tunes—a favorite among *Power Hour* listeners.... A video feed of the concert was also streamed live over the internet to a 'world-wide' audience via VonKleist's production team."[iii]

According to the article's author, most of the signs that had been put up were torn down "by unknown antagonists."[iv] In photographs published with the article, VonKleist is shown on a makeshift stage singing into a microphone while wearing a shirt fabricated to look like the U.S. flag. Randy Weaver is pictured sitting on the lawn next to Elaine Brown in one of them. The article mentions that "Ruby Ridge survivor, Randy Weaver, had spent nearly a week with the Browns and was able to put off last-minute commitments to stay for the concert."[v]

Within a couple of days of the concert, the investigative team learned that Randy Weaver had, in fact, left New Hampshire and was headed home.

The Marshals arranged with the U.S. Customs Border Protection for a CBP plane equipped with long-range photo capabilities to do a fly over of the "picnic/concert" on Saturday, June 23rd. Between twelve and fifteen vehicles and approximately thirty to fifty people were observed at the Browns' property during the "picnic/concert." The CBP provided the Marshals Service with a DVD of the photos taken during the event. A confidential source for an OGA also attended the "picnic."

Chief Dimmitt and Deputy Ken Nunes' team members were in the area conducting loose surveillance in unmarked SUVs, while Plainfield PD kept an eye on Center Town Road. Plainfield PD reported that there were no problems, and no cars parked on the road.

Not long after this concert, the investigative team learned that a second concert was being planned for July 4th, and that invitations had gone out on social media to show up and support the Browns during the "July 4th Freedom Fest." This was not good news from a community perspective, as it was bringing more people in who were giving the

Browns moral support for an immoral cause. Of course, the concern from people in the community ramped up as well.

After the June attempt to arrest Ed Brown at the mailbox, Ed and Elaine stopped taking phone calls from Chief Deputy Gary DiMartino. The chief, however, devised a method of getting information to and from the Browns by meeting with a key local Brown supporter from Weare, New Hampshire. This individual had known Ed Brown for many years and was a member of the Constitution Rangers, yet was open to meeting with Gary DiMartino for a discussion about the Browns' situation.

"This is something I actually started doing before the attempt to arrest Ed. It was another way of gathering information and establishing some rapport with people who were visiting with Ed and Elaine on a regular basis," DiMartino said. "We would meet at Remi's Place, the lunch place across the street from the U.S. district courthouse, and talk about Ed and Elaine's situation.

"In the beginning, Joe Haas would join in a couple of times, but after Ed Brown told Joe not to come back to the compound, I met just with this member of Ed's inner circle. He was a supporter, but he was willing to meet with me," Gary said. "I told him that nothing had changed about the Marshals Service finding a peaceful solution to this situation, that it was necessary to take Danny Riley, the 'Dog Walker,' into custody when he discovered our team at the end of the driveway. I also told him that no one fired live rounds at Riley."

As DiMartino explained to Monier and Chiefs Dave Dimmitt and Andre LaBier following these meetings, "I was confident that the information I was telling him was being relayed back to Ed and Elaine. It was also an opportunity for me to receive a message back from the Browns. In a conversation, this particular Brown supporter would give me a sense of what the mood was at the compound and who else was there. He still supported Ed Brown's beliefs about the courts and the government, but he was someone I could talk with.

"It was," Gary said, "one more added piece to the puzzle. One more way of getting some messages to and from Ed and Elaine, and of having someone I could call, when, and if, we needed another intermediary. The marshal had spoken with Bethany Hatch, Elaine's daughter, and I had this guy available as well."

On or about the 19th of June, the Marshals got wind that Reno Gonzalez's father, Jose Gonzalez, and Reno's brother, who was a local police officer on a Texas police department, were going to travel to Plainfield. Marshal Monier spoke with Jose Gonzalez on the phone before they made the trip north.

The marshal bluntly told Jose that his son, Reno, was exposing himself to potential criminal liability by his conduct and the assistance he had been, and was, providing to the Browns. "The best thing you can do for your son right now, Jose, is get your son out of there. This is serious stuff."

Chief DiMartino spoke with the police chief of the local Texas police department where the brother worked and explained the situation to him as well. "He's your officer, but if he goes there to support the Browns and not to get Reno out of there, then he's at risk of committing federal crimes himself," the chief said. DiMartino added, "He and the father, Jose, better not be bringing any guns to the Browns' property. Fair warning."

Interestingly, on the Monday following the "picnic" at the Browns', Chief Gillens called Marshal Monier at about eight forty-five a.m. to say that there were rumors that Ed and Elaine Brown had skipped town. An anonymous call was placed to Plainfield PD's dispatch center, and a second call went to Plainfield's town administrator saying the same thing, that the Browns had skipped town overnight.

Both the marshal and Chief Gillens agreed that it was highly unlikely that Ed and Elaine had left town but also promised to share any new information that might develop about that.

On Tuesday, June 26th, the Marshals Service also got word that

Reno Gonzalez, his father Jose, and the brother had all left the compound, though there was some uncertainty whether just the father and brother left and Reno was still there with the Browns. The investigative and surveillance teams worked to confirm what may have developed on that front.

By the following day, the team had confirmed that Ed and Elaine had not left the compound, but that Reno Gonzalez, his father, and the brother had left and were returning to Texas. Further information indicated that Ed Brown had gotten into a dispute with Jose and the brothers over "security" and that Ed got angry and told them to leave.

Meanwhile, Chief Gary DiMartino talked with his contact agent from another governmental agency (OGA) about their confidential source going back into the compound within the next few days. The agent's supervisor also called the marshal and asked if the USMS wanted this agency's Texas field office to conduct an interview of Reno Gonzalez when he was back in Texas.

After discussing this with his leadership team, the marshal told the supervisor that the Marshals Service wanted to hold off on that until we had a better picture of what might develop with Reno and other Brown supporters in the near future. The marshal also expressed his great appreciation for all the assistance this sister federal law enforcement agency was providing to the USMS on the Brown case.

Given the community unrest with the Browns holding a "picnic" and attracting more people to their compound, the ratcheted-up media attention, the calls to the governor's office, and even to the White House, it was inevitable that USMS HQ wanted daily updates. Between June 25th and July 1st, Marshal Monier fielded several calls to and from USMS HQ. There were discussions about the protective details, plans going forward with respect to the second planned "Freedom Fest" on July 4th, and what assets were needed.

In a rather unusual and direct call from the Department of Justice, which bypassed the ordinary chain of command, the chief of staff to the

Deputy Attorney General of the United States (DAG) called Marshal Monier directly for a status update on the armed standoff. The marshal gave a brief overview and update on the situation. At the end of the call, the chief of staff told the marshal, "You may need to come to Washington in the near future, Marshal, and together with the director of the Marshals Service brief the senior leadership of Main Justice about this case. Just be prepared." It was a pointed message that the heavy hitters in the Department of Justice were aware of the armed standoff with the Browns, and they were concerned.

In each of these discussions with the USMS HQ people, and with the DOJ, the marshal repeated his and the team's assessment that the best way to end this without violence was from the inside out. "The Marshals Service," Monier said, "needs to get an undercover operative inside who can then introduce a USMS team of deputy U.S. marshals, posing as 'Brown supporters,' into the compound.

"We need to drive up the driveway and be invited in," Monier would point out during these calls. "Everyone else does."

This was, in essence, the Trojan Horse strategy that Chief Deputy Gary DiMartino had devised early on. It would involve another ruse, by which deputies could be invited into the compound at the most opportune moment and preferably when Ed and Elaine were alone. Getting there would take some more work, and the right undercover operative needed to be found to have it succeed. At the beginning of July, there were still too many people visiting the Browns and hanging around. Things needed to quiet down again.

During this busy period, another issue cropped up that consumed a good amount of time on the part of the Marshals Service HQ staff and Marshal Monier. Who could possibly predict that the longest armed standoff in the Marshals Service history, in the rather remote hills of New Hampshire, population 1.3 million, would take place—as the crow flies—within a mile of the summer residence of a U.S. Supreme Court Justice? If there wasn't enough to keep the marshal, the chiefs, and their team awake at night, this was one more straw on the camel's back.

During every one of the Supreme Court's summer breaks, the justice would travel with his family to enjoy their vacation home, which was nestled in an idyllic setting on a small private lake in Plainfield, which was accessed by some of the same roads that led to the Browns' property. The home was surrounded only by the quiet woods of the upper Connecticut River Valley area. They weren't neighbors in the conventional sense, but it was close enough to cause the Marshals Service discomfort.

While many in the small town of Plainfield knew the justice and his family would regularly spend several weeks in the area, no one bothered them, and they gave them their space to enjoy the quiet woods and the splendor of a New Hampshire summer on a beautiful lake.

New Hampshire boasts some of the cleanest and clearest lakes in the nation and has been the summer home—or permanent home—to many well-known people throughout its rich history. There's a reason the Oscar-winning film *On Golden Pond* was filmed at one of New Hampshire's hidden gems. There are many hidden lakes in the Granite State, and the justice owned a quiet place on one of them. He wanted him and his family to spend the summer of 2007 there, just as they had for many years before.

The problem, of course, was that the Marshals Service was dealing with the Browns, and armed folks of all stripes were traveling to and from the compound while threatening members of the U.S. court system.

When Supreme Court Justices are at work in Washington, D.C., they are protected by the U.S. Supreme Court Police. If there is a specific threat against a justice or when the justices travel, it is the Marshals Service that is tasked with doing an assessment of the risk involved in that travel and with determining if additional security steps are warranted.

In this case, the USMS talked with the Supreme Court chief of police and made the recommendation, with the concurrence of the Supreme Court police chief, that the justice NOT travel to Plainfield during the court's summer break.

Understandably, the justice was not happy about this, and there ensued much back and forth as to what could be done about it. Calls were made to the U.S. Attorney General's Office, which resulted in calls to the director of the Marshals Service.

Ultimately, after much back and forth, HQ senior staff drafted a letter with Marshal Monier's input that was sent to the Supreme Court Justice. Director John Clark recalled speaking directly with the justice. "He called me," Director Clark later reported. "He was very polite and respectful and after our conversation understood what we were dealing with. He was gracious and offered his wishes that we succeed in safely taking them into custody."

In the end, the justice and his family did not travel to Plainfield that summer. Sadly, the justice was yet another victim of the Browns' continued criminal conduct to obstruct justice.

The other issue the marshal worked on during this time and into mid-July was getting some financial assistance to the Plainfield Police Department and the other state and local agencies that were having to contend with the prolonged armed standoff.

Having been a local police chief, Monier knew the burden this case placed on a small police department's budget. Chief Gillens was having his full-time officers work overtime, and he was bringing in part-time officers to cover extra patrols. Could anything be done to help them out? the Town of Plainfield asked.

The marshal said he would see what he could do but made no promises. After several discussions and memos to HQ senior staff, the district was authorized to provide $6,500 in overtime assistance to the

Plainfield Police Department, and authorized $20,000 to assist state and local agencies as needed. It wouldn't cover all the costs involved, but it was a help, and showed that the USMS appreciated the local and state agency support.

At the end of June, word went out from the Browns that the "July 4th Freedom Concert" was being postponed until July 14th. This information was disseminated on several online postings. The messages were for people to show up and "show their support for the Browns!"

On Thursday, July 5th, the Marshals Service confirmed that another online supporter of the Browns, James Hobbs, aka "Old Buck," had made it to Plainfield in an RV. Hobbs stayed in semi-regular contact with his ex-wife in Texas but had left in his RV from Phoenix, Arizona, to travel to Plainfield to help the Browns in "their struggle with the federal government."

He actually stopped by the Lebanon PD before heading up to the Browns' compound. Hobbs was known to "drift" and travel extensively in his RV. He had access to the internet and supported the Browns' resistance to any federal or court authority. The Browns allowed him to set up his RV and stay on the property. At about the same time, New Hampshire State Police got word that Ed Brown was installing additional motion-activated security lighting around the house and some of the outbuildings.

By this time, the marshal and members of the district's leadership team were having weekly conference calls with the Plainfield police chief; the Lebanon police chief; Lt. Jerry Maslan, the area troop commander for the New Hampshire State Police; and the sheriffs of both Sullivan (Plainfield) and Grafton Counties (Lebanon). This was an effort to ensure that there was an open line of communication between the Marshals Service and the local agencies on the ground in and around Plainfield.

In the lead-up to the Browns' planned July 14th Freedom Fest Concert, Sullivan County Sheriff Mike Prozzo brought up in one of the calls that his county attorney (the equivalent of district attorneys in most states) was questioning why we were allowing the Browns to have yet another concert on their property since it could endanger public safety.

The sheriff of Grafton County, Doug Dutile, said that the same question was being asked by the Grafton County attorney, who believed that under existing state law, and with an order from the county superior court, the road leading to the Browns' could be shut down and concertgoers turned away. The county attorney was frustrated with the whole situation, and he wanted to be proactive. While Plainfield was located in Sullivan County, there had apparently been some joint conversations between the two county attorneys about the armed standoff with the Browns.

Marshal Monier told both Sheriff Mike Prozzo and Sheriff Dutile that he understood the concerns. He knew that the Grafton County chiefs of police were meeting on Wednesday, July 11th, and he proposed that he attend the meeting, as he understood the Grafton County attorney would be there. Given all of the circumstances currently, and the fact that the USMS got some good intelligence from the first concert, the USMS did not believe that attempting to shut down this concert was the best plan, but he would meet with the sheriffs, the chiefs from the area, and the county attorneys—if both were able to attend—on the 11th. The marshal said he would ask U.S. Attorney Tom Colantuono to attend as well.

On the morning of the 11th of July, the marshal traveled to Grafton County to attend the county chiefs of police meeting. The U.S. attorney also attended but traveled there with his USMS protective detail. The Grafton County attorney, New Hampshire's Attorney General Kelly Ayotte, and many of the area police chiefs were in attendance. The marshal gave a briefing on the USMS response thus far and an overview of the current situation.

Without getting into specific operational details, he attempted to assure everyone that the Marshals Service intended to execute the warrants on Ed and Elaine Brown, but in a way that would ensure there was not an armed, violent confrontation leading to serious bodily injury or death to any law enforcement officers, the Browns, or others.

"The Marshals Service is mindful," Monier said, "that even the best of plans can fall apart given an unforeseeable event or the actions of a third party, such as one of the Browns' supporters. To that end, the USMS Special Operations Group has contingency plans in place should the need arise to enter the property directly."

Monier continued, "We are extremely grateful for the support the Lebanon and Plainfield Police Departments, the county sheriffs' offices, and the New Hampshire State Police have given to us. I know we are all concerned about the safety of the communities in the Plainfield and Lebanon areas. I can also tell you that we are getting that same kind of support from every one of our sister federal law enforcement agencies, including the IRS, the FBI, the ATF, Customs and Border Protection, the U.S. Postal Inspectors, the Treasury Inspector General for Tax Administration (TIGTA), the U.S. Attorney's Office, and from the U.S. Department of Justice in Washington, D.C."

U.S. Attorney Colantuono added to that and said that his intelligence officer was working closely with the Marshals Service on developing information and that several of his assistant U.S. attorneys were coordinating with the Marshals' investigative team on getting the necessary subpoenas and warrants, as needed, for the collection of evidence.

The chiefs asked a few specific questions about the upcoming concert on the 14th and what plans were in place for community safety. The marshal discussed the extra USMS personnel that would be in the area supporting the Plainfield PD, the New Hampshire State Police, and the Sullivan County Sheriff's Office. There would be air support and surveillance again from Customs and Border Protection, and other "assets" would be in place.

The Grafton County attorney spoke and said that he and the

Sullivan County attorney were very concerned that this standoff had been going on for so long. He said that he and his counterpart had been getting calls from many people who were outraged that the Browns were being allowed to thumb their nose at the judicial system. His basic message, rather forcefully expressed, was that "*you* need to end this now."

The marshal calmly repeated that the U.S. Marshals Service and the district office intended to end this, but in the right way, and at the right time, so that no one got hurt. "We believe that we know how to do that," Monier said, "but it's going to require a little bit more patience on everyone's part."

Monier ended by pointing out that "*everyone*, I'm certain, wants this to end the right way. The right way is to find a better way to prevent anyone from getting hurt. The last thing anyone in New Hampshire could possibly want is for 'Plainfield' to join the American lexicon of 'Waco' and 'Ruby Ridge.'"

When Marshal Monier left the chiefs of police meeting, he traveled to Plainfield and met up with Deputy U.S. Marshal Ken Nunes and one of the USMS Task Force deputies assigned to work with Chief Dimmitt and Ken's team. They were working loose surveillance of the Plainfield area and the Browns that day. The three of them then met with Chief Gillens and Cpl. Roberts from Plainfield PD about the "concert," and they reviewed the plans to keep the community safe, with eyes on the event and ears to the ground.

Members of the investigative team had been meeting with Chief Gillens on a regular basis, and USMS team members had been quietly present at a number of community meetings in Plainfield.

After the stops in Plainfield, the marshal headed back to his Concord office. On the way, he received a phone call from the commissioner of safety, John Barthelmes. "The governor would like to meet with you again tomorrow at five p.m. in his office. Would you be able to make it?" the commissioner asked.

"Certainly, Commissioner, I'll make sure I'm there at five p.m." He added, "Though I am a *federal* employee in the U.S. Department of Justice, *not a state employee*, the governor has been very supportive, and it's important that we answer all of his questions and keep him up to speed on the situation. I'll see you folks at the State House tomorrow at five p.m."

When he got back to the USMS office, he sat down with Chief Gary DiMartino and summarized the meetings he had that day. Then he told him about, once again, being summoned to the governor's office the next day at five p.m. "I phrased my response to the commissioner the way I did, just to politely remind everyone that we're a federal agency and that my boss is the director of the U.S. Marshals Service. But I also wanted it clear that I'm happy to oblige. No doubt, we're going to need additional support from the state in the near future. And the governor and state agencies have been supportive."

"Besides," he told Gary, "I've known John Barthelmes since he was a New Hampshire State Trooper. John rose quickly through the ranks because he was a very good investigator and a very smart guy. The governor saw these qualities, too, since he appointed John the colonel of the state police and then appointed him the commissioner of safety for the state. Both of these important positions require the concurrence of New Hampshire's Executive Council," the marshal explained.

"Moreover, John's been quite supportive of our go-slow approach to this whole case. So we need to keep the commissioner informed as well."

On Thursday, July 12th, Chiefs Dimmitt and LaBier met with Chief DiMartino and the marshal, and they updated everyone on their work in preparation for the concert and developments on what the Investigative Services Division and the Judicial Security Division from HQ were considering. Dave Dimmitt said the Technical Operations Group was still working on getting cameras up in Plainfield.

Chief Andre LaBier reported that he and Deputy Jamie Berry were reviewing everything that'd been collected off the web and were talking with the assistant U.S. attorneys (AUSAs) about a list of targets—those people most involved with the Browns in the conspiracy to obstruct justice. DiMartino reported that his contact with an OGA told him they would have a confidential source—or sources—at the Browns' during the concert. He also said that one of our deputies would be in the camera-equipped CBP aircraft for the overflight during the event.

DiMartino added, "The 'concert' will once again be live streamed by an internet radio station, which is one of the 'sponsors' for the event, so we can all tune in."

There was slight pause, then the marshal asked, "Gary, are they going to have *any* good music this time?"

There was a back and forth then about what the best lineup of tunes should be. Somebody suggested that we have Jamie Berry hack into the live feed and play the theme song from the reality show *Cops*. After a few chuckles, everyone went back to work.

The marshal made follow-up calls to Chief Gillens, Sheriff Prozzo, Commissioner Barthelmes, and Chief Jim Alexander at the Lebanon PD. He sent a summary memo/situation report to Assistant Director Art Roderick at HQ, with a copy to Chris Dudley (who had been promoted from chief of staff to deputy director of the USMS), and then spoke again with U.S. Attorney Tom Colantuono. He complimented Tom on the great work his intel analyst Tim Hanes was doing. At about four thirty p.m., the marshal left the office and headed to the State House for the meeting with Governor John Lynch.

At five p.m., he was ushered into the governor's corner office. In attendance for the meeting was the governor's chief of staff, Rich Siegel; his legal counsel Mike Delaney; New Hampshire Attorney General Kelly Ayotte; and Commissioner John Barthelmes. The governor opened by saying, "I'm sure you know, Marshal, that I've been getting a lot of calls from people concerned about the Ed and Elaine Brown matter."

"We have been, too, Governor, and I'm sure that some of mine have been a bit more colorful than some of yours, but I completely understand the concerns. We're going into the seventh month of an armed standoff with the Browns, so with that let me give everyone a briefing on where we're at…"

Monier then summarized for everyone what the USMS had been doing and, without getting into operational specifics, discussed what the USMS wanted to do in the near future. The marshal and commissioner then outlined for the governor what the plans were for this weekend's second concert at the Browns', with a particular focus on the steps being taken to make sure the community was safe. That involved support to the Plainfield PD from the U.S. Marshals, other federal law enforcement, the state police, the sheriff's office, and from neighboring Lebanon PD.

The marshal also informed the governor that the USMS was providing $6,500 in direct assistance to Plainfield PD to help with Chief Gillens' overtime and other expenses. Both Chief Gillens and the town administrator had been informed of this, he reported.

"We have also been holding weekly conference calls with the chiefs, both sheriffs, and New Hampshire State Police Troop Commander Lt. Gerry Maslan to share any developments," Monier informed the governor.

Once again, both General Ayotte and Commissioner Barthelmes told the governor that they believed the Marshals Service was taking the right approach to resolve the armed standoff. The governor asked a few questions. He listened and was supportive.

Toward the end of the meeting, the marshal noted that he had been getting a lot of calls from the media who generally asked the same thing. "That is," he said, "what is the Marshals Service doing about the concert, and more importantly, what are the plans going forward?"

"I'm sure each of you are going to get the same inquiries, if you haven't already. I've put together some talking points I use to frame all of my responses to these inquiries, and I'd like to share them with you. I think it would be helpful if we all are on the same page, so I brought a copy for everyone, so you know what the U.S. Marshals are saying when these questions are asked."

With that, Marshal Monier passed around his "talking points." The sheet read:

Talking Points on the Edward and Elaine Brown Matter

July 13, 2007

- It has been three months since Edward and Elaine Browns' April sentencing in the United States District Court. They were tried and convicted by a jury of their peers for income tax evasion charges and sentenced to a 63-month term of imprisonment in the United States Bureau of Prisons. There are active warrants for their arrests.
- The United States Marshals Service continues its careful effort to resolve this peacefully. It has no intention of creating an armed, violent confrontation with the Browns.
- The Marshals Service is proceeding in a purposeful, methodical, and deliberate manner. Access to power, telephones, and other utilities at the Browns' property in Plainfield has been shut off. Other steps may be taken in the near future to convince the Browns that they must turn themselves in, and stop threatening the use of violence towards law enforcement. Lines of communication with the Browns remain open.

- Because the Browns are inviting people to visit them at their property, and because they have indicated that they will violently resist efforts to arrest them, local, county, state, and federal law enforcement officials are working in close partnership to ensure that public safety is preserved.
- Area law enforcement will have a heightened presence during any gathering at the Browns to ensure that the well-being of the public is maintained.
- The security of the greater Plainfield community is the highest of priorities as officials work to successfully resolve the situation the Browns have created.
- Anyone actively engaged in aiding and abetting the Browns in their continuing obstruction of justice is committing a separate federal felony offense and may be subject to arrest and prosecution.

The marshal's "talking points" ended with this:

Edward and Elaine Brown can do the right thing and end this today. All they need to do is call and make arrangements to turn themselves in.

With that, the governor thanked the marshal for coming to meet with him and for the updates. He said that they would stay in touch and assist in any way they could.

Not long after the marshal met with the governor and his department heads, the Marshals Service became aware of a letter Ed and Elaine Brown had sent to their neighbors. It was in response to a letter the Browns had received signed by many of their neighbors who expressed their concern that the continuing armed standoff with the Marshals Service, with armed supporters coming and going, was making their community and neighborhood unsafe. The letter pointed out that there were children in the area, and this ongoing armed standoff put them at risk.

The Browns' letter was long and rambling and reiterated their erroneous interpretations of state and federal law. It assured the neighbors that it was not the Browns they had to fear, but the government they were resisting. At the end, there was a handwritten postscript that invited the neighbors to attend their gathering on July 14th. The Browns' letter read:

To our concerned neighbors,

We have read your letter and appreciate the way it was written, as we know you would have liked to express yourselves in a very different way.

We are aware of your concerns, and you are right to fear for your children's safety, although not for the reasons you stated. We also are concerned for our children, all our children; that is what we are fighting for. If you have not followed our case through the true media, you will not know that we are not doing this because we do not want to pay taxes.

Our stand is against the corruption and criminal activity in our administration. There are millions like us across this country, who know that we must return our country to the republic it was intended to be, or live in slavery. These are the choices our children face, it is their future we are all fighting for.

Think about REAL ID, the North American Union, the decline of the dollar and the replacement of it with the Amero, the Transatlantic Union, the fact that even now all new hires must be approved by Homeland Security, the corruption in our courts.

We have chosen the IRS as our means to fight this battle because it affects all of us; because so many people have been persecuted, their lives ruined, their businesses destroyed, their homes confiscated, their families lost, even their lives lost, in the name of a law that does not exist. Remember, since 1994, we have been asking the IRS to show us the law. Show us the law and we will pay. Even at our trial, we said, show us the law and we will pay. No one has shown us or anyone else such a law.

We all have been lied to, tricked, defrauded into believing something that does not exist. "I pay my taxes, why shouldn't they pay theirs?" We hear this often from those who have not studied the law and do not know they don't have to pay these taxes, that the right to labor and the fruits of that labor come from our Creator, and cannot be taxed.

We are thankful for the thousands of friends and supporters who have stood with us, people like ourselves from all over the country, who want nothing more than to be able to live in freedom and peace, to go about our lives without interference and tyranny from our public servants. This stand, this fight is not about just taxes; it is about our children's future. All that is necessary for evil to abound is for good people to do nothing.

We know you are all good people, but lack of knowledge leads to fear, which leads to inaction. We only ask that everyone learn and get together to fight for our liberties, to remove the criminals within our administration. The law-breakers and the ignorant serve at all levels of our government, from local to federal. Just last week, our own select-board stated that they would not protect us, even after being shown the law that shows how the feds have violated RSA 123:I by not registering in the state, and thereby having no authorization to conduct any business in New Hampshire. Sheriff Prozzo has violated the law also by refusing to do his duty to keep the feds out of Sullivan County as he is supposed to do. Chief Gillens has said he will take his orders from the state. He is supposed to take orders from us, here in Plainfield.

Friends, it is up to us, as we are the government, to hold our employees to task, to insist on accountability, and to see to it that they uphold the laws of our land or remove them. Thomas Jefferson said, the price of freedom is eternal vigilance. We have not been vigilant, and have thus allowed the deterioration of our wonderful country to its present condition. We have lost too many of our freedoms, allowed our God-given rights to be taken from us, many in the name of security. As such, we have neither.

Your children are safe from us; their only danger is from a government out of control. We know many of you think of us as kooks, conspiracy theorists, anti-government, etc., and wish we had never moved to Plainfield. Others around the country feel the opposite; people have come from as far away as California and Washington, Florida and Texas, just to shake our hands. Even Ron Paul has acknowledged us as true patriots. Ask yourselves why would we put everything, including our lives, on the line for this. Why would anyone place themselves in our position? certainly [*sic*] not to avoid paying some 'lawful' tax. We do it because we love our country, as do millions of others, and have taken a stand hoping to give courage to others to fight injustice. When people in a locality stand together for justice, there is no need for others from distant places to come to their aid.

All of you are always welcome in our home; we invite you all to come, whether individually or all together, for coffee and a chat. You see how many come; it is heartening to see some of our neighbors starting to respond now, also. The scriptures say that most resistance will be seen in our own families/neighbors. Hopefully you will start to question what you have heard and seen in the media, and will come by for enlightenment. You might be surprised to find that we are not evil or crazy people, but are only doing what Americans are supposed to do, are demanded to do in the Declaration of Independence.

We pray daily to Yahweh for enlightenment of the people, that they may see the truth and act on it. May He be with you always. Your neighbors

Edward-Lewis

Elaine Alice

Post script (handwritten)—You are cordially invited to our gathering on Sat., July 14.

As one neighbor confided to Marshal Monier after receiving the letter, "It's hard to wrap your head around their beliefs about the income tax, and Ed's conspiratorial rants to the media and online…. Before all this, we just thought that Ed Brown was a bit of a nut, but now he and Elaine are putting many people's lives at risk…. They need to knock it off and turn themselves in to you guys."

The neighbor added, "People in Plainfield are tired of it all."

On Saturday, July 14, 2007, the Browns hosted their gathering, the invitations to which welcomed "all freedom-loving people and honest media."[vi] There were Brown supporters at the end of the Browns' driveway directing traffic onto the property, while Plainfield police officers were present nearby to ensure that the town roads remained open.

Marshals Service deputies were nearby in unmarked SUVs to support Chief Gillens and his officers, as were additional area patrols from the sheriff's office and the New Hampshire State Police. The USMS teams had communication with the deputy U.S. marshal in the CBP aircraft.

According to an article from the *Concord Monitor*, the Browns were not allowing reporters from the more mainstream media on the property: "While the invitation to yesterday's party welcomed 'all freedom-loving people and honest media,' two men directing the traffic at the end of the Browns' driveway said reporters weren't allowed and denied access to the *Monitor*."[vii]

Several people from Plainfield were quoted in the same article and gave similar statements to the *Monitor*'s reporter as one of the Browns' neighbors privately expressed to Marshal Monier.

We the People Radio Network, Genesis Communications, along with *GCNLive.com*, and *WTPRN.com* all helped to host the "Live Free or Die Jamboree" as it was alternately called that day, via the live online radio broadcasts. There was a makeshift stage, generators, microphones, and amplifiers for the various musical presentations to go with the food.

Those in attendance heard remarks from Ed and Elaine Brown, Danny "the Dog Walker" Riley, and Jack Blood (a blogger), along with Mike Knaar from *WeAreChange.org*, Ted Anderson of *GCNLive.com*, and others.

The Marshals Service learned that the CBP plane with the long-range camera was unavailable that day. Instead, Deputy U.S. Marshal Gene Robinson and an IRS agent were picked up in a Department of Homeland Security (DHS) helicopter. While a chopper offers certain advantages to fixed-wing aircraft in some situations, it was not the ideal aircraft Chief Deputy Gary DiMartino had in mind for the event. He wanted the air surveillance to be lowkey, with a good standoff distance.

To get good photographs from a chopper with handheld telephoto lenses, it needs to be closer to the ground, and of course, a helicopter is not as quiet as a plane at altitude. In the late afternoon, the chopper buzzed the event several times.

Learning of this, DiMartino communicated to the deputy to have the DHS pilot stand off. "Remind the pilot," the chief deputy told his deputy, "there are people in the crowd that have ready access to long guns, and some of them might be crazy enough to fire at them."

Radio host Mike Rivero of the *GCNlive.com* broadcast reported that people wrote down the tail number from the chopper, and while he was broadcasting live from the event said that, after an internet search, he could confirm it was a Department of Homeland Security chopper. He also reported that Ed Brown called the FAA and warned them that the chopper was flying too low. It's unverified whether Ed actually did talk with the FAA.

According to reports the next day from confidential source(s), the chopper's appearance at the jamboree elicited more conspiracy theories about how the federal government may have dispersed a biological or chemical weapon over the crowd during the time it was hovering over the compound. Many worried that they would become stricken in some manner in the ensuing days.

At the end of the gathering, the "guests" were treated to a fireworks display before finally departing the compound. There were no arrests or incidents directly related to the concert. Chief Andre LaBier, Deputy U.S. Marshal (DUSM) Jamie Berry, and the investigative team chronicled many of the statements Ed, Elaine, and Dan Riley made during the live broadcast.

In a subsequent debrief in the "war room" about the weekend's activities, the district leadership team agreed on several things for their situation reports (sitreps) to HQ: one, a lot of good information had been collected; two, people the Browns didn't know were still allowed to drive up the driveway; and three, the music still wasn't very good.

CHAPTER 12
THE LONG SUMMER CONTINUES

On July 17th, at approximately 9:50 a.m., the marshal had a debrief with Chief Gillens to see what the chief was hearing from the community about the concert. The chief told him that after observing the flow of traffic to and from the Browns', talking with a number of the neighbors and a few people who had attended the jamboree, he believes there were approximately100 people at the event. Overall, the chief said, the neighbors were pleased with how it went and were pleased with how law enforcement handled it.

"There's another thing I was told, Marshal," Gordon said. "A number of the people at the event were folks that followed the bands that played at the concert. They weren't necessarily all people supporting the Browns. I don't know if that's true, but I thought it was interesting I was told this."

Chief Gillens also said that the Sullivan County Sheriff's Office was unhappy to learn that someone stole their traffic counter that they had placed on Center Town Road. "They cut the chain that had been used to secure the machine to a telephone pole and took the whole thing. The sheriff is unhappy," the chief said.

"Yes, I know, Chief. I've already heard from the sheriff about that," the marshal replied.

Later that morning, Deputy Ken Nunes notified Chief DiMartino and the marshal that a sergeant from Lebanon PD had just called. "The green Chevy Blazer that Ed and Elaine Brown own was just involved in an accident in Lebanon. Jason Gerhard was driving it," he said.

Unfortunately, the young female driving the other vehicle was injured. Fortunately, the report was that her injuries were not serious. After discussing it briefly with the team, Chief DiMartino told the Lebanon PD to tow the vehicle to a secure impound lot, that the U.S. Marshals Service was impounding the vehicle.

Ed Brown was talking on his *Ed Brown Under Siege* daily internet radio show when he got word that his vehicle had been impounded. He said that the "Marshals have 'arrested' the car" and that "he needs another SUV now, because they just stole this one."

The *Concord Monitor* contacted Marshal Monier that afternoon about the vehicle. The marshal acknowledged that the USMS had impounded the vehicle. "It's a vehicle belonging to fugitives," he told staff reporter Margot Sanger-Katz, "and we are investigating it further. Moreover, we are investigating several of the Browns' supporters, and we expect that charges may be forthcoming for those who have engaged in a continuing course of conduct to aid and abet their obstruction of justice."

In the mid- and late summer, Monier was taking every opportunity to warn people assisting the Browns that they were criminally liable if they engaged in a conspiracy to help the Browns evade arrest.

On July 20, 2007, the district leadership team met with a Judicial Security Division chief inspector from HQ. He had been in the state with a small team of deputies to work with the district's Judicial Security Inspector Brenda Mikelson. They were there to update the threat assessment on Judge McAuliffe, U.S. Attorney (USA) Tom Colantuono, and the prosecutor, Assistant U.S. Attorney (AUSA) Bill Morse.

During the time in the District of New Hampshire, for what was termed Operation Granite, the chief inspector and his team conducted counter-surveillance to determine whether there were any efforts to follow or surveil the protectees or their family members. They worked with the district and Chief LaBier's investigative team to determine the whereabouts and current activities of some of Ed Brown's supporters, particularly those who had caused concern with either a direct threat or some type of inappropriate communication or other concerning activity.

In his summary report to the district's leadership team, he provided the following overview of his findings:

- All recent noteworthy communications by the Browns, or their supporters, are primarily directed at law enforcement and not the court family.
- Counter-surveillance during Operation Granite found no evidence of any surveillance efforts directed toward the three protectees.
- No protective detail had reported an unusual circumstance or suspicious occurrence since their start in January of 2007.
- William Miller, one of the individuals who first caused the district concern, was no longer involved with the Browns and hadn't been for some time.

The Judicial Security Division had coordinated the installation of alarm systems at all of the protectees' residences. They also made some additional suggestions for home security and schooled each of the protectees and their family members on exercising sound personal protective measures, which would afford the family protection while at home.

Accordingly, the Judicial Security Division recommended that the protective details be stepped down. HQ concurred with this. After discussion, and a few questions from the marshal and other district team members, the marshal also concurred with this. He turned to Judicial Security Inspector Brenda Mikelson and asked if she was comfortable with the findings.

"I am, Marshal," she replied, "and I know that the protectees are probably quite ready to have the 24/7 nature of the details end." She added, "While each of the protectees have expressed their appreciation for the security the USMS had provided them, I think they believe it's time to step it back. Each of the installed alarm systems has a 'panic button' feature, which allows them to summon immediate assistance, if required."

"Sounds good to me, Brenda. Please meet with each of them to let them know what's happening, and give them the end date. And remind them to contact you immediately if they, or family members, see or hear anything concerning. We'll certainly do the same," the marshal said.

At the conclusion of the meeting, Monier called USA Tom Colantuono to let him know that Brenda would be reaching out and that the 24/7 details would be ending. He also wanted to give him an update on the Brown case. They discussed a few details of the ongoing investigation and talked about some next steps. The U.S. attorney thanked the marshal for the call.

"All of the deputy U.S. marshals that have been on my detail have been terrific, Steve," Tom said, "but I have to tell you two quick stories. At one point, the members of my detail were parked at night on a street that intersected with mine but diagonally across from my house. As you know, I live in a fairly dense residential area of the city, but I keep a pretty low profile when I'm home. After a while, with them sitting there, a neighbor from that street came out of his house and walked up to the SUV they were in," Tom said.

"The neighbor said, 'You guys must be cops; you're watching that house aren't you?' And the deputies replied that yes, they're keeping a close eye on things; the neighbor blurted out and said, 'I knew it! I knew that guy was a drug dealer!'

"Both deputies told me that they had a very hard time not laughing when the neighbor said that," Tom told the marshal.

"More recently," the U.S. attorney said, "I had to attend a morning Coos County [the northernmost county in New Hampshire] Law Enforcement meeting in the north country. At the time, I had a deputy on the detail from New York, and he had never seen a moose. He told me that he was really hoping that he could see a moose while he's in New Hampshire.

"So I told him that this might be the perfect opportunity since we were traveling to the north country [the northern border of Coos County in New Hampshire is Canada] on roads where moose crossings were pretty frequent. In fact, I told him that you had to be careful driving on these roads because an accident with a moose could be quite serious, sometimes fatal, because moose are huge," Tom said.

He continued, "However, on the early morning drive all the way up to the meeting, we didn't spot any moose. The deputy was pretty disappointed. When we left the meeting, I told the detail that we needed to stop at the Franconia Police Department and that the small PD was located on the Main Street of Franconia, population about nine hundred twenty-five."

Franconia is still in the "north country" of New Hampshire.

"You wouldn't believe what happened next," Tom said. "As we pulled into a parking place [in] downtown Franconia and got out of the SUV, we see this huge female moose walking up an embankment onto the Main Street with two calves in tow. They're just a short distance from us. I thought to myself," he told Steve, "*This is great, the deputy from New York gets to see not one, but three moose up close!*

"So the other deputy, who was from Illinois, and I are standing there quietly just watching the moose walk near us on the street, when I realize the New York deputy was missing. I look around, and I see that he had run back to the SUV and was sitting inside the vehicle. Apparently, he wanted to see a moose, just not that close up!

"As you might imagine, Steve," Tom said, "on the way back, we had a pretty good laugh about his close encounter with not one, but three, New Hampshire moose."

At approximately eleven thirty p.m. on July 28, 2007, Danny "the Dog Walker" Riley sent out a panicked email from the Browns' compound saying they were at "Red Alert!" In the broadcast, which was quickly picked up on the various web pages devoted to Ed and Elaine Brown, Riley said that thirty to forty shots had been fired in the woods and that "'federal agents' had banged on an RV on the property."

Presumably, since James "Old Buck" Hobbs was still camped out there, this was Old Buck's RV A short while later, Riley also reported that a motion sensor light by the garage had been activated.

These reports kept the internet world abuzz for about twenty-four hours and prompted several calls from the media to the Plainfield Police Department and the Marshals Office the next day.

"There were NO law enforcement actions at or near the Browns' compound last evening. We have no idea what people at the Browns' may have heard or seen," the marshal told reporters who called him.

Chief Gordon Gillens said the same thing, that if someone was in the woods near the Browns', it wasn't law enforcement.

Unfortunately, however, the chief did report that once the "red alert" went out via the internet sites, about sixty calls from all over the country came into the dispatch center in Hanover late that Saturday evening and well into the next morning.

"This totally disrupted emergency services and clogged the 911 lines," Chief Gillens told the *Associated Press*.[i]

. . .

On July 31, 2007, Marshal Monier, Chief Deputy Gary DiMartino, and Chief Inspectors Andre LaBier and Dave Dimmitt convened to discuss the developing plans to facilitate an arrest of Ed and Elaine Brown and to discuss the Technical Operations Group's progress with respect to cameras and other requests.

Chief LaBier and Jamie Berry had been working with the U.S. Attorney's Office to get the necessary subpoenas and/or search warrant(s) necessary for the cell phone records on the individuals being investigated for aiding and abetting the Browns. The list of targets was narrowing and now focused on those who were bringing weapons, ammunition, or IED components to the Browns and/or who were actively engaged in trying to thwart the Marshals' efforts to serve the arrest warrants.

The leadership team then joined Investigative Services Division HQ Chief Bill Sorukas and others in a conference call to discuss investigative developments. There had been progress in getting access to cell phone records, but the USMS had still been unable to get a set of cameras up by which to monitor the compound from a line-of-sight tower near the Browns' hilltop complex. They were still working to find a solution to that.

The district leadership team then discussed getting an order under the All Writs Act, which would provide the USMS with the authority to warn and arrest people going to the Browns' and to further contain the property, when and if necessary. It was agreed that Attorney Cedric Bullock from the Office of General Counsel at USMS HQ would work with Chief LaBier, the IRS, and the assistant U.S. attorneys assigned to this case to develop the appropriate language for such a court order. The order would need to be signed by a judge from the U.S. District Court in New Hampshire.

The conversation then focused on the next steps and immediate goals. After discussion, everyone agreed that the immediate goals were to:

- Quiet the Browns down so that fewer people travel to the property.
- Execute arrest warrants on the targeted supporters, when appropriate.
- Get a writ signed by the judge.
- Develop additional information on conducting a ruse.
- Implement the plan to make the arrests.

The leadership team and the HQ senior staff on the call also agreed that should circumstances on the ground dictate it, the criteria for having to completely shut down the Browns' property may include but would not be limited to:

- Learning that more people were heading to the Browns' than could be controlled.
- An increase in the danger level/threat to community safety.
- Facts and circumstances that indicated a situation was spiraling out of control.

The conference call with HQ ended, but the team at the district office continued to flesh out more details about the ruse necessary to take Ed and Elaine into custody.

"We need an undercover operative to go into the Browns' first—ideally someone who has been introduced to them through someone they've already met or have conversed with through the internet," Chief DiMartino said.

"Agreed, Chief, we need someone from the inside to invite other 'supporters' into the compound," the marshal said. "Our task in the next few weeks is to get this done. And we need to convince HQ this is the best way to go." Monier continued, "And Andre, your team, working with the assistant U.S. attorneys on this case, needs to let us know when everyone thinks we should arrest the targeted supporters."

The first week in August, a confidential informant cooperating with the USMS conversed on the phone for about an hour with Old Buck. The district's investigative team set up a recording device and was with the CI during the conversation.

At one point, Old Buck said that Ed was becoming despondent about the situation. The team got some additional information about who had been coming and going from the compound. They also learned that another Freedom Fest may be in the planning stages for September 8, 2007.

On August 9th, Cedric Bullock from the USMS Office of General Counsel and the U.S. Attorney's Office agreed to the language for a new court order under the All Writs Act. This was presented to Judge Steven McAuliffe, and he signed it.

The language gave authority to the U.S. Marshals Service, at their discretion, to keep people off the Browns' property, when and if necessary, and to delegate that authority to other agencies as the Marshals Service deemed fit. The order also renewed the prior orders to shut down their utilities, mail, and other delivery services in furtherance of the execution of the arrest warrants.

On the same day, the Marshals learned from blog postings on several websites that the date for a fall Freedom Fest at the Browns' compound was now September 15, 2007, not the 8th as originally discussed.

A couple of days later, Chief LaBier stuck his head into the Marshals Office and said, "Marshal, Elaine is opening up a new dental practice."

The marshal took a moment to see if the chief was being serious, then asked, "How exactly, Chief, is Dr. Brown opening up a new dental practice?"

"They are making over one of the areas or rooms in the house into some kind of a dental 'office,'" Andre replied, "and we got word she will shortly be sending out computer-printed invitations to former patients that says she has resumed seeing patients at her new 'home office' in Plainfield. We acquired one of the invitations. Here it is." And with that, Chief LaBier handed the marshal a printed folding mailer, which read:

I am pleased to announce that I have resumed seeing patients at my new home-office in Plainfield, New Hampshire. I invite any of my previous (or new) patients who would like to continue with me to come here for your dental care.

The invite continued with detailed directions on how to find the entrance to their driveway from Rt. 12A south from West Lebanon.

The invitation closed with, "No need to phone ahead. I look forward to seeing you soon." The heading at the top of the fold read, "Elaine Alice: family Brown, DMD, Center of Town Road, Plainfield, NH."

"So, Chief, how does Elaine have access to Novocain and all the other things she might need in a dental office?" the marshal asked.

"Well, she doesn't, Marshal," Andre replied, "but it appears that some things may have been retrieved from the office before we seized it. Apparently, she also had some kind of chair suitable for working on a patient. But she doesn't have access to what a modern dental suite would have, of course."

Andre added, "If you want dental work without Novocain, Elaine is your go-to dentist."

"And to be clear, Chief, the invite says 'new' patients can go to the compound without calling ahead? Am I reading this right?"

"That's how it reads, Marshal," Andre replied.

"Amazing. This is what I've been telling HQ. Everyone else just drives up the driveway," Monier said.

A word is in order here about "driving up the driveway." Marshal Monier used this phrase often when meeting with his leadership team and when conversing with the senior leadership at USMS HQ.

His point was to emphasize that Chief Gary DiMartino's Trojan Horse strategy developed early on would be the most effective way of arresting the Browns with the least risk possible to everyone involved. That is, an arrest from *inside* the compound, by people invited to be *on the compound.*

That did not mean that strangers were never challenged if they drove up the driveway and that they weren't taking a risk by doing so. In some manner, most strangers were challenged when they just showed up.

When Ed had supporters with him at the property, Ed would rely on one of the supporters to approach a vehicle before they got to the house. More often than not, these supporters were armed. This was the case with each of the concerts that had been held at the property. Ed's supporters would greet each vehicle at the bottom of the driveway before they were directed to head up to the compound.

If Ed and Elaine were alone on the property, Zoe, the German Shephard, would alert the Browns to the approach of a vehicle (or other event undetectable to her human companions), and Ed would come out onto the front porch to see who was approaching.

When this happened, he was always armed, either with the .45 semi-auto pistol tucked into his waistband or with a long rifle (usually an AK-47 or SKS rifle) or with both. Sometimes, when Ed Brown challenged people, he would tell them to stay where they were and to lift up a jacket or overshirt and to turn around to demonstrate (visually) that they didn't have a weapon on them.

These facts were the reason that Monier would say to members of the media wanting to interview Ed and Elaine at the compound, "Look, the Browns are allowing the media—for the most part—onto their property. Mainly because Ed likes to talk. But that doesn't mean that going there is without risk. Be aware that law enforcement can't protect you while you're on the property. And under no circumstances should you send a reporter there alone."

This was the standard admonition he gave to the legacy, mainstream, even the "alt-media" when asked about interviewing the Browns. Most listened to the advice the USMS gave them. Some didn't. Fortunately, during the nine-month standoff, none were injured or, worse, taken hostage.

In early to mid-August, Ed continued to make contingent threats against law enforcement. In statements on his internet radio show and to media, he threatened to kill Sullivan County Sheriff Michael Prozzo and Plainfield Chief of Police Gordon Gillens.

He was displeased that the local and county law enforcement CEOs were cooperating with state and federal law enforcement in protecting the greater Plainfield communities and working with the U.S. Marshals Service.

During this time, Ed, along with some of his supporters, made frequent reference to the "list" of people who would be targeted should the Browns be arrested. This "list," Ed boasted, had the names of fifty people on it. "Should Elaine and I be arrested or killed by government agents," he would say, "there are people who have this list and are ready to go, to act on this list."

This was so troublesome to Sullivan County Attorney Marc Hathaway that his office issued a press release on August 10, 2007, which read:

The Sullivan County Sheriff's Office, the Plainfield Police Department, and the Sullivan County Attorney's Office are disappointed that Edward Brown has, by his recent contingent threat to kill Sullivan County Sheriff Michael Prozzo and Plainfield Chief of Police Gordon Gillens, attempted to increase the tension arising from his continued refusal to obey the law.

The contingent threats by Edward Brown will not prevent the Sullivan County Sheriff's Office and the Plainfield Police Department from focusing on the safety and welfare of all the residents of Plainfield and the neighboring communities impacted by Edward and Elaine Brown's irresponsible behavior.

The contingent threats by Edward Brown will not prevent law enforcement from taking whatever action is appropriate with respect to Edward Brown and Elaine Brown. Likewise, the contingent threats by Edward Brown against local law enforcement officials have not altered law enforcement's commitment to have Edward and Elaine Brown taken into custody without injury to any member of the public, law enforcement or to Edward and Elaine Brown.

Law enforcement views Edward Brown's most recent threats as a continuation of his efforts to rally support to his failing cause.

Marshal Monier received a copy of the release when it was sent out to local and state media. The marshal was pleased that the Marshals Service oft-stated intention to take the Browns into custody "without injury to any member of the public, law enforcement or to Edward and Elaine Brown" was repeated in the release from the county attorney.

On Saturday, August 18, 2007, a USMS confidential informant (CI) reported that James Hobbs, aka "Old Buck," had left the Browns' compound. Old Buck, the CI said, was increasingly concerned that Ed was more despondent and was talking about "ending it." Old Buck left during the night. On Monday, the 20th, USMS air surveillance confirmed that Hobbs' RV was no longer parked on the compound.

During this same timeframe, Deputy U.S. Marshal (DUSM) Jamie Berry was tracking reports that a militia group from North Carolina may be preparing to send some members to Plainfield to support the Browns. This was reported to the Southeast Regional Task Force and HQ to gather more information on any movements north, should they occur.

He and Chief Inspector Andre LaBier were also putting reports together for Assistant U.S. Attorneys Bob Kinsella and Arnie Huftalen on at least four targeted individuals who were most involved with the Browns in a conspiracy to obstruct justice. They were also meeting with them regularly to prepare criminal indictments.

To this end, subpoenas were prepared and served on local businesses, such as the Lebanon Home Depot, and on delivery services, for their records related to purchases and deliveries to the Browns' property. The Home Depot was a frequent stop for Jason Gerhard, Reno Gonzalez, Dan "the Dog Walker" Riley, and Robert Wolffe. Some of the purchases showed that they were picking up electrical components, pipe fittings, and other materials suitable for making IEDs or adding extra security components to the Browns' house and outbuildings.

Robert Wolffe had also been identified as the individual to whom people could send supplies based on the list of "needed items" that Ed had posted on his Myspace page. Wolffe would collect the donated materials at his Vermont mailing address and bring them to the Browns.

On a couple of occasions, Wolffe was also conducting counter-surveillance on Chief Dimmitt's and Ken Nunes' teams in the Plainfield area and was suspected in the tampering of the cameras that had been placed in the woods across from the driveway entrance to the Browns' property.

The investigative team was considering possible charges on Old Buck as well, but his forays into town and/or Lebanon often had more to do with picking up groceries than bomb-making materials, as evidenced by his blog posting of August 11, 2007:

> Today, I went into town to pick up some groceries. My supply
> was running low. Ed and Elaine being the generous people that
> they are have offered me anything I need but I do not want to
> take from their provisions so I supply all my own food, coffee
> etc. After being here 6 weeks, I had a lot to pick up. Elaine used
> my computer to go on the net and reviewed the local grocery
> stores [sic] sales brochures. So I left here with a list (She says I
> should only shop with a list, that way I don't get sucked into
> overspending) but she had me going to 3 different grocery
> stores with all the sales prices written down and what store I
> should buy this or that in. I left with my head spinning but
> promised I would be thrifty and follow her directions.

This was also the day that Wolffe was doing counter-surveillance on
the deputies who were tracking Old Buck as he left the compound for
this trip. Wolffe ended up filming the deputies at one point, and he and
Old Buck conversed by cell phone on the presence of the deputy U.S.
marshals.

While in one store, Wolffe "tells Hobbs to go out a side entrance
and he would pick him up." Wolffe then took Old Buck to another
store, walked back to the first store, and got in Old Buck's vehicle in an
attempt to have the deputies follow him.

In the same posting about his trip to the grocery stores, Old Buck
posted that the Marshals had "no idea where he is now, as they are
following Wolffe in his vehicle." Toward the end of his very long post
about this trip to Lebanon for groceries, he wrote, "This was more fun
than I have had in years we had them agents going in circle(s)…"

Little did he know that the deputies had figured out what he and
Wolffe were up to and knew where they both were. After some more cat
and mouse, Wolffe and Hobbs met back at the Browns' compound

with the groceries.

After reviewing the evidence that Chief Andre LaBier had accumulated, organized, and presented in a concise format to the U.S. Attorney's Office, the decision was made to first move forward with a secret indictment against Jason Gerhard. His purchases of semi-automatic rifles and ammunition, including a .50-caliber rifle, which he brought to the Browns', made his indictment a priority.

The Marshals had also received information that he was planning to enter the U.S. Army as a recruit. Gerhard was indicted on August 8, 2007.

Assistant U.S. Attorneys (AUSAs) Bob Kinsella and Arnie Huftalen were preparing complaints on Daniel "the Dog Walker" Riley and Reno Gonzalez as well. They were also looking at the evidence on the activities of Robert Wolffe, James "Old Buck" Hobbs, "Free Stater" Rob Jacobs, William "Bill" Miller, and perhaps one or two others.

Bill Miller, who had issued the January 13th online threat against the judge, the U.S. attorney, and the prosecutor who handled the tax trial, left the Browns' property in early February and developed his own difficulties with the Farmington Police Department not long after. After that, Miller had not been involved to any significant degree with Ed Brown, but for an occasional statement or posting about Ed Brown's activities.

In one email sent on or about August 20, 2007, Bill Miller wrote: "Brown has ignored, on many occasions throughout the years, the good council [sic] of some valiant, focused, hard-working freedom fighters whom, unfortunately, exemplify a larger spiritual vision, and a more finely tuned sense of balance and reason than does Brown."

Given that Miller ended the relationship with the Browns early on in the armed standoff, and lacking other sufficient evidence to show a continuing conspiracy to aid and abet the Browns, the AUSAs, with input from the USMS, decided not to pursue charges against Bill Miller.

They were still weighing the information about Old Buck, since he lived in his RV on the Browns' property for a good period of time, ran errands for them, and was observed on several occasions doing "security work" on the compound.

The errands usually involved shopping trips to Lebanon for household and food supplies, and the "security work" involved checking people coming on to the property for the concerts or other events. Hobbs, too, decided that Ed was becoming unstable and left the property during the night of August 18th, thus removing himself from further involvement with the Browns.

Robert Wolffe, however, had been a U.S. Constitution Ranger with Ed for several years and had been making frequent trips from Vermont to the compound since the beginning of the armed standoff. He became the conduit for supporters to send many of the "supplies" Brown was requesting on his Myspace page. Wolffe offered his Randolph, Vermont, address as the site of the "Liberty Defense Project" and said he would deliver any mailings to the Browns.

In this role, he brought the Browns camouflage outfits, fishing weights, fishing line, flashlights, solar-powered security lights, and more than 500 pounds of dehydrated food, among other things.

When interviewed during the June attempt to arrest Ed Brown at the mailbox, Daniel "the Dog Walker" Riley of Cohoes, New York, had given the USMS and another governmental agency (OGA) detailed information about the Browns. He described the weapons at the compound and the explosive devices, what they looked like and where they were. He described the rifles, the handguns, and the two black powder devices in the house that could be used as "grenades."

He also told the USMS and OGA team there were ten to twenty other similar black powder devices on the property and that he had brought a number of supplies to the house that Ed had requested. This included a .50-caliber rifle and twenty-five fire extinguishers. Riley had also ordered twelve pounds of Tannerite, a chemical agent for explosive devices.

When he was released to go back to the Browns' late that June afternoon, he had agreed to cooperate with the Marshals in trying to resolve the armed standoff. Of course, that promise evaporated after about twenty-five yards into the Browns' driveway on the way to the house.

From that point on, Riley continued to actively engage in aiding and supporting the Browns. He would travel back and forth to the compound from New York and would often stay at the compound. He ran errands for them and did armed patrols of the cleared acreage around the house. He brought them weapons. Not long after the Marshals Service had the utility company cut the power to the compound, Riley, an electrician by trade, climbed the utility pole at the end of the Browns' driveway and turned the power back on.

The Marshals knew this right away, of course, but opted to "pretend" that they didn't. Their foremost consideration in doing so was that they didn't want to further endanger the line workers from the utility company by having them go back up near the driveway to cut power again and possibly be engaged by an armed Brown supporter. When the linemen had cut the street power to the property, deputy marshals provided overwatch for them.

For all of Ed Brown's talk about the "ability to live off the grid," he knew that relying on stored solar battery power at night and relying on whether there was wind or not was not all it was cracked up to be. So, Riley the "Dog Walker" was tasked with heading to the end of the driveway, climbing the pole, and restoring the utility company's transmitted power.

Zoe, the dog, stayed home. Smart dog.

Moreover, as to electric power from the street, the Marshals weren't all that concerned that it had been restored. The strategy wasn't to lay "siege" to the compound. The strategy was to conduct another ruse to arrest the Browns from the "inside out."

The landlines for the phones were never restored, but people brought cell phones for the Browns to use, and the Browns had wireless access to the internet. There were many public comments urging the Marshals Service to deny them access to the internet.

But, as previously stated, the ability to monitor the websites, Ed's daily internet radio show, blog postings, and emails provided invaluable information in real time on what was occurring at the compound each day.

At the end of August, the district made a request of HQ to deploy a six-person SOG team (a team leader + five) to the district so that they would be quickly available to the New Hampshire Marshals. They also asked that the USMS aircraft be sent to the district. Things were progressing with a possible opportunity to introduce an undercover operative to the Browns'.

The district leadership believed that when the next opportunity to arrest the Browns developed, it must be "lean and mean." They learned from the June attempt to arrest Ed Brown at the mailbox that too many people, and too many agencies, had been brought into the planning process. This led to "leaks." Though the leaks were inadvertent and not intentional, it still could have seriously compromised the operation.

Having a SOG team immediately available, without involving too many agencies, would be beneficial, the district leadership team argued. HQ approved the request.

Chief DiMartino got word that another Freedom Fest was planned for Saturday, September 15, 2007. The invitations were going out over the various internet webpages that focused on the Browns. On Sunday, September 9th, the *Keene Free Press* ran a story titled "Party/Fundraiser at Ed and Elaine Brown's 9/15." It read:

Ed and Elaine Brown invite everyone to their home on Saturday September 15, 2007 from noon till 10 pm for a celebration of freedom. It will include the talents of David VonKleist playing his hit music "Show Me the Law." Pokerface will also be entertaining the crowd. There will be food and drink along with games: horse shoes, bocce ball and others. They ask if you could bring some food items of your own. There will be a grill for cooking. Camping on the grounds will be permitted, RV and trailers are welcome. Come and enjoy the only government-free zone in the US!

In a postscript to the article, the address on Center of Town Road, Plainfield, New Hampshire, was provided, along with this: "*Follow the trail of police cars and helicopters buzzing overhead,*" an apparent attempt at humor and a reference to the last concert.

Meanwhile, on August 22, 2007, the five SOG team members from the Regional Fugitive Task Force arrived at the District of New Hampshire's office. Chief Inspector Dave Dimmitt and District Deputy Marshals Ken Nunes and Steve Bartlett briefed them in the training room.

As an experienced member of the Special Operations Group (SOG), District Deputy U.S. Marshal Steve Bartlett would serve as the team leader during their deployment to New Hampshire.

In their briefing packets, SOG team members learned the layout of the compound and reviewed the strategy for making the arrests. Deputies Ken Nunes and Steve Bartlett discussed the best method for conducting covert surveillance and the entry points to the property.

Deputy Marshal Steve Bartlett was "almost" a New Hampshire native. His family moved to the state when he was six years old. After graduating high school, Steve attended St. Anselm College in Goffstown, New Hampshire, from 1974 to 1978, where he majored in Criminal Justice. Following graduation, he worked for a time at the Youth Development Center in Manchester, New Hampshire.

When an opportunity arose to work for the U.S. Marshals Service as a contract employee in the District of New Hampshire, he took it. He transitioned to a full-time deputy U.S. marshal position and graduated from the USMS Academy in 1984.

The Marshals Service sent him to the Southern District of New York for his first assignment. It was there that he met Gary DiMartino for the first time. Gary was also working in New York in the Southern District.

Bartlett worked in New York for approximately three years, when he got a notice to report to the Denver, Colorado, district office, where he spent another three years. That's when an opportunity arose to move back to the District of New Hampshire in 1992.

"The marshal in New Hampshire called me and asked if I wanted to come back home. Of course, I said yes," Steve said. By then, he was also an experienced member of the Special Operations Group (SOG). He applied to SOG when he was still working in New York, was accepted, and went to the March 1985 SOG class. It was as a SOG team member that he met Billy Degan.

As the team leader for the SOG team brought in to assist the District of New Hampshire with rapidly developing situations, Steve Bartlett and the team members settled in to closely monitor events with district leadership, assist in covert surveillance, and be prepared to deploy to support the planned arrests and transport of the Browns from the compound.

The U.S. Marshals Service does not *per se* have trained deputy U.S. marshals to conduct undercover work. The FBI, the DEA, the ATF, and one or two other governmental law enforcement agencies do train select personnel for undercover operations, given their particular missions. The Marshals Service does not, and its mission doesn't usually require it.

The USMS enforces court orders, plans arrests, engages in

subterfuge to make arrests of fugitives, and as noted earlier in this book plans a ruse or arrest scenario in high-risk or other unusual circumstances so as to minimize the risk to the law enforcement officers involved, the targeted fugitives, and/or any civilians in the area. They also cultivate and work with confidential informants and other operatives.

The issue was how could the USMS get someone inside the Browns' with the training and skillset necessary to gain their confidence and bring in a team of deputies posing as supporters? The USMS had confidential source(s) visiting with the Browns, as did other federal law enforcement agencies in New Hampshire. They were providing important information back to the Marshals, but they were not trained operatives, and none were appropriate for what needed to be done.

Both USMS HQ personnel and district leadership had reached out to two other governmental agencies to see if they had the availability of an undercover agent who could insert themselves into the Browns' compound.

On August 31, 2007, U.S. Marshal Steve Monier and Chiefs DiMartino and Dimmitt met in Boston with the regional office of another governmental agency (OGA) for this request: "Can you assign one of your undercover operatives/agents to us to visit with the Browns, gain their confidence, and bring a team of deputies in to make the arrest?"

The U.S. Marshals Service HQ leadership team did the same from their end to the HQ of this OGA. They listened. They were polite. They understood the request, and they knew of the Ed and Elaine Brown case from the intense media coverage of the armed standoff. At the end of the Boston meeting, they told the marshal and the chiefs they would get back to them within a few days.

As the marshal and the chiefs headed back to New Hampshire, the marshal asked both Chief DiMartino and Chief Dimmitt a rhetorical question. "I don't have any sense that this agency has any desire to get involved in this case, do you?"

Both chiefs felt the agency's answer to the request would be "no."

On Monday morning, August 27, 2007, U.S. Marshal Steve Monier boarded a plane and headed to the USMS HQ in Washington, D.C. A meeting was scheduled for three p.m. with the director of the USMS and senior staff about the planning for the Browns' arrest from the "inside out," along with contingency planning for a Special Operations Group plan should the Trojan Horse strategy fail.

Marshal Monier's meeting with the director was also to prepare for a briefing at the main Department of Justice office in Washington, D.C., scheduled for the following morning, with the deputy attorney general (DAG) and senior members of his staff.

Main Justice was closely following the armed standoff with Ed and Elaine Brown (as the call directly to Marshal Monier the previous month had informed him).

People at Main Justice were concerned. The memories of Ruby Ridge, Waco, and the fallout from both—including the bombing of the Alfred P. Murrah building in Oklahoma City—were fresh on the minds of the leadership at Main Justice. They *did not want* a repeat of *any* of that.

The deputy attorney general's office had called the director of the Marshals Service and told him, "The DAG wants a briefing; please be here at the prescribed hour on the morning of Tuesday, August 28th." Hence, the call to Marshal Monier to report to HQ on the 27th to meet with the director and staff to prepare for, and then attend, the briefing on the 28th with the DAG.

The "big boss" of the heads of the law enforcement agencies in the U.S. Department of Justice is the Attorney General of the United States, who, of course, reports to and serves at the pleasure of the chief executive of the U.S. government, the President of the United States. Thus, the directors of the FBI, the DEA, the ATF, and the U.S. Marshals Service are answerable to the attorney general.

In terms of the chain of command, however, their *immediate report* is to the Deputy Attorney General of the United States, or the DAG. The DAG reports to the attorney general.

At the Monday afternoon meeting with the director of the Marshals Service, the deputy director, and senior staff, including the chief of staff, Commander of the Special Operations Group David Robertson, Chief Inspector Billy Sorukas, Assistant Director Mike Earp, and other senior members, Marshal Monier gave a brief summary of the Ed and Elaine Brown case to date.

He concluded with his belief—and that of the district leadership—that the best way forward to safely arrest the Browns was the Trojan Horse strategy from the inside out. He also said, "If we find the right confidential operative to be invited into the Browns' compound, then that person can invite a team of deputy U.S. marshals in posing as supporters."

Monier acknowledged that they had not yet identified that person but repeated his oft quoted admonition that "we need to drive up the driveway, everyone else does." He reported that they had spoken with and met with other governmental agencies about using one of their undercover agents for this purpose.

One agency had already said no, but they had not heard back yet from the other. He noted, however, that he did not have the sense this agency was willing to participate, either.

SOG Commander Robertson outlined a four-phase tactical plan to arrest Ed and Elaine should SOG be needed. It would include moving team members into place when Ed and Elaine were alone on the property, shutting down access, and moving armored vehicles into place to negotiate their surrender. Depending on the time of the operation, this could involve as many as forty to sixty people from the Marshals Service.

The director ended the briefing by noting that the USMS needed to be slow and methodical with their approach but that they also needed to be mindful of the Department of Justice's concerns about this prolonged armed standoff. "We need to keep pursuing good intelligence, including being careful about how this case is discussed in emails." He asked everyone to keep it general.

For the meeting the next day, he said that they would have about ten to fifteen minutes to talk about their approaches to this case and their developing plans about a ruse and their tactical options. Then there would be eight to ten minutes for a Q&A with the DAG and his staff.

The marshal asked the director if he was willing to give the undercover operative route, the Trojan Horse strategy, a chance with SOG support there. The director said yes. "I do want to give the undercovers/the ruse a chance," he said. "I think this is the best way to reduce the risk to everyone involved, but I also understand that this might not be possible.

"One thing you should all know," the director continued, "the deputy attorney general has expressed some urgency and concern over letting concerts go on at the Browns'. But he also doesn't want to 'make heroes out of the Browns' by having an outcome that leads to loss of life. I told the DAG that I agreed with that."

At nine thirty a.m., on August 28th, Marshal Monier entered a government SUV with the director and deputy director. They were followed in a second SUV occupied by Chief Inspector Billy Sorukas and Assistant Director Earp and others, along with the director's security detail in a third vehicle. The convoy made the short trip from the U.S. Marshals HQ to the main Department of Justice office.

At ten a.m., the Marshals Service personnel met in a large conference room with the deputy attorney general and members of his senior staff, including the chief of staff and Frank Shultz, also from the DAG's office. Also in the room was a marshal from the U.S. Supreme Court Police. Additionally, linked by secure video, was U.S. Attorney Tom Colantuono, his intel analyst Tim Hanes, and a senior member of the

Criminal Division in the District of New Hampshire, Assistant U.S. Attorney Bob Veiga.

The marshal was surprised that a Supreme Court marshal was in the room and that three people from the New Hampshire District Office of the U.S. Attorney's Office had joined in the meeting via video link. This had not been discussed at the meeting yesterday at USMS. It appeared that it was a surprise to the director and deputy director as well. It had been agreed at the briefing that the current operational plan to insert an undercover operative into the Browns' compound was a "close hold" and not to be shared widely in the Marshals Service or beyond the group at the district office with the need to know.

The meeting opened with the director giving a brief general update on the Brown armed standoff and what the strategy was moving forward, i.e., to conduct a successful ruse to arrest them safely. He mentioned that the Special Operations Group (SOG) had developed a plan should that fail.

A Q&A followed. The DAG asked why people were going onto the property, particularly to attend concerts and supply the Browns with additional supplies. The response was that completely shutting the property down up to this point was counter-productive, given that confidential informants were also going in and out and supplying the Marshals with valuable intelligence.

Director Clark discussed that the USMS, working with the U.S. Attorney's Office, had worked out an order for the court to sign under the All Writs Act. Judge McAuliffe had signed it, and it gave the USMS the authority to shut down access when and where needed.

The DAG seemed satisfied with the discussion and gave three broad admonitions:

- Don't turn Ed and Elaine into heroes; don't do anything that will create a bigger problem, e.g., with militias.

- Don't engage in a rash action that will cause additional problems.
- And don't take an action simply because we here at Main Justice are overly concerned about this standoff. Do what's best.

U.S. Attorney Tom Colantuono brought up the issue of undercover agents going into the compound and mentioned the intel the local offices of the ATF, the FBI, and his office were also supplying to the Marshals Service.

The USMS leadership team felt constrained in the meeting to discuss further any details about getting an undercover operative into the compound due to the additional people who were brought into this meeting. None of them were expecting such a large group of people to participate.

For operational security purposes, the USMS wanted to keep the detailed planning process to as few people as possible, having learned that the operation in June to arrest Ed at the mailbox had involved too many agencies and too many people.

The DAG, once the undercover was mentioned, said, "Don't lose the opportunity to get someone inside."

"With that, the meeting ended, and people filed out and the video link with the USA's office in New Hampshire ended. The director and I spoke briefly with Frank Shultz as the DAG and other members of his staff left," Monier reported.

The director said, "We wanted to give the DAG some more information about an undercover going in, but there were some unexpected guests invited to this briefing."

Frank said, "Well, let's catch up to them and have a quick aside with them."

They rushed out of the room and caught up with the DAG's chief of staff and an assistant DAG as they were returning to their offices.

The director told them that they had some more to tell the DAG about the current plan. The assistant deputy attorney general snippily told the director, "Well, then the whole meeting was a waste of time."

The director looked at this person, spoke confidently, and said, "No it wasn't," and explained why. "There were people in that room, in particular, that did not have a need to know of the more specific plans we were working on. Operational security keeps law enforcement officers from getting killed."

The assistant didn't say any more, and the director quickly briefed the chief of staff on the more detailed planning going into getting an undercover inside. The chief of staff said he would call the director in a bit to get some more information and would meet with the DAG about it in private.

With that, the convoy headed back to USMS HQ. Marshal Monier spoke a bit more with the deputy director of the USMS at HQ, then left to board a plane for the return flight to New Hampshire.

While the marshal was in D.C. for two days, the district office troops were busy. Upon the marshal's return to the district office, the team briefed him on several important developments.

Chief Inspector Andre LaBier told him that they had executed a search warrant on Wolffe's computer hard drive(s), and they had served a "ton of search warrants and subpoenas" on phone and emails connected with the principal supporters for the Browns."

Andre learned that Shaun Kranish from Illinois, who was running the webpage *Make the Stand* for Ed and who had visited the Browns on a couple of occasions, had set up a physical mail drop to help the Browns. Andre had a subpoena out to PayPal for information about this.

Chief DiMartino and Chief Dimmitt told the marshal that a lieutenant from New Jersey working with the regional fugitive task force had reached out to Chief Dimmitt and that Gary DiMartino was given the name of an undercover operative by the name of "Dutch" who had been talking with Shaun Kranish online. The indication was that this operative may have the skillset and experience necessary to go into the Browns' compound. More work to completely vet Dutch was needed, both chiefs told the marshal.

In the interim, the district was also concerned that, where probable cause existed to do so, the timeline for arresting the supporters of the Browns may need to be moved up. Jason Gerhard had already been secretly indicted. He was now in basic training with the U.S. Army at Ft. Leonard Wood in Missouri. Everyone was concerned about this.

Gerhard had told the army that he wanted his career path to be in combat engineering and explosives. This was the same career path Timothy McVeigh followed after he did his basic training at Ft. Leonard Wood.

The staff was also concerned about the upcoming September 15th Freedom Concert at the Browns'. While the various agencies with confidential informants were planning to have their CIs attend, it was concerning that it was more of an opportunity for people to lend the Browns additional moral support and bring supplies to them. The DAG had mentioned his concern about this in his briefing with the director and senior staff from the Marshals Service.

More importantly, the wide online live broadcast of yet another concert at the Browns' would only give them an even broader national audience to spout their nonsense about the income tax laws and the federal government.

Marshal Monier circled this in the notes he was taking during the meeting. It was an excellent point and needed to be explored further.

It was time, he thought to himself, to send a very strong message to the Browns' supporters.

CHAPTER 13
THE SEPTEMBER 12TH ARRESTS

On September 6, 2007, in a conference call with Assistant Director Art Roderick, Chiefs Dimmitt, LaBier, and DiMartino and Marshal Monier outlined why the USMS needed to move forward now with the arrests of Jason Gerhard (now in basic training at Ft. Leonard Wood), Cirino "Reno" Gonzalez of Texas, Daniel Riley of New York, and Robert Wolffe of Vermont.

Originally, the district had planned to arrest supporters who had aided and abetted the Browns after the Browns were in custody. "But recent events require us to move forward now," district leadership told Roderick. "We have confirmed that Jason Gerhard joined the army and is stationed at Ft. Leonard Wood in Missouri for basic training. All concur that, given his recent (sealed) indictment, and his volatility, he can't be left there."

Moreover, "Reno Gonzalez is the subject of a Joint Terrorism Task Force (JTTF) investigation in Texas and reportedly had plans to go to, or has been at, Camp Casey and may join the movement," district leadership told Roderick. (Camp Casey was the name given to the encampment of anti-war protesters established outside the Prairie Chapel

Ranch in Crawford, Texas, during U.S. President George W. Bush's five-week summer vacation there in 2005.)[i]

"In all probability, he is still in possession of a .50-caliber rifle," Chief LaBier said. "He, too, is a volatile individual and should not be left on the streets. Riley and Wolffe are continuing to supply and assist the Browns on a regular basis, and we need to stop the flow of such supplies into the Browns' compound. This will help do that."

The marshal added, "I've been saying all along in my statements to the media that people actively engaged in supporting the Browns in their obstruction of justice are subject to arrest and prosecution. This will send the strong message that we're serious about that."

The U.S. Attorney's Office was on board with serving the warrants for the arrests of these four individuals at a date and time to be determined by the USMS.

Roderick agreed with the rationale to move forward and said he would meet with Assistant Director Mike Earp and the director to get the green light. Toward the end of the meeting, and given the need to move forward, everyone also agreed that once the arrests occurred:

1. They needed to set up a checkpoint system to control access to the Browns', pursuant to the authority given them in the recent court order.
2. The checkpoints would be random and on a rolling basis, not a complete shutdown, utilizing existing personnel already in New Hampshire from the Regional Task Force, SOG, and district, in coordination with local and state law enforcement partners. (On a random basis, the district would still be able to have a confidential operative go into the property.)
3. Should circumstances arise which would require it, they would need to be prepared to shut everything down

completely; planning for this would be coordinated with the SOG commander.

4. They would coordinate the arrests and any follow-up investigation(s) with the districts where the targets were located.

5. They would coordinate the charges, indictments, search warrants, appearances, and bail questions with the U.S. Attorney's Office.

USM Monier and AD Roderick also agreed that it would be helpful to move forward with bringing additional charges against the Browns, to include the obstruction, their conspiracy with others for the obstruction, threats, and any weapons charges. Chief Andre LaBier would coordinate this possibility with the U.S. Attorney's Office.

The meeting participants agreed that should circumstances require the USMS to completely seal off the Browns' property, the additional charges should set forth how the Browns, *by their actions*, had elevated this from a tax case. Everyone concurred that the Browns continued to engage in activity that violated the rule of law, they had resisted efforts to end this the right way, they continued to arm themselves and make threats, and they continued to encourage others to engage in a conspiracy to obstruct justice, all while the USMS had been thoughtful, deliberate, and methodical in its approach.

Any such action to completely seal off the Browns' property would be necessary to protect the community and bring this lengthy armed standoff to a conclusion.

With that, the team at the district office jumped into planning the arrests. The chiefs and marshal determined that these arrests should take place on the same day for the greatest impact. This would involve a lot of planning for each arrest, as it would involve coordination with each of the Marshal Service district offices where the targets lived or were currently located.

Chiefs DiMartino and Dimmitt worked on coordinating this. Chief LaBier worked with the U.S. Attorney's Office to get search warrants to go with the arrest warrants.

At HQ, Assistant Director Art Roderick phoned the marshal and told him that Chief Billy Sorukas was working to bring three to four deputies from the Southeast Regional Fugitive Task Force in to assist with the undercover operation. Art Roderick told the marshal that SOG was also working on plans to support that operation. SOG discussed a team in the woods for surveillance.

"I'm not keen on having our people in the woods. It's too big a risk," Monier told Art. "The Browns still have Zoe the dog, and she's already demonstrated her ability to alert to the presence of even heavily camouflaged deputies in the woods. I think it would be better to have them equipped and ready to go in an armored SUV, hidden somewhere nearby to the Browns' compound." Art Roderick agreed with this.

As to the undercover operative, Chief Gary DiMartino had already spoken on the phone once with Dutch in the late afternoon on August 29th. DiMartino told the marshal that Dutch fit the bill as an experienced undercover operative who could insert himself into the Browns' property and had the "hook" to do that since Dutch was already communicating with Shaun Kranish over the internet. Gary told the marshal that Chief Dave Dimmitt was working with the Southeast Regional Fugitive Task Force to begin vetting him, since he was from that area.

"If Dutch clears the vetting process, Marshal," Gary said, "this guy looks very promising. He's a big guy and has a special forces background. We should know soon."

This was important since they still hadn't heard back from the Boston office of an OGA on using one of their undercover operatives. The marshal was convinced that when they did that, the answer would be no. (HQ confirmed this on or about September 10th. The OGA declined to devote one of their undercover agents to this planned operation.)

By Friday, September 7, 2007, plans were continuing for the four arrests. Chiefs Gary DiMartino and Dimmitt were reaching out to their counterparts in the districts where each arrest would occur. Since both Wolffe and Riley were within driving distance from the District of New Hampshire, it was decided they could both be brought directly back to New Hampshire for their arraignments.

Chief Andre LaBier was working with the U.S. Attorney's Office on getting search warrants for Wolffe and Riley's homes, in Randolph, Vermont, and Cohoes, New York, respectively; for Gerhard's mother's home in Brookhaven, New York; and Gonzalez's father's mobile home in Alice, Texas.

The leadership team decided it would be beneficial to have deputies from the District of New Hampshire to directly participate in two of the arrests. Deputy U.S. Marshal (DUSM) Jamie Berry, who was a U.S. Army veteran, was assigned to travel to Ft. Leonard Wood, Missouri, to work with deputies from that district and with the military police for Gerhard's arrest.

DUSM Gene Robinson was assigned to travel to Alice, Texas, to work with deputies and local law enforcement there for the arrest of Reno Gonzalez. Chief Andre LaBier was going to closely monitor the arrests in the Districts of Vermont and New York where Wolffe and Riley were and be available to answer any questions that might come up with them. The same would be true of the search of Gerhard's room at his mother's home in Brookhaven, New York.

In what may have been a first for the U.S. Marshals Service, the USMS was the lead investigative agency for all of the criminal charges being brought against each of these four Brown supporters. The district, in consultation with HQ and the U.S. Attorney's Office, decided that the arrests would have the biggest impact on the Brown armed standoff, if all the arrests were coordinated to occur on the same day, at approximately the same time (given the time zones involved). This was a huge undertaking.

Wednesday morning, September 12, 2007

In a tightly coordinated effort, the U.S. Marshals Services executed arrest and search warrants on all four of the indicted individuals stemming from their activities to aid and abet the Browns and obstruct justice. Although there were some very tense moments during the arrests, each of the four takedowns were successful, and valuable evidence was recovered in the process.

With the concurrence of HQ and the U.S. Attorney's Office, and once word was received that all four were in custody, the district issued a press release that afternoon. It read:

ASSOCIATES OF NEW HAMPSHIRE TAX EVASION FELONS INDICTED BY GRAND JURY AND ARRESTED BY LAW ENFORCEMENT AUTHORITIES

Concord, New Hampshire – Today, teams of state, county, local and federal law enforcement officials, led by the U.S. Marshals Service, arrested four individuals on charges stemming from their association with convicted felons Edward and Elaine Brown of Plainfield, New Hampshire. The indictments were issued by a federal grand jury in Concord, New Hampshire, and made public today. The four arrests were made in different locales and were conducted without incident.

Cirino "Reno" Gonzalez, 30, of Alice, Texas; Daniel Riley, 40, of Albany, New York; Jason Gerhard, 22, of Brookhaven, New York; and Robert Wolffe, 50, of Randolph, Vermont, are now in U.S. Marshals custody, and face charges that range from

Accessory After the Fact (aiding and abetting) to Possession and Use of a Firearm in Relation to a Crime of Violence. The indictments allege that each of these men has helped obstruct justice in the Brown case. Officials believe that at certain times, the men participated in various efforts to assist the Browns in avoiding justice at their rural home in northwestern New Hampshire and conspired to impede federal agents.

U.S. Marshals conducted all four arrests in a manner consistent with this continuing operation since the Browns' sentencing five months ago. "We are acting with an abiding concern for the safety of surrounding communities, neighbors, and law enforcement officers," said U.S. Marshal for New Hampshire, Stephen Monier.

The arrest of Gonzalez occurred in Alice, Texas; Riley was arrested in Cohoes, New York; Gerhard was arrested at Ft. Leonard Wood, Missouri; and Wolffe was arrested in Hartford, Vermont.

The Marshals Service made clear that it is a crime to aid and abet convicted felons who are avoiding justice. "In this case, these men are alleged to have helped the Browns in their ongoing refusal to surrender to authorities," said Marshal Monier. "The Browns have engaged in a course of conduct that has led to further criminal investigations into their activity. Anyone who aids the Browns is subject to investigation, arrest, and prosecution for serious felonies, which carry very heavy prison sentences."

"This was a tax case," Monier added, "but over the last seven months, the Browns have allegedly: obstructed justice and encouraged others to assist them. Ed Brown has threatened to kill law enforcement officers and other governmental officials. So our message to the Browns is clear: do the right thing, call us, and surrender peacefully."

The U.S. Marshals and their law enforcement partners have taken purposeful and methodical steps to convince the Browns to surrender. In June, utility access and deliveries to their property were cut off.

The Marshals will continue to assist local authorities by exercising the authority to control access to the property. "We will work with our law enforcement partners to ensure these efforts are conducted in a safe manner, and with minimal intrusion to the Plainfield community," said Marshal Monier.

As Chief DiMartino later explained it, "Chief Andre LaBier and I coordinated most of the four arrests with the other districts, Andre from the investigative case and evidence side, and me from the operations side working with each district management team for the support and resources necessary to safely make the arrests."

"All the districts were great," he reported. "I believe Assistant U.S. Attorney Bob Kinsella was hooked up with Andre on the evidence side for any on site issues relating to evidence collection."

Chief DiMartino continued, "This was a big deal, and I don't recall the USMS ever taking the lead on the investigation into significant charges and coordinating the effort of four nationwide hits like this at one time. I remember talking to district management for assistance and the resources needed. All of them were surprised we were the lead agency on the criminal investigation into such major cases. We weren't just hitting locations executing arrest warrants like we usually do!"

DiMartino recalled, "I remember advising some about the situation, but most everyone had at least heard about our armed standoff, and many had sent support to us. I asked that each district ensure that ATF be onboard, due to the possibility of explosives; and again, most initially thought ATF was the lead agency on the gun charges, and I'm like NO, the USMS is.... We got this!

"For Reno [Gonzalez]," DiMartino continued, "a chief deputy U.S.

marshal that Dave Dimmitt and I knew well and worked with was great helping out. After we spoke, the chief hooked me up with one of their supervisors who coordinated on their end and assisted our deputy, Gene Robinson," Chief DiMartino said.

He added, "As I recall, Alice, Texas, was near Corpus Christi, which was this chief's district. But the supervisor that was our POC, I seem to remember, told me that Alice, Texas, actually sat in the adjoining district. Nevertheless, they said they would take the lead on this for us. Everyone was working hard to get this done!

"For Jason Gerhard, who was in basic training at Ft. Leonard Wood," Chief DiMartino said, "I reached out to another great friend of Dave Dimmitt and me, Chief Deputy Tony Gasaway. Tony was in our SOG class, and we were instructors at the academy together. Tony was also surprised about our lead overall on the case and assigned one of his supervisors to coordinate the assistance on their end. Ft. Leonard Wood was in their district. Although our deputy, Jamie Berry, did a bang-up job, he was still relatively new to the USMS. So having one of their supervisory deputy U.S. marshals there was a good thing," Gary recalled.

DiMartino continued, "In Albany for Danny 'the Dog Walker' Riley, I remember talking to a senior supervisory deputy and asking again to include ATF for explosives, and same deal there; the question was the USMS is the lead investigative agency?? YES, I said. Moreover, I remember after the arrests went down, the chief there briefed me. It was at Riley's home we found a rifle that had been at the Browns', because it was *signed by both Randy Weaver and Ed Brown*. It was seized, along with other weapons."[ii]

Chief DiMartino also reported, "I don't remember too much about the Wolffe takedown. I talked to the district, but again, I think Andre being from Vermont worked on a lot of that."

Gary DiMartino added, "The overriding message from this major op was the coordination and exceptional support provided by ALL of the districts where the arrests occurred. This was crucial to success and the way the USMS has done business over the years."

The deputies involved in two of the arrests were able to add more detail about two of the more tense moments during these operations.

Deputy U.S. Marshal Jamie Berry from the District of New Hampshire was assigned to travel to Ft. Leonard Wood, in Pulaski County, Missouri. There he met up with the supervisor Chief Deputy Tony Gasaway had assigned to work on the arrest of Jason Gerhard. Gerhard was in army basic training at Ft. Leonard Wood. The team then met up with the Judge Advocate General's Office and the military police to safely affect Gerhard's arrest.

Deputy Jamie Berry is a native of New Hampshire. Following his graduation from high school in 1993, he joined the U.S. Army and served ten years as a military police officer and investigator. He attained the rank of sergeant and transitioned to the USMS following his honorable discharge from the army. Jamie was recruited to the District of New Hampshire following his graduation from the basic USMS Academy. An IT expert, Jamie was an innovator and helped develop essential tools and templates for the Marshal Services' use nationwide. He would go on to serve as the assistant chief of data governance at the USMS. His knowledge of the U.S. Army and his experience as a military police officer and investigator made him the best person to be on the team to arrest Gerhard at Ft. Leonard Wood.

Deputy Jamie Berry later said, "When I arrived in the district where Ft. Leonard Wood was located, we went to the Criminal Investigative Division (CID) office on the army post. The district had a good relationship with the military law enforcement people. The drill instructor [DI] for the platoon Gerhard was in was brought into the loop for his arrest, so that we could coordinate where Gerhard would be.

"When we arrived at Gerhard's barracks," Jamie continued, "the DI had it set up beautifully. The privates were on their knees facing away from the entrance, and Gerhard had his back to the door we entered.

NO ONE HAS TO DIE

They were all folding army-green blankets with their feet crossed, so Gerhard didn't see us approaching him."

Deputy Jamie Berry explained what happened next. "When I was right behind him, I touched him on his shoulder and whispered in his ear, 'U.S. Marshals, you're under arrest.' He tried to get up. He began to struggle immediately. So we forced him to a prone position and placed the handcuffs on him. The DI even jumped in to help secure Gerhard. Then the DI asked, 'Do you want to take any more of them with you?' I chuckled to myself but said, 'No, we're just taking Gerhard.'"

Berry continued, "We took him back to the CID office to interview him. But as a ten-year army veteran myself, I refused to interview him while he was wearing the uniform of the United States. He was against the United States, in my view, so I made him change into the civilian clothes he was wearing when he reported for basic training before I would talk to him. I noticed then that he had pissed his pants."

"I also remember," Berry said, "that Gerhard had a T-shirt in his personal belongings that had a quote from Timothy McVeigh on it. I don't remember what the quote was, but I remember that he seemed obsessed with McVeigh. We read him his rights, but he didn't want to say anything, so we packed him up to move him to the courthouse."

Deputy Berry continued, "On the ride to the courthouse, we were making small talk with Gerhard about the army. He just started talking about McVeigh. Gerhard wanted to complete combat engineer school like McVeigh did and then eventually become a 'sapper' like McVeigh had become." (Sappers work with frontline combat troops and often work with explosives.)

"Not long after, I got a call from the New York/New Jersey task force guys who were conducting a consent search at his mother and stepfather's house in Long Island. They found a pipe bomb there. They were a bit unnerved by it, as they shook the container or box it was in. They ended up shutting down the neighborhood and part of the highway then to have the bomb unit deal with the pipe bomb," Berry said. "It was a crazy-busy day, with the four arrests being coordinated all over the country."

Chief Andre LaBier had arranged with the New York/New Jersey Task Force to have people from the task force go to Gerhard's mother and stepfather's home in Suffolk County, on Long Island, New York, and attempt a consent search of the property. Deputy U.S. Marshal Roy Wright and Joe Thomas, a Suffolk County law enforcement officer assigned to the Regional Fugitive Task Force, went to the home. Gerhard's mother consented to a search of the property.

Deputy U.S. Marshal Roy Wright later told Chief Deputy Dave Dimmitt what happened. "After Gerhard's mother consented to the search," Wright said, "we were in the basement apartment of the home, which Jason Gerhard occupied when he was there. At approximately four fifteen p.m., we discovered a locked metal box. Gerhard's mother gave them the location where to find the key to the box, and we opened it."

Deputy U.S. Marshal Wright continued, "Much to our surprise (and concern), we found what appeared to be a small pipe bomb with two end caps wrapped in duct tape. We immediately notified ATF and a local HAZMAT team, and they responded. At that point, we stopped any further search and applied for a court-ordered search warrant for the entire seven-acre property. We executed that search warrant the next morning, but nothing more was found. For a while, the whole area was shut down."

The U.S. Attorney's Office from the Eastern District of New York wanted to hand off the case from the USMS, ATF, and Suffolk County to the FBI, but they were informed that the District of New Hampshire USMS and ATF were handling the criminal investigation and that the District of New Hampshire U.S. Attorney's Office would be handling any subsequent prosecution. Deputy U.S. Marshal (DUSM) Roy

Wright would later testify at the supporter's trial in the District of New Hampshire.

Meanwhile, District of New Hampshire DUSM Gene Robinson had been assigned to travel to Corpus Christi, Texas, to meet up with the district supervisory deputy U.S. marshal assigned to the arrest team, which Chief DiMartino had arranged with the district's chief deputy there, Lisa Saenz.

Gene Robinson, a New Hampshire native and U.S. Marine Corps veteran, had begun his law enforcement career with the Manchester, New Hampshire, Police Department before being hired as a deputy U.S. marshal. He had assignments in New York and Connecticut before returning to New Hampshire during Marshal Monier's tenure. Robinson said, "As a descendant of several generations of Black Americans growing up in the Granite State, I was proud of my state and nation and was very pleased to return home."

As he explained it, "The Brown armed standoff in 2007 was huge, of course, in the district. We were a small district and everyone had a hand in trying to solve this the right way.

"During the standoff, I was often on the team with Ken Nunes and various New York/New Jersey Task Force members that Chief Regional Inspector Dave Dimmitt sent up to Plainfield to do covert surveillance or to change out batteries on the cameras we had set up in the wood line across from the Browns' driveway entrance, or to provide support to the Technical Operations Group people trying to get a camera set up on a tower," Robinson said.

"A couple of times," he continued, "we were paired with deputies from the New York/New Jersey area who were clearly raised in the city. Several were 'very anxious' when we were in the vast woodlands of the Upper Connecticut River Valley area.

"These were great deputies, fearless in the city, but put them in the woods, and some would just jump at every little sound. 'There's coyotes and bears out here!' they would say.

"I told them that both the black bears and coyotes in New Hampshire's woods ran away from people, not toward them," Robinson said. "They still didn't like it. Some would also become easily disorientated in the woods, even though we were never very far from a road. One time, we were carefully walking a line spaced not far apart when one deputy got separated somehow. It took us a good twenty minutes to find him. We had a good laugh at his expense."

When DUSM Gene Robinson arrived in Corpus Christi, Texas, for the arrest of Cirino "Reno" Gonzalez, he did a briefing at the Corpus Christi District Office with district management and the arrest team.

"Reno Gonzalez was living in a single-wide trailer in Alice, Texas, about forty minutes away from the district USMS office," he said. "We left at three thirty to four in the morning on September 12th to go make the arrest. We were worried about Reno's brother, who was a police officer on a local PD in the area, and we were concerned about Reno's father. The brother had a police scanner, so I insisted on radio silence as we approached the trailer Reno was in, which we believed was owned by the father, and we knew the father lived in the area."

Robinson continued, "We went by the father's house first on the way to Reno's trailer. The father's car wasn't there, but shortly after, the state police stopped the father's vehicle. Jose was driving it. I immediately told the officers on the stop to take the father's cell phone so he couldn't alert Reno that we were coming.

"Then," Robinson reported, "we entered the trailer park where Reno was located. We were in a small convoy of several vehicles. The SWAT team that was with us overshot the trailer where Reno was. On the way by, we noticed a male sitting outside a trailer on a picnic table having a smoke. It turned out it was Reno's brother, the cop.

"And it was good that we had overshot the trailer, because as we came back to the trailer Reno was in, the brother was coming around the corner to see what was going on elsewhere, and we were able to take him by surprise at gunpoint and secure him before we hit the trailer.

"When we entered the trailer, we entered into the kitchen-living room area," Robinson said. "There was a hallway leading from there back down to the bedroom and bathroom area. We could hear water running. Just then, Reno emerged in the hallway from the bedroom area. He was completely naked. Once he saw us, he turned quickly to go back to the bedroom area. In that gap we saw several weapons sitting on a side table—what looked like an SKS semi-auto rifle and a handgun.

"In just seconds, Reno first tried to close the door on us to the bedroom, but we piled up and pushed it open against him. Reno then went running and dove toward the coffee table with the guns on them. I jumped on him, as did the others with me. There were three or four of us. The table collapsed with Reno on it, and us on top of Reno," Robinson said.

"Remember," he continued, "I was worried about the guns on the table, which were now underneath Reno with us on his back. I wanted to secure his hands and the guns. But it was already hot and sticky, and Reno was all sweaty. As we worked to secure his hands, I heard someone screaming. I thought it was Reno, but it turned out to be another deputy from the Texas district we were in," he said.

"The screaming was because Reno had shit himself, and he shit all over the deputy that was closest to the stream! We finally got Reno's hands behind his back and handcuffed him.

"To add to the chaos, the water we heard running was Reno's girl-friend, who just then stepped out of the shower and opened the door to the bedroom. She was naked. Then... she screamed," Robinson said. "It turns out they had just had sex before we arrived."

He continued, "So we told the girlfriend to wrap herself in a towel, told Reno to grab some shorts, and we had three people outside in handcuffs—Reno, his brother, and the girlfriend.

"Then we pulled twenty or thirty weapons out of the trailer, including a .50-caliber rifle that Reno had brought up to the Browns', an SKS rifle, and a bunch of handguns.

"Reno also had a laptop, which I wanted to seize for evidence, but after conferring with the assistant U.S. attorneys in New Hampshire, we left the laptop but turned all the guns over to the ATF," Robinson reported.

"The brother and the girlfriend were eventually released. Reno was first transported to the local PD to be processed before we brought him to the U.S. courthouse for a first appearance."

"Needless to say, it was quite the experience arresting Reno at the trailer in Alice, Texas. Reno was ordered held and remanded to the custody of the U.S. Marshals, and the USMS flew Reno and me back to New Hampshire on a chartered jet. Reno didn't say too much during the flight. Only that the government was really 'F...ed up.'"

That same day, on the morning of September 12th, Marshal Monier conducted a briefing at a meeting in Grafton County at the Lebanon, New Hampshire, Police Department for the Plainfield and Lebanon Police Departments, the New Hampshire State Police, the Grafton and Sullivan County Sheriff's Offices, and area police departments about the arrests and the concert scheduled for September 15th.

The marshal shared the news about the arrest of the four individuals. He made them aware of the All Writs Act and the order signed by Judge Steve McAuliffe. The Plainfield police chief argued, "We have to shut down people from trying to attend the concert at the Browns'. It's simply too dangerous now to allow people up there." Others said the same thing.

"We need your help to do this, Marshal," Chief Gillens of the Plainfield PD said. "Even though you can delegate that authority to us, the USMS needs to be there with us. This is your case."

"I completely understand what you're saying, Chief, and we will have additional deputies and SOG team members in the area. I'm sure you've noticed them already. Unfortunately, I haven't gotten the green light yet from HQ to conduct a 'static' or stationary checkpoint, only a 'roving' one," Marshal Monier said.

"Well, we need a static checkpoint on Center Town Road, probably the night before and the day of the advertised Freedom Concert. Otherwise, people will get through," Gillens responded.

"We need to stop everyone. We can let people up the road who live there and who have a legitimate reason to be there, but we need to turn away people who have no business driving up there," Chief Gillens said. All the other local, county, and state law enforcement officers at the meeting agreed with that assessment.

"I'm with you, Chief, and I will be speaking with the director of the Marshals Service to relay our concerns. In the interim, reach out to us with anything that comes up. Talk with the deputy U.S. marshals that are assigned to roving patrols over the next few days. Introduce yourselves. We'll get this done," Marshal Monier said.

With that, the marshal returned to the USMS office in Concord and conferred with staff and made a phone call to HQ to speak with the director. Monier hadn't heard back yet on establishing a static checkpoint to prevent anyone from going to the Browns' for their so-called Freedom Concert.

A briefing with the director was scheduled for the next day, September 13th, which was also when Danny "the Dog Walker" Riley and Robert Wolffe would be making their first appearance in U.S. district court in Concord, following their arrests.

Given the media interest and large volume of calls from the press to the news that four of the Browns' supporters had been arrested, Marshal Monier had staff schedule a press conference in the large meeting room at the courthouse following Riley and Wolfe's first appearance. There, the press was informed, Marshal Monier would answer a few questions about the developments outlined in the press release about the arrests.

At the eight thirty a.m. conference call on Thursday, September 13th, with the director and senior HQ staff, the marshal and the senior leadership team in New Hampshire briefed them on the outcome of the four arrests.

"Dan Riley from Cohoes, New York, and Robert Wolffe from Vermont are being arraigned today in our courthouse," Monier said to the director. "We were able to transport both of them directly back to our district given their proximity to where they were located. Both Gonzalez and Gerhard will be transported as quickly as possible through our system to New Hampshire after making brief appearances in the U.S. district courts where they were arrested."

The leadership team then briefly outlined the circumstances surrounding their arrests and some of the evidence collected from the locations for which the USMS had search warrants.

"Chief Inspector Andre LaBier and Jamie Berry, among others, have done a terrific job working with our U.S. Attorney's Office here in New Hampshire to put the affidavits for the warrants together," the marshal said. "Moreover, Assistant U.S. Attorneys Bob Kinsella and Arnie Huftalen have been outstanding in their work with us, as have others in the U.S. Attorney's Office."

Next, the district leadership team discussed the upcoming concert, which had been advertised for Saturday, September 15th. "Director, it appears that HQ may have some misgivings about our people conducting a static checkpoint on Center Town Road in Plainfield to prevent people from going to the Browns' for the concert," Monier said.

"We need to do both roving stops and the static checkpoint come Saturday morning. We need to shut this concert down," Monier argued. "Judge McAuliffe has signed the court order under the All Writs Act giving us the authority to do so, and I met with the local, county, and state agencies. They all very persuasively argued for not letting people onto the property for another concert. We know there are explosive devices on the property, some of which are hanging in the tree line around the open areas; we know there are high-powered weapons on the property; we know that we can't guarantee the safety of people who go there," Monier said. "So it's time to send a strong message to supporters—in concert with the arrests we just made—that people aren't going to be allowed to continue supplying the Browns. For our plan to arrest them 'from the inside out,' we also need the Browns to be more isolated and alone most of the time."

The answer from HQ on the static checkpoint so far had been NO. There was a long silence from the D.C. end. The marshal, the chiefs, and others sitting in at the district office looked at each other and were shaking their heads.

Chief DiMartino was very frustrated with this, so he said, "Okay, I'd be remiss if I don't say this, but we know what's up there, and families are going to be up there, and if some kid gets an arm or a leg blown off, or worse, besides it being a tragedy, we'll [the USMS] never recover from the fallout!"

There's another long silence before Director Clark says, "Okay, so you guys think it's best to shut it down?"

"Yes," everyone in the district said.

The director then said, "Okay, then work out the details, and shut it down."

Everyone in the district breathed a sigh of relief. As Chief DiMartino later recalled, "I don't think some of the management crew at HQ were all that happy since they were advocating to let the concert go on, but to the director's credit, he gave us the green light.

"Between the SOG members currently on location and our deputies, we had the resources to work with local, county, and state law enforcement to shut down the concert," Chief DiMartino said. "An operations plan had been developed, and we had talked with all our local partners. We were ready to go."

The New Hampshire leadership team added that the U.S. Attorney's Office was on board with the USMS shutting down the concert and would be available on Saturday for questions about any arrests or other legal issues that may arise.

The plan to shut down the concert and move forward with trying to isolate the Browns further was on.

At their first appearance in the U.S. district court in Concord on that Friday, September 14th, both Riley and Wolffe entered pleas of not guilty in front of Magistrate Judge James Muirhead. They were remanded to the custody of the U.S. Marshals pending their detention hearings set for the following Monday, September 17th.

At a press briefing in the large meeting room in the courthouse following the defendants' first appearance, U.S. Marshal Stephen Monier outlined the developments so far in the case. He emphasized that the four supporters were alleged to have aided and abetted Ed and Elaine Brown in their continuing efforts to prevent the USMS from arresting them.

In preparing for the press briefing, as he always did, Monier wrote up talking points. Here's what he wrote:

Talking Points: Following the Arrests of Persons Aiding and
Abetting the Browns

- From the time Edward and Elaine Brown absented
  themselves from their criminal proceedings in the U.S.
  District Court, and certainly since they were convicted and
  sentenced, we have cautioned anyone who may be

considering aiding the Browns in their obstruction of justice that they are exposing themselves to criminal liability.

- Aiding and abetting convicted felons in avoiding justice—in this case the Browns refusal to surrender to serve their sentences of 63 months each in the U.S. Bureau of Prisons —is a crime, a very serious crime.
- Unfortunately, some people didn't get the message; others still haven't.
- Yesterday, the USMS arrested the following individuals after the Federal Grand Jury returned indictments:

Cirino "Reno" Gonzalez, age 30 LKA [last known address] of Alice, TX, on an indictment alleging he has committed violations of 18 U.S.C. §3 (Accessory After the Fact), 18 U.S.C. §372 (Conspiracy to Impede or Injure an Officer), and 18 U.S.C. §924(c) (Possession and Use of a Firearm in Relation to a Crime of Violence).

Daniel Riley, age 40, of 62 Younglove Avenue, Cohoes, NY, on an indictment(s) alleging violations of 18 U.S.C. §3 (Accessory After the Fact), §372 (Conspiracy to Impede or Injure an Officer) and §924(c) (Possession and Use of a Firearm in Relation to a Crime of Violence).

Jason Gerhard, age 22, of Brookhaven, NY, on indictment(s) alleging violations of 18 U.S.C. §3 (Accessory After the Fact), §372 (Conspiracy to Impede or Injure an Officer) and §924(c) (Possession and Use of a Firearm in Relation to a Crime of Violence).

Robert Wolffe, age 50, of 22 Highland Avenue, Randolph, VT, on indictment(s) alleging has engaged in the crime of accessory after the fact, in violation of Title 18, USC, § 3, by supplying the Browns with material and supplies so that the Browns may continue to avoid apprehension.

- For months, the USMS has proceeded in a purposeful, deliberate, and methodical way to convince the Browns that they must stop threatening the use of violence against law enforcement, and submit to justice. Thus far, they have refused.
- We have no wish to have a violent encounter with the Browns. This was a tax case; but over the last seven months, the Browns have allegedly:
- Obstructed justice, and encouraged others to assist them in obstructing justice;
- Ed Brown has threatened to kill law enforcement officers and other governmental officials; and
- They have armed themselves and attempted to acquire additional weapons and ammunition.
- The Browns have engaged in a course of conduct that has led to further criminal investigations into their activity.
- In June, the USMS shut off access to all of the Browns' utilities and deliveries and took other steps to isolate them, while still trying to keep lines of communication open. We sent them two letters outlining how they could end their ordeal in a peaceful and dignified way.
- We will continue to work closely with the Plainfield Police Department to ensure that the public's safety is maintained.
- While we have no desire to engage in a violent confrontation with Mr. and Mrs. Brown, we are not going away, and they will serve their sentences. The Browns' actions—and those of some of their supporters—are only delaying the inevitable.
- From the very beginning, we have repeatedly asked them to surrender peacefully. So far, they haven't.
- Continuing on the course they have chosen thus far only adds to their complicity in ongoing criminal conduct.

- Our clear message to any of the Browns' supporters is this:
  If you are thinking about aiding the Browns in their
  obstruction of justice; if you are considering supplying them
  with weapons, ammunition, or other supplies: **Don't do it**.
  You will be subjecting yourself to investigation, arrest, and
  prosecution for serious felonies, which carry very heavy
  prison sentences.
- People have every right to criticize our tax laws. Work to
  change them, if that's what you desire. But aiding and
  abetting convicted felons is a crime. *A very serious felony*.
  Conspiring with others to obstruct justice is a crime. *A very
  serious one*.
- Our message to the Browns is also clear: do the right thing
  and end the ordeal you have created for yourselves—
  surrender peacefully. All you need to do is call us. We will
  continue to keep all lines of communication open.
- Ours is a nation of laws. We will continue to work
  diligently to resolve this.

While it was Monier's habit to have talking points with him for
use during any press briefing, he would not read from them.
Rather, he would use them as notes and salient points that he
wanted to be sure to make during his statements from the
podium. He would then offer to take a few questions. He
would also make a list of anticipated questions from the media
for each press briefing. Here are the ones he anticipated for
this one:

- "What happens if they don't surrender after this course of
  action?"
- We won't discuss future operational plans, but all possible
  law enforcement options are being considered.

- "How long are you prepared to wait?"
- We're going to proceed in a methodical way, as we have demonstrated from the beginning. I won't speculate on the length of time.
- "Are you communicating with the Browns?"
- Without getting into any specifics, we're going to keep all lines of communication open.
- "Where are the people who have been arrested and what will happen now?"

As the *Associated Press* reported the following day, "Wearing ankle chains, 40-year-old Daniel Riley of Cohoes, N.Y., and 50-year-old Robert Wolffe of Randolph, Vt. made separate, brief appearances in a federal courtroom to plead not guilty to charges of supporting the convicted couple during their self-imposed exile at their fortress-like home in Plainfield. Both were appointed lawyers for trials [scheduled] in November."[iii]

The article continued:

Bail hearings were scheduled for Monday. Meanwhile, authorities on eastern Long Island [NY] reported seizing a pipe bomb and rifles from the Brookhaven home of 22-year-old Jason Gerhard, a supporter of the Browns and a recent army recruit. Gerhard was arrested Wednesday at Fort Leonard Wood in Missouri.

A fourth man, 30-year-old Cirino Gonzalez, was arrested in Alice, Texas. Gerhard and Gonzalez are awaiting extradition hearings before they can be brought to New Hampshire to face the charges.[iv]

The Browns, who were convicted in January and have refused to turn themselves in to authorities, claim the federal income tax is not legitimate. They've drawn supporters from across the country. Some of those relationships ended bitterly after the Browns squabbled with bloggers, radio hosts, and several spokesmen and assistants.

The hearings for Riley and Wolffe drew a small handful of supporters to the federal courthouse, including a couple wearing T-shirts reading, "I support Ed and Elaine Brown, Show me the law" and one person holding a painted sign with the slogan, "Free the Ed Brown Supporters."

Wolffe's wife also was present. She declined to speak to reporters after the hearing.

Stephen Monier, the U.S. Marshal for New Hampshire, warned Thursday that anyone helping the Browns could face prosecution, and that the Browns themselves face deepening criminal charges as they continue their monthslong refusal to report to prison.[v]

Monier told the assembled reporters at the briefing that Ed and Elaine Brown had threatened law enforcement and other government officials and that they'd encouraged people to provide them with supplies, weapons, and ammunition, among other things. "The Browns received assistance from supporters to patrol the compound while armed, to warn them of law enforcement attempts to monitor or approach their hilltop fortress, and to add layers of security or target hardening to do the same," the marshal said.

Marshal Monier admonished anyone engaged in such conduct that they were subjecting themselves to possible arrest, prosecution, and incarceration. "The arrests from September 12th should send a strong message to everyone that we are serious about that," he said.

Monier continued, "By their own actions, and by some of the steps the U.S. Marshals Service has taken, the Browns' support has begun to diminish. We have said all along that we're going to take a deliberate and methodical approach to ending this armed standoff the right way. The right way is for the Browns to call us and arrange their surrender. They can end this today."

Shaun Kranish posted a call to action on the *MaketheStand.com* website. In it, Kranish called for "emergency action" to help the men the Marshals arrested for supporting Ed and Elaine. "Harmless supporters of harmless Ed and Elaine Brown have been harmed by agents of the de facto, illegitimate, autocracy calling itself the Federal Government," Kranish said.

The site also continued to announce the Fall Freedom Fest concert on Saturday at the hilltop compound. The leadership team at the New Hampshire District Office of the USMS was aware of this.

Monier told the gathered reporters he was strongly discouraging anyone from attending the so-called "concert." "It's not safe to go there," Marshal Monier said. "We're aware that there are hazardous conditions on the property. It's a safety issue, and we will be taking proactive steps, along with our state and local partners, to ensure the community remains safe."

Following the press briefing, the district USMS leadership team continued its operational planning to shut down the event. Plans were reviewed with Plainfield PD Chief Gordon Gillens.

Chief Deputy Gary DiMartino would be the USMS on-scene commander for the duration of the event. Marshal Monier would also be on scene and would respond to any inquiries from any law enforcement agency, the public, or press. Anyone attempting to go to the Browns' concert on Saturday would be greeted by a phalanx of local, county, state, and federal law enforcement officers at the checkpoint on Center Town Road.

Chief Gary DiMartino and Regional Chief Inspector Dave Dimmitt wrote the September 11, 2007, Operations Plan for the checkpoints that weekend. It opened with the description of the situation, and the action to be taken:

Situation

1. **Type of action:** The United States Marshals Service (USMS) will set up checkpoints in conjunction with state and local police. These checkpoints will allow access control to the BROWN residence prior to and during a planned "concert". These checkpoints will be established after the planned arrests of four BROWN supporters. These checkpoints will limit access and provide safety warnings to persons attempting to access the BROWN property.

The USMS, working with the U.S. Attorney's Office, prepared flyers for distribution to people who showed up to attend the concert. It was also a warning to any would-be supporters. It read in part:

By order of the United States District Court, no one may enter or remain on the property known as Center of Town Road, Plainfield, New Hampshire, which is the defendants' residence, without the express authorization of the U.S. Marshals Service or its designee. Whoever enters or remains on the property without the express authorization of the U.S. Marshals and/or refuses to leave the property may be criminally prosecuted; see 18 USC 111 (assaulting, resisting or impeding certain officers or employees), 402 (contempt constituting crimes, 1501 (assault on a process server) and 1509 (obstruction of court orders).

. . .

Late that afternoon, Marshal Monier phoned U.S. Attorney Tom Colantuono and updated him on the investigation and on shutting down the Browns' Freedom Fest concert the next day.

Everything was in place. There would be no concert at the Browns' hilltop compound on September 15, 2007. In fact, there would never again be a large gathering of any kind at the Browns...

CHAPTER 14
NOT THIS TIME...

September 2007

Exercising the authority from Judge McAuliffe's order, the U.S. Marshals Service and local law enforcement establish a checkpoint on Center of Town Road in Plainfield on the morning of Saturday, September 15th. The purpose of the static checkpoint was to prevent people from going to the Browns' compound for the Fall Freedom Festival.

In addition, the "roving checkpoints" throughout the weekend would help ensure the safety of the Plainfield community and surrounding areas.

Beginning early on the morning of September 15, 2007, USMS deputies and members of the Plainfield Police Department and the Sullivan County Sheriff's Office established a checkpoint in a safe area of Center Town Road, well below the driveway entrance to the Browns' compound. Chief Gordon Gillens and his officers quickly identified residents of Center Town Road who were allowed to come and go through the checkpoint.

All other vehicles were stopped, the occupants identified, and a photograph taken. The occupants were then handed one of the flyers warning them they were not allowed to go to, enter, or remain at the Browns' property. The local Boston TV affiliate of Fox News showed up, as did a British documentarian who gave the name of Johnny Howorth.

Howorth had called the Marshals Office the day before and had a conversation with Marshal Steve Monier. Howorth told the marshal he was a successful, independent documentary filmmaker. "The armed standoff with Ed and Elaine Brown has garnered international attention," Howorth told the marshal. "I've traveled here to get an interview with both the Browns at their hilltop home and have already met with them twice." Monier gave him his standard admonition about going there, and then the marshal asked him what his reception was like when he arrived at the Browns' house.

"It was interesting," Howorth said. "The first time I arrived, I drove up the driveway and expected to meet people, possibly armed, along the way. Instead, there was no one. I honked the horn when I got to the house, and still, no one appeared. I went up and knocked on the door, and Ed and Elaine and the German Shepard dog finally came to greet me. I told them who I was and why I was there," he explained.

Howorth then added, "Ed, Elaine, and I then sat in the kitchen, and we talked for three or four hours. I got a good interview from them. I went there again last night, and there was another guy there. I believe he said he was from Pennsylvania."

The marshal asked Howorth if any weapons were displayed. Howorth said, "The only weapon I noticed was that Ed was wearing a semi-auto pistol, which was clipped to his belt in his back. Ed told me it was a 1911. I didn't get a full tour of the house."

Howorth was returning today to attend the concert. When he encountered the checkpoint, he asked to speak with the marshal. The marshal told him that they were not allowing the concert to go on, and they were turning people away. Howorth asked, "Well, can I interview you, Marshal?"

"Maybe later, but not right now. We're a bit busy," the marshal told him. "Give me a call at the office on Monday."

Shortly after Howorth left, at approximately 2:05 p.m., Lauren Canario and her friend Jim Johnson drove up. Johnson was driving the van they arrived in. Canario, a Free Stater and activist from the Keene, New Hampshire, area, had visited the Browns on several occasions, had posted stories and videos about the case on the *FreeKeene.com* website, and as noted earlier was very active in protesting against the federal government.

Chief Deputy Gary DiMartino described what happened next. "So they roll up in the van. Her friend Jim Johnson is driving. At some point, she exits the vehicle with a video camera in hand. I say to her, 'You're not going to stay here,' and Lauren responds, 'That's right, I'm not,' and starts walking up the road. That's when I tell her to stop. Stop right now!

"By that point," DiMartino explains, "other deputies and officers are telling her the same thing. That's when Deputy U.S. Marshal (DUSM) Jeff White steps in front of her and he stops her. And she immediately drops into a sitting, passive resistant posture. (This is typical for a seasoned demonstrator.) We take the camera and later (when it's reviewed), you can hear me say, 'Make sure it's off!'"

DiMartino recalled, "DUSM Jeff White cuffs her and she's transported to Lebanon PD for processing. We call the assistant U.S. attorney (AUSA) designated as the point of contact for this operation, I think it might have been AUSA Bob Kinsella, and after discussion, we end up releasing her. The AUSA told us we can review the case later to see if any charges should be filed."

Not long after Canario was arrested, Marshal Steve Monier left the checkpoint and traveled to Lebanon PD. The marshal had spoken earlier with Lebanon PD Chief Jim Alexander. The chief said he'd make office space in the PD available to the marshal for any landline phone calls or other work that needed to be done.

The marshal had several phone messages by the afternoon, and he wanted to make them from a landline since cell phone service was spotty in the area. Moreover, Monier wanted to brief the Lebanon PD deputy chief who was working that day on how the checkpoint was going. Lebanon PD had detailed personnel to assist Plainfield if and when needed.

Moreover, the department had been an excellent partner to the Marshals Service and to neighboring Plainfield PD throughout the entire course of events with the Browns. The cooperation was outstanding. Marshal Monier took extra steps to ensure that Chief Alexander and his command staff were kept in the loop.

After meeting with the deputy chief at Lebanon PD and returning several phone calls—mostly from the media—the marshal agreed to an interview in the police department's parking lot with the local ABC affiliate, WMUR TV-9, from Manchester, New Hampshire. This was late in the afternoon. He also gave a phone interview about the checkpoint and shutting down the concert to the *Concord Monitor*. And he agreed to in-person interviews in the Lebanon PD lobby with both the *Valley News* and the New Hampshire *Union Leader*.

In each of these interviews, Monier talked about the decision to shut down the concert and the arrests of the four supporters just three days ago. "There are known hazards on the property," the marshal said, "and we simply are not going to allow any more gatherings there."

As to the arrest of the four supporters, "We've said all along that if you aid and abet convicted felons—Ed and Elaine Brown—in their continuing obstruction of justice, then you are subject to arrest and prosecution for very serious crimes. I hope anyone contemplating further assistance to the Browns considers this very seriously."

Shortly after the last interview in the lobby with the media, Lauren Canario was brought out from the PD's booking room to sit in the lobby. She was waiting for a ride home. The marshal sat down with her to engage her in conversation.

"I'm sure you know why we had no choice, Lauren, but to take you into custody," the marshal said to her. "We have an order from the court to keep people off the property at our discretion, and, certainly, we're not going to allow any more gatherings there."

When Canario didn't respond, the marshal continued, "You may think you're helping the Browns fight against an unjust or unconstitutional law, Lauren. But you're not. That's not what's going on in Plainfield. This has become a very dangerous situation. Serious threats have been made to kill people. Deadly weapons have been provided to the Browns. Armed people are patrolling the property for them. There are explosives there. That's not civil disobedience, Lauren. That's planning for a violent confrontation with law enforcement. That's law enforcement like myself, and the deputies who work in the District of New Hampshire, who have a duty and obligation to enforce valid orders of the court. The Browns are convicted felons," Monier said.

"Lauren, what you did today is civil disobedience. You walked past us at a checkpoint and refused to stop. You're an activist. You think the government overreaches. I get that. But when you were stopped, you didn't threaten violence," the marshal said. "You didn't assault a law enforcement officer. You didn't brandish a deadly weapon. You didn't say you were going to kill the officers or their offspring. You simply sat down, and you peacefully submitted to an arrest. You accepted the consequence of being arrested," the marshal told her.

Monier continued, "The kind of peaceful civil disobedience that Dr. Martin Luther King advocated was to fight against the civil rights violations and discrimination of the 1950s and '60s, and Lauren.... You know that's not what the Browns are doing. So I'm going to politely tell you this. Don't go there again. Don't bring them any more food.

"This will end," the marshal told her, "and the U.S. Marshals are determined to end it without anyone getting hurt, but the Browns are making things very dangerous for everyone. Don't. Go. There. Again. This is the wrong cause, and the Browns are the wrong people."

Lauren said little during this time, but toward the end of his little soliloquy, the marshal noticed that she did nod her head.

Then the marshal asked her how she was getting home. "Do you have a ride home, Lauren?" he asked.

"Yes, I've made a call, and I should have a ride coming," she replied.

"Okay. If that changes, let me know," the marshal told her. "I'll be here at the PD for a bit more, so just ask at the window to talk with me if that changes, and we'll see if we can get you a ride if yours doesn't show up."

With that, the marshal went back inside the PD and called the checkpoint for a situation report (sitrep). By 7:40 p.m., sixty-one people in thirty-five cars had been turned away. Two of the vehicles that were stopped were unregistered. Local law enforcement agencies had those vehicles towed away, and they dealt with the state violations.

Marshal Monier returned one more phone call from the *Boston Globe* and then headed back to the district office at approximately eight p.m. when everyone cleared the checkpoint in Plainfield.

On Monday, September 17th, Robert Wolffe from Vermont was scheduled for a two p.m. detention hearing in the court. That morning, the district USMS leadership team was busy filing reports from the shutdown of the concert and following up on details from the weekend.

Marshal Monier sent an email to Assistant Director Art Roderick and the deputy director. He also spoke with the ATF special agent in charge about working with the ATF to handle evidence collection, the guns, and rendering safe any IEDs on the property post-arrest of the Browns.

DUSM Gene Robinson reported that the identification hearing for

Reno Gonzalez in Texas took place and that he would be traveling back to New Hampshire with Gonzalez tomorrow.

Early in the afternoon, Johnny Howorth, the independent film-maker and documentarian from Great Britain, arrived at the courthouse and asked to speak with the marshal. Marshal Monier and Deputy Jeff White interviewed him in one of the conference rooms on the second floor of the courthouse.

Howorth told the marshal and Deputy White that he had a few more days he could stay in the state and that he wanted to visit the Browns several more times before he had to leave. The marshal asked Howorth if he'd be willing to talk with the Marshals Service after each visit. He said that he would. The marshal gave Howorth an overview of what the USMS approach to this situation was, specifically that it was their intention to exercise restraint and to end the armed standoff without anyone getting injured or, worse, killed.

It was the same information Monier had been giving in all of the Marshals Service's statements to the press.

Howorth agreed to stay in touch and provide information on what he saw and who was there during his visits. He said he understood that the USMS wanted this to end the right way. Deputy Jeff White would be his point of contact for this, and they exchanged cell phone and contact information before Howorth left the courthouse.

At the two p.m. hearing in the U.S. District Court, Robert Wolffe agreed to detention in the custody of the U.S. Marshals and agreed to a cooperating debrief with the U.S. Attorney's Office and investigators from the Marshals Service.

But it was an interesting hearing. Wolffe's wife, Valeri Wolffe, was in attendance for the hearing and according to an AP report of the proceeding was surprised halfway through when her husband agreed to his continued custody.

Associated Press writer Beverley Wang's report of the proceeding follows:

. . .

Concord, N.H. (AP) – A Vermont man charged with helping convicted tax evaders Ed and Elaine Brown evade authorities left a trail of evidence all over the Internet showing his allegiance, authorities said Monday. Robert Wolffe showed his devotion to the Browns and his wish for an armed showdown with authorities via blogs and e-mail, even e-mailing a manual on how to kill government officials to his wife at work—an employee in the Vermont division of the Federal Highway Administration—a federal prosecutor alleged.

Assistant U.S. Attorney Arnold Huftalen also read from a blog with a supply list and instructions for sending packages to the Browns in care of Wolffe, an Army veteran. The list, giving Wolffe's name and address, sought items ranging from cardboard to night vision goggles and camouflage clothing, but the "number one most important thing" is "people to come and make a stand to their death if necessary."

The Browns insist there is no law requiring payment of federal taxes. Ed Brown has said he will resort to an armed confrontation if authorities try to take him and his wife by force. Regardless of their views on taxes, "the supporters of the Browns… have been energized by the desire to force the government into an armed confrontation," Huftalen said Monday as he argued for Wolffe to be jailed until a November trial.

Defense lawyer Paul Garrity at first disputed Huftalen's characterization of Wolffe as a dangerous flight risk with a potential for violence. He said federal authorities had mischaracterized earlier statements by Wolffe and asked that Wolffe be released under supervision to return to his job as a technician for a propane company.

Garrity said Wolffe wanted a peaceful end to the Browns' self-imposed siege. "[Wolffe's] not one who's going to outwardly lash out at anyone," he said.

But Garrity did not get far. Wolffe decided midway through the hearing that he would not contest authorities' wish to keep him in custody. The decision was announced just as the hearing was reconvening to play video of an interview between Wolffe and a deputy U.S. marshal, and an Internet radio interview with his wife, Valeri Wolffe.

Valeri Wolffe appeared shocked by her husband's decision, exclaiming, "What!" as the judge made the announcement.

She refused to speak to reporters at the hearing.

Robert Wolffe is one of four men arrested last week and charged with providing supplies and other help to the Browns, who each face prison sentences of more than five years following their conviction on federal tax evasion charges in January. His Web site, bobwolffe.com, was disabled Monday. He is being held at the Strafford County Jail.

Huftalen said Valeri Wolffe told authorities that she and her husband had visited the Browns more than a dozen times together and shot guns with Ed Brown. Marshals had observed Wolffe's car on the Browns' property and observed Wolffe on armed security patrol there, Huftalen said.

Huftalen said authorities visited Valeri Wolffe at home on the day of her husband's arrest and saw a loaded AK-47 on a couch and a loaded Ruger rifle propped near a doorway. Hours later when they returned with a search warrant, they didn't see any guns. Deputies searched Valeri Wolffe's car and found three rifles and four handguns hidden in the rear of the car, four full boxes of ammunition and two suitcases packed with the couple's clothes, Huftalen said.

"The defendant was intending to flee, most likely to the Browns' residence," Huftalen said. Garrity said all of the guns were legally owned.[i]

Daniel "the Dog Walker" Riley's detention hearing was continued until nine thirty a.m. on Wednesday, September 19th.

Chief Gary DiMartino reported that they had identified the woman from Pennsylvania who had been at the Browns over the last week, and they were working on identifying the man from Pennsylvania who had been there. A confidential source from another government agency was providing the information.

Late in the afternoon, Marshal Monier received a phone call from HQ informing him that Chief Billy Sorukas was en route to the district, as was Dave Robertson, the SOG commander.

The marshal was informed that Chief Sorukas would be the designated incident commander for the operation going forward to arrest the Browns.

"Marshal, we need you and the district leadership team to fully brief him once he arrives in the district. He will be directing the arrest operation going forward, beginning first with the plan to get an undercover operative inside with the Browns, and then bringing a team of deputies posing as supporters in. But, if that doesn't pan out, Dave Robertson will also be on site with a compliment of SOG operators to go to plan B," the marshal was informed.

"This is what the director has approved, so please give Sorukas every courtesy you can extend to end this armed standoff," the caller said.

"I understand," the marshal said. "Just keep in mind that I want this to end the right way. That is with no one getting hurt. It appears we have a good opportunity to get an undercover operative into the Browns' now that they have been further isolated. If this operative checks out, and he gets in, please understand that Plan B—having SOG move in—is a *last* resort," Monier said. He added, "Let me emphasize that—Plan B is **NOT** the first option."

Monier continued, "HQ also needs to be aware that Wolffe has agreed to a debrief with our investigators and with the U.S. Attorney's Office, and Riley may do the same. So we're going to get additional information about what is going on at the Browns' compound and what additional hazards may be on site. We'll bring Chief Sorukas and Commander Robertson up to speed as soon as they arrive in district."

With that, the marshal informed Chiefs DiMartino and LaBier of the phone call. Chief Dimmitt was also due back in district by Wednesday, and there would be a full briefing when everyone was at the district office, the marshal told the leadership team.

Chief William "Billy" Sorukas, Jr., arrived at the district office on Wednesday morning, September 19, 2007. He met first with the marshal and Chief Deputy Gary DiMartino for a briefing.

Chief William J. "Billy" Sorukas, Jr., from the Investigative Operations Division of the USMS, was a seasoned veteran of the USMS, having served from 1986 to 1998 in the San Diego, California, office and rising to the position of supervisor and coordinator for the Fugitive Group of the San Diego Violent Crime Task Force. From 2006 to January 2014, he served as the chief for both Domestic and International Investigations. He had earned a bachelor's degree in criminology from Indiana State University in 1982. Sorukas had graduated from the Indiana Law Enforcement Academy, the USMS Basic Academy, and the USMS Special Operations Group basic training, and from the DoD Technical Surveillance Counter Measures Course.[ii]

At about nine thirty a.m., the district got word from the U.S. Attorney's Office that at the detention hearing, Daniel Riley said he would agree to a cooperating debrief about the Browns. The assistant U.S. attorneys handling the case and USMS investigators would do the debriefing. This was followed shortly by Robert Wolffe, at his detention hearing, also agreeing to a cooperating debrief. Both stipulated to their continued detention, subject to a further hearing.

Chiefs DiMartino and Sorukas and the marshal held a conference call with state and local agencies in the Plainfield area to debrief from shutting down the concert on Saturday and to share any information about new developments. On the call were Chief Gordon Gillens and Sgt. Larry Dore from the Plainfield Police Department; Lt. Jerry Maslan, Troop C Commander from the New Hampshire State Police; and a representative from the Sullivan County Sheriff's Office.

Overall, Chief Gillens said, the community was very pleased with the operation to shut down the concert last Saturday. The residents of Center Town Road were especially complimentary. Sgt. Dore said that he got a tip that one of the residents, however, may be sympathetic to the Browns and may be passing along information in phone calls to them as to what's going on in the area. The Marshals said it's safe to assume that some local people had been talking with the Browns during the entire standoff.

Everyone on the call agreed that the Browns knew very early on the morning of the planned concert that law enforcement had set up a checkpoint and was not allowing anyone to go to the Browns' compound. The marshal shared that Elaine had made a statement to this effect on Saturday morning in a call in to the *Power Hour* internet radio show on the *WTPR Network*.

The marshal said that the next weekly conference call with local, county, and state agencies would be at ten a.m. the following Wednesday.

Shortly after, the USMS received word that the debriefs from both Wolffe and Riley were instructive. Among other things, the U.S. Attorney's Office and the USMS learned that there were at least two cans of black powder rigged with simple fuses in the kitchen area of the house, and there were an unknown additional number of black powder cans with fuses in the garage.

There were also at least six types of explosive devices that Brown and supporters made and placed in and around the Brown property, which included three different types of pipe bombs, Tannerite bombs, back powder cans with fuses, and different-sized propane tanks hung from trees. The pipe bombs had been constructed in the garage, which was attached to the house.

It was said that Brown sent Gerhard to stores in Lebanon, New Hampshire, to purchase materials needed to make the explosive devices, while Wolffe also supplied pipe materials for the improvised explosive devices, or IEDs. Some of the pipe bombs were reportedly made of 2 ¾" pipe filled with 1 ½ cans of gunpowder designed to be detonated by a fuse. Others, using ¾" pipe with a spring-loaded triggering mechanism, were designed to be detonated by a trip wire armed with shotgun shells, some of which were in the wood line around the property.

In addition, Tannerite bombs were hung from trees and on outbuildings around the Brown compound. Tannerite, often described as a binary explosive, is designed to be detonated by a gunshot. In low-volume amounts, these are the "exploding" targets sold to sporting enthusiasts to be able to "see" when a round hits a target at longer range. The Tannerite bombs were made with much larger amounts of Tannerite and were marked with orange dots on them to make them easy to spot in the trees.

According to the information received from the debriefs, Jason Gerhard had provided the Browns with a variety of long rifles, including the .50-caliber Serbu "heavy-duty" rifle. Brown had also obtained .50-caliber incendiary rounds, night-vision goggles, and at least three video surveillance cameras attached to the main house and fed to monitors inside the house. There were also fish line barriers in the wood line around the house to serve as an alarm system and line of defense to the smaller spring-loaded pipe bombs.

There was a bunker beneath the kitchen area of the house, which was accessible through the floor of the pantry in the kitchen. There were thousands of rounds of ammunition and packaged food in this bunker. It was also believed (but not seen) that there was a second bunker somewhere else under the home.

The bunker under the kitchen had an "escape" tunnel and hatch that led away from the house to a section of the driveway. The "hatch" was secured from inside, and the top of it was covered by gravel on that section of the driveway. To access the hatch, the ladder from the pantry to the bunker would be moved to the accessway leading up to the hatch.

It was also reported that Ed Brown was difficult to get along with and became verbally abusive with people who came to know him. He was reportedly also verbally abusive with Elaine Brown. This caustic behavior had caused a number of "supporters" who came to know Ed Brown to part ways with him.

On September 20, 2007, Jason Gerhard and Reno Gonzalez both made their first appearance in the District of New Hampshire U.S. District Court. Gerhard refused to enter a plea, and Magistrate Judge James Muirhead entered a plea of Not Guilty on his behalf, scheduled a detention hearing for Tuesday, September 25th, and remanded him to the custody of the U.S. Marshals. Gonzalez was likewise remanded to the custody of the U.S. Marshals.

As Cirino "Reno" Gonzalez was being processed in the cell block area of the U.S. Marshals space in the courthouse, Marshal Monier met him for the first time after overhearing him say that Gonzalez's father had a "deal" with the marshal.

Monier introduced himself to Gonzalez. He made it clear to Reno that there was no deal with his father, Jose.

"Let me make this clear, Reno. I did talk to your father while you were up at the Browns' supporting their efforts to avoid arrest. I told your father he should get you out of there. Instead, it appears your father and your brother went there and at first were willing to help you in aiding the Browns. Instead, within a couple of days, Ed Brown apparently threw all three of you off the property, and you left," the marshal said.

"There was no deal with your father," the marshal said. "You all made your own choices when you were at the Browns'. All of you have been posting things on the various social media sites about the Browns. We've seen those postings, too."

The court ordered Gonzalez detained, and following Gerhard's detention hearing on September 25th, he, too, was detained pending trial.

. . .

On September 26th, a conference call was made from the district office of the USMS to the director and senior staff. At the district office, participating in the call were U.S. Marshal Stephen Monier and Chiefs Gary DiMartino, Dave Dimmitt, and Billy Sorukas, and SOG Commander David Robertson.

Chief Sorukas outlined a two-phase plan to take the Browns into custody. The first phase involved sending a developed confidential source—an undercover operative—in to do a security "sweep" for the Browns.

Once in, the undercover operative would require assistance from his "team" to conduct the "sweep." The "team" would be comprised of USMS personnel from their Southeast Region Task Force. This ruse to arrest the Browns would occur at their property at the appropriate point (with nearby SOG officer extraction support and backup).

Should this phase be unsuccessful, the USMS would move forward with SOG shutting down access to the property, a carefully coordinated approach to the house, and a systematic effort to negotiate the Browns into surrendering.

The marshal quietly arranged to have New Hampshire State Police SWAT backup for phase two, if needed. SOG Commander Dave Robertson would meet with his counterpart from the state police to coordinate this. The state police would not be on point but provide support. The New Hampshire National Guard Armory in Lebanon would once again serve as a command post for the operation, and the New Hampshire National Guard Civil Support Team would be on standby.

Director Clark approved moving forward with these plans and with the SOG move order.

During this time, Dutch was being vetted as the undercover operative to go meet the Browns and insert himself into the compound.

Chief Gary DiMartino was the first to speak with Dutch on the phone. This occurred mid-September. As Chief DiMartino later explained it, "Dave gave me a contact number to a local New Jersey officer that worked with the USMS New York/New Jersey Fugitive Task Force that had some info regarding the Brown case. At the time, I wasn't that optimistic about it and made a sticky note to get back to it and make the contact. I sat on it a couple of days, hitting on the many other priorities at the time," DiMartino said. "Dave Dimmitt followed up with me about it, and I told him I hadn't got to it yet but would. So I called the officer, and he gave me some limited information about Dutch and a contact number."

Chief DiMartino continued, "I called Dutch, and we started to talk about the Brown case. Dutch mentioned the *MaketheStand* site and Shaun Kranish. We talked about his background and the different cases he had worked on (initial vetting). He talked a good game. We also talked about some possible scenarios, and he mentioned a Trojan Horse–type ruse. Not really trusting him at this point, I was guarded about sharing too much information. But the fact was that is exactly what we wanted to accomplish. I continued to talk to him to develop rapport and gather more info about him.

"We talked about him working with the FBI," DiMartino said, "and he gave me some information to help with the vetting process. My contact on this case at the FBI and I had numerous conversations about how Dutch might be useful and different ways we might be able to capitalize on the situation. I gave my FBI contact all of Dutch's info, and he checked him out with the Bureau, and I believe talked to his handler and case agent."

DiMartino added, "My FBI contact got back to me and said that Dutch's story checked out and that in fact he had successfully helped with a difficult FBI case. Once this was confirmed, we had the task force in Atlanta do more vetting. I believe Chief Dave Dimmitt arranged this.

"From that point on," Gary DiMartino said, "I talked to Dutch a couple more times cultivating him while continuing to build some rapport. I created a 'file' on him, and when Billy Sorukas arrived in district, he told me that he was going to 'handle' Dutch going forward. I briefed him and gave him the file."

Once Chief Sorukas arrived in the district and had a briefing with Chief DiMartino and the marshal and had Dutch's information, Sorukas called him. Chief Sorukas wanted a face to face. Dutch was in Long Island, New York, at the time, so he made arrangements to meet him there.

As Chief Billy Sorukas said, "It was early Sunday morning, September 23rd, and I drove down to Long Island from New Hampshire. We met, and I spent several hours with him. He gave me his background and enough information on what law enforcement agencies he had worked with to do some follow-up on him. Although Dutch didn't know this at the time, I had gotten approval from HQ to pay him some expense money should this work out. A deputy U.S. marshal from our New York/New Jersey Task Force was positioned outside the hotel where we met and was able the grab the plate number of the truck Dutch got into when he left the hotel.

"After meeting with Dutch," Sorukas said, "I drove back to New Hampshire and the next day made several calls—to the FBI and to the local New Jersey agency that he had done some work with. Everything he told me checked out, and he had the bonafides to be the undercover operative to go in to the compound. His 'hook' to do so was Shaun Kranish, with whom he had been communicating over the internet.

"Once we completed the vetting process, I spoke with my bosses at HQ and said we should give Dutch the greenlight to make arrangements to meet with Kranish and convince Kranish to take him to the Browns to introduce Dutch to them. HQ gave me the green light," Chief Sorukas reported.

The vetting process, both through the face-to-face interview and a discussion with the FBI, proved positive.

Shortly thereafter, Dutch, who had been conversing with Shaun Kranish over the internet, made arrangements to meet up with Kranish in South Bend, Indiana (the hometown where Chief Sorukas grew up). Sorukas was convinced that once Dutch told him where he was meeting Kranish—in South Bend—that Dutch had been doing his own "research and vetting" on Sorukas.

At the meeting in South Bend, Kranish and Dutch talked for several hours. Kranish then agreed to ride first to New York (Dutch supposedly had a "job" to do there) and then to New Hampshire. They were traveling in Dutch's truck.

When they got to New Hampshire, Kranish—who had visited with the Browns on several occasions—introduced Dutch to Ed and Elaine. Dutch was introduced as a "security expert" and someone sympathetic to the Browns' cause. They all talked for some time. When Kranish said that he had to return to Illinois, the Browns invited Dutch to stay. Dutch drove Kranish to the airport in Boston, Massachusetts, and paid for his one-way return ticket to Illinois, then returned to Plainfield. This was on or about Saturday, September 28, 2007.

During his time off the property, Dutch made contact with Chief Billy Sorukas when needed. Sorukas set himself up in the north country—Lebanon area—and along with David Robertson set up the command post at the National Guard Armory with a link to a virtual command and control center at HQ.

In the interim, a four-person team selected from the Southeast Regional Task Force began their move from Atlanta to northern New England. This was in anticipation of the opportunity for Dutch, and the team, to conduct a ruse to arrest the Browns.

By September 28, 2007, things were quiet at the Browns', and the only ones reported to have visited the Browns were a couple of reporters from media outlets. On that same day, at approximately 3:26 p.m.,

September 28th, Bethany Hatch, Elaine's daughter, called Marshal Monier to let him know that she and her brother were going up to Plainfield tomorrow, the 29th, to visit their mother. Bethany and the marshal talked for a bit, and he thanked her for letting him know.

The marshal informed Chiefs DiMartino, Sorukas, and Dimmitt of this.

By October 1st, Dutch had established himself with the Browns. He smoothly became a confidant of Ed and Elaine. They sent him to do errands in Dutch's white crew-cab pickup truck and do other chores around the property.

During his time with the Browns, Elaine agreed to do some dental work for Dutch in the "dental office" they'd constructed inside the house where, on occasion, she had been treating a few of her former patients. Dutch had the dental work done and paid her for this.

On October 1st, Chief Sorukas briefed the marshal and Chiefs DiMartino and Dimmitt on Dutch successfully inserting himself into the Browns' home. At nine thirty a.m., Director Clark called for an update for the acting attorney general. Monier sent Sorukas some talking points for that purpose, and Chief Sorukas sent the summary update to the director.

By this time, on October 1st, the four members from the Atlanta task force assigned to assist with the arrest of the Browns were flying into airports in Maine and Vermont. They avoided the Manchester, New Hampshire, regional airport out of an abundance of caution. A number of Free Staters who supported the Browns were known to hang out at Murphy's Taproom in Manchester, and several of them had visited and communicated with the Browns. The team members had been warned of some countersurveillance by Brown supporters.

Once assembled, Chief Sorukas would meet with the four-member undercover team for a full briefing.

Chief Dimmitt recalls that before the full team from Atlanta was ready to meet with Dutch, he, Chief Sorukas, and another USMS member met Dutch after dark "at a wooded and rural ice cream stand in Vermont near a park just east of the Quechee Gorge. The location was on the west side of the White River about ten to fifteen miles west of Lebanon, New Hampshire. "Myself, Sorukas, and someone else (don't recall who) met at the ice cream stand," Chief Dimmitt said.

"It was the first time that I met Dutch, as I had only talked to him on the phone before this. He was a big guy with a beard. The briefing ended and contact information was confirmed," Dimmitt later reported. This would have been on the evening of October 1st.

The next two days were very busy at the district office of the USMS. In addition to the concern about arresting the Browns, there were growing concerns about the aftermath of a successful arrest of Ed and Elaine. Supposedly, Ed had a "hit list" of fifty people on it and agreements with several of his ardent supporters that the list would be acted upon should the Browns be arrested or killed.

Confidential informants had said that no one had actually seen this list but that Ed talked about it frequently. It was his "insurance policy," he told them.

Ed said several times that the list included Judge McAuliffe, AUSA and prosecutor during the tax trial Bill Morse, U.S. Attorney Tom Colantuono, Marshal Monier, Chief Deputy U.S. Marshal Gary DiMartino, Plainfield PD Chief Gordon Gillens, and Sheriff Michael Prozzo, among others, along with the IRS criminal investigative agents involved in the tax prosecution.

Ed repeated many of these statements during internet radio shows and during interviews with the press.

Given this, the district office had to be prepared to once again stand-up protective details on the judge, the U.S. attorney, and the prosecutor Bill Morse. Deputy U.S. marshals would be sent out to interview anyone who had made concerning statements in the past about such activity and would work with their partners in federal law enforcement to follow up on any perceived or potential threats.

The anticipation grew, and the teams prepared...

CHAPTER 15

THE INTRO, A BURGLARY, THE SOLDIER LEFT BEHIND, AND THE TAKEDOWN

October 2007

O nce the team of four Task Force members from Atlanta were assembled, they made plans to meet with Chiefs Billy Sorukas and Dave Dimmitt along with Dutch, the undercover operative, to discuss what ruse would take down the Browns.

Critical to the success of any ruse to arrest the Browns was the composition of the selected team members brought to New Hampshire from the Southeast Regional Fugitive Task Force from Atlanta. They needed to be convincing as people supportive of the Browns' views, and they needed to be fearless. They would be going into a heavily armed compound with a couple who had repeatedly said they would either walk out as a free man and a free woman or they would come out in body bags.

Fortunately, for the USMS, the district, and the people of Plainfield, New Hampshire, Chief Billy Sorukas and AD Mike Earp had selected the right team members. Comprising the arrest team were:

Supervisory Deputy U.S. Marshal W.S. Robertson. Robertson was a criminal justice major at Georgia Southern University and first became a narcotics agent with the Georgia Bureau of Investigations when he began his law enforcement career. In December of 1983, W.S. joined the U.S. Marshals Service. He was stationed first in Illinois and then sent to Atlanta in 1986 through 1988. Completing many assignments, he worked fugitives with the Atlanta task force and warrants, and ended his career with the Southeast Regional Fugitive Task Force (RFTF) in 2019, after thirty-five years with the USMS.

Special Deputy U.S. Marshal Jeff May, who at the time of the Browns' arrests was a deputy sheriff from Georgia assigned to the USMS-led Southeast RFTF as a task force officer. Jeff first became a law enforcement officer as a deputy sheriff in 1976 with a northern Georgia county sheriff's office and spent eleven years with the University of Northern Georgia as the deputy director of the university's law enforcement agency. In 1990, he worked fugitive cases with the Georgia Department of Corrections. In 1992, he spent seven years with the metro fugitive squad, and in 2003 was assigned to the USMS-led Southeast RFTF until his retirement in 2007. However, he was retained as a deputy sheriff in Georgia after retirement and stayed with the RFTF through 2019.

Chief Inspector Joe Parker joined the U.S. Marshals Service in January of 1991. In 1996 or '97, he was collaterally assigned to the Technical Operations Group (TOG) and in 1998 was assigned full-time to TOG. In 2007, he became the chief of TOG, was assigned to the Southeast RFTF in 2010, and served as the RFTF deputy chief until his retirement in 2016.

Inspector Wayne Warren is the son of a career military officer. Wayne ended up in the tidewater area of Virginia for high school and college. Originally a business major, he switched to criminal justice as his interests changed. Before graduating college, he was hired as a local law enforcement officer in a fifty-person Virginia agency, worked for a time, then went back to college and finished his degree. After graduation, the same agency rehired him. He later joined a larger, 450-person

Virginia agency where he worked uniform, SWAT, then in detectives and vice/narcotics. It was in this position that he trained as an undercover officer and worked undercover assignments. He spent nine-plus years in local/state law enforcement.

In 1998, the U.S. Marshals Service hired Wayne. After graduating the academy, he was sent to the D.C. Superior Court. In 2000, Wayne did a lateral transfer to the DEA for one year, then transferred back to the USMS in 2001. He became a member of SOG in 2002. In 2005, Wayne was promoted to inspector and assigned to the Southeast Regional Fugitive Task Force in Atlanta when he was selected as part of the team to arrest the Browns. Following that, he was an instructor at the academy until his retirement from the USMS on December 31, 2018, after twenty-one years of federal service and nine-plus years with local law enforcement. Wayne currently serves as an instructor at the Federal Law Enforcement Training Center in Georgia for the Department of Homeland Security (DHS).

These were the team members selected from Georgia to be the "Brown supporters" brought in to conduct the Trojan Horse ruse.

The original thought for the ruse to arrest the Browns was to call in a team of "security experts" to sweep the house for bugs, since Ed Brown was very paranoid about being surveilled. But Ed Brown expressed that he was satisfied with all the security upgrades they had been making, and Dutch assessed that approach would not work out.

When the team assembled in New Hampshire, Chief Sorukas arranged a meeting with them, Chief Dave Dimmitt, and Dutch in Vermont. Dutch was already in place at the Browns' and had earned Ed and Elaine's confidence.

Early on the morning of Thursday, October 4, 2007, they met at a park in Vermont near the same ice cream stand where Dimmitt and Sorukas had met with him a few days before. After a lengthy discussion, everyone agreed the "security sweep" was not viable.

Finally, Dutch was asked, "Has Ed asked you to do anything for him?"

Dutch replied, "Well, he did ask me to burglarize Elaine's dental office yesterday, since the Treasury Department had seized the property and alarmed it."

"Ed wanted the refrigerator," Dutch said, "along with some dental supplies from the office, and he wanted to leave a 'manifesto' or 'warrant' at the office for the authorities to find."

Once he said that, the USMS team members looked at each other. They all thought, *Bingo!* Because this was Ed's idea, this was a feasible plan.

A plan was formulated right then for Dutch to call Ed and tell him he had a team in to "burglarize" the dental office, and the team could bring Ed and Elaine the materials they wanted from the office.

The plan included the deputies hiding their weapons in a compartment in the back of Dutch's pickup, in the event Ed asked them to raise their shirts to prove they weren't armed.

As Chief Dimmitt later explained, the decision to send the undercover team into the Browns' compound to arrest them on October 4, 2007, was *huge*. "The fact that Ed's supporters had been openly bringing firearms and IED components into the compound was extremely disconcerting to those of us at 'the tip of the spear.' With the exception of a taser and a small semi-auto handgun, we were sending the team in virtually unarmed. The sentiment was we might be outgunned, but we won't be outsmarted."

Chiefs Sorukas and Dimmitt, and the other senior people on scene trusted the Georgia crew to pull it off. *Why?* Because of each of the undercover team's reputation in the U.S. Marshals Service. As Dimmitt explained, "Reputation means a lot in the USMS. What are you bringing to the table and can you back it up?"

In an extensive interview for this book, with all four members of the undercover USMS arrest team, they relayed the following about the rest of that day, October 4, 2007:

Dutch called Ed and told him that he had people up that could "burglarize" the dental office and that he had a four-member team in his truck to do it. Ed told Dutch to go ahead and do the burglary.

While Ed was on the phone with Dutch, he told them to be careful. "There's a vehicle with Virginia license plates that's been in the area of the office, and you and your crew may be surveilled by the Marshals Service," Ed told him. This turned out to be a Virginia-plated vehicle driven and occupied by Chief Sorukas and Chief Buck Smith.

Indeed, one of Ed's supporters *was* doing counter-surveillance in the Lebanon area.

When the team arrived at the dental office in Dutch's pickup, Dutch and W.S. went to the front door, and Joe and Wayne Warren went to the back door. W.S. said he had been given the code to the alarm system, which was supposed to be 1789, the year the USMS was established.

When W.S. punched the code 1789 into the alarm system, the alarm started counting down, but it never went to green.

"Uh oh," WS said, "we knew that the alarm was tripping and the local PD would be notified. So we made a quick phone call to the command post and told them to alert the PD that it was us and not to respond, then quickly left the area."

Unbeknownst to the Marshals, the Treasury folks had reset the alarm code.

Both Chief Dave Dimmitt and Chief Gary DiMartino made frantic phone calls to Lebanon PD Chief Jim Alexander and said, "The PD is going to get an alarm in from Elaine's dental office—please don't respond. Trust us. It's us, please don't respond!"

"We regrouped," W.S. said, "and went back to the office. Joe Parker actually picked the lock to the back door to get us in. We really did break in."

Meanwhile, Jeff May had been dropped off to do counter-surveillance and overwatch nearby. He picked up that there was a truck driving by two or three times and it was probably counter-surveillance. He later learned the spot he was sitting in was apparently also a pickup spot for gay men. He said one guy drove by and winked at him.

Back at the office, W.S., Wayne, Joe, and Dutch loaded the refrigerator and other things into their truck. Ed also wanted them to leave his "manifesto" or "writ of possession" at the office for the feds to find. This was very important to him. He had given this to Dutch in a folder, and they'd gone to a CVS to make copies of it before going to the office.

Dutch, Joe, Wayne, and W.S. drove the truck back to Ed and Elaine's. Earlier, when Dutch had told Ed Brown he had four guys to help him burglarize the office, Ed said, "That's too many guys to bring back here." As a result, Jeff May was left behind in Lebanon.

What happened next was very important, as members of the team reported:

When the team arrived at Ed and Elaine's house, Ed came out on the front porch and told them to pull around to the garage in the back. They did so.

When the door to the garage opened, Ed was sitting on a tractor holding either an AK-47 or an SKS semi-automatic rifle. He was pointing it at the team. He said to Joe Parker as he's pointing the rifle at him, "And what have you done for your country lately?"

Joe was not expecting a semi-automatic rifle to be pointed directly at them—particularly since they were essentially unarmed. Only Wayne Warren had a small handgun concealed in his pants and a taser tucked inside his boots. And neither was readily accessible.

Nor did Joe expect that kind of an introductory statement from Ed. Joe kind of mumbled a response to the, "What have you done for your country" query. In reply, Ed said something like, "Sorry, but I don't know you guys."

Elaine also made an appearance at the door leading from the house into the garage. She, too, was carrying a long gun.

At Ed's direction, they unloaded the stuff from the truck into the garage. Ed—still holding the rifle—told them to pull back around to the front. He also said he had some beer.

Wayne Warren asked if he had any Coors Light. Ed said he'd see what he had.

Later, Wayne said the team members razzed him about this. "He's holding a rifle on us and you ask if he has Coors Light?"

"Well, that's what I like. And it seemed like the natural thing to say to put him at ease," Wayne said.

When they pulled the truck back around to the front, Ed came out of the house and met them on the porch. He did not have the rifle with him; rather he had his 1911 semi-auto handgun tucked in his waistband. Elaine also came out at one point holding her Glock pistol, while she was talking on a cell phone.

On the front porch, they got to talking, and Ed seemed to relax a little bit. Soon, the team told Ed Brown that they had left one guy behind in Lebanon.

Ed quickly said, "We don't leave soldiers behind. Go back and get him!" He also placed an order for pizza for them to pick up in Lebanon, while they were getting the "*soldier left behind.*"

By this time, Ed had brought some beer out to the front porch. As they were discussing going back to get the "soldier left behind," Joe Parker remembered saying something like, "Well, W.S. likes beer; he'll stay."

So Joe Parker and Dutch left in the truck to go pick up Jeff May and the pizza, while W.S. and Wayne Warren stayed behind.

While watching Joe and Dutch head out in the truck, W.S. remembers thinking, *Well, there go all our guns!*

W.S. started talking with Ed and remembered saying things like,

"You guys have a lot of guns here, and guns make me a little nervous."
Then, he said, "Are there really U.S. Marshals that could be watching us
right now?"

Ed said, "Yes, it's possible."

W.S. played that up and said, "Well, you know, I really can't afford
to get involved with the Marshals if they come here, because I have
some paper [warrants] on me in Georgia, and I'd be locked up."

Ed said, "You don't have to worry about that. The U.S. Marshals are
afraid to arrest me. They're afraid to come here."

(It was for that reason that no SOG members were positioned in
the tree line near the house; they didn't want to inadvertently do
anything that would make Ed and Elaine tell the team or Dutch that
they needed to leave.)

Dutch and Joe headed back to Lebanon to pick up Jeff May. Joe
Parker felt that there was a vehicle following them at one point and the
vehicle could be supporters of Ed and Elaine conducting counter-
surveillance.

Back in Lebanon, once Chief Dave Dimmitt and SOG
Commander Robertson heard Dutch and Joe were on the way to pick
up pizza *and* Jeff May, they dropped Jeff off near the Dunkin' Donuts
so he could be picked up by Dutch and Joe.

In the event Joe Parker and Dutch *were* being followed, they wanted
to be sure that any counter-surveillance saw that Jeff was picked up
alone by the dumpsters at Dunkin' Donuts, and *NOT* dropped off by
people who could be federal law enforcement.

With Jeff May and the pizzas in tow, Joe Parker and Dutch headed
back to the compound.

In the planning phase, the team had discussed that once they were
in position and when the best opportunity to take down Ed and Elaine
arose, the code word, or prompt, to quickly take Ed and Elaine into
custody would be "*Party!*"

When *WS* said *party*, the team knew that they would have to move *fast and hard* to stop Ed and Elaine from grabbing their firearms while they were forcing them down to the floor.

When Dutch, Joe, and Jeff May arrived back at the compound, Jeff was introduced, and they all sat down on the front porch to eat some pizza and drink some beer with Ed, Elaine, and the dog, Zoe.

At one point into a few more minutes of conversation, W.S. felt that Ed and Elaine were a little bit relaxed and that the time was right.

"So I stood up," WS said, "and I moved sort of in between Ed and Elaine so that I was positioned on Ed's gun side. I kind of made a slight eye motion to Joe Parker, and I think Joe knew that I was about to give the code word. That's when Wayne Warren said, 'I have to pee.'"

We said, "Well, go pee!"

When he came back and everyone was positioned properly again, W.S. was feeding Zoe the dog some of his pizza crust when Ed said something like, "Hey, stop feeding Zoe pizza. It'll make her sick."

That's when WS said, "Well, it sure looks like Zoe is enjoying the *party!*"

Actually, both Joe and Jeff May remembered that W.S. actually *screamed* the word *party!*

On hearing *party*, Joe, W.S., Dutch, Jeff, and Wayne all quickly swarmed the Browns.

Joe and W.S. took Ed down. Both remembered Ed put up a good fight.

The district had briefed the team about the first ruse to arrest Ed and Elaine at the dental office. Supervisory Deputy U.S. Marshal Brian Hughes told the team to expect that Ed would go for his gun and that he was "scrappy."

"We first reached and grabbed the gun to control that while Jeff and Wayne took Elaine down."

Jeff May and Wayne Warren also reached to first control Elaine's gun, as Elaine tried to get to her fanny pack where the Glock was. "Elaine was cussing at us and did try and reach into her pack for her Glock." Elaine was stunned with the taser when she did this.[i]

When Ed continued to physically resist the deputies, he, too, was stunned with the taser.

Dutch quickly stepped in and took control of both of the handguns once Ed and Elaine were on the ground.

All of this activity took place within seconds.

W.S. remembered that he had placed a set of handcuffs in his crotch, next to his "junk." "When I went to get the cuffs, I started pulling out everything but the cuffs! It took me a bit to retrieve them."

Joe Parker did a quick security sweep of the porch and inside the hallway to the house.

While being held down, Ed Brown told W.S., "You have no idea what you have done."

W.S. responded, "I'm a U.S. marshal and you're under arrest."

At approximately 7:40 p.m., on October 4, 2007, the arrest team made the phone call to the command post and said 10-95, meaning both Browns were in custody. The heavily armed SOG extraction team, hidden not far down the road in armored SUVs, responded quickly and then took control of both Ed and Elaine.

Upon the SOG team's arrival, the undercover deputies were asked to step away from the front porch area, and they did so in order for the SOG team members to shackle both Ed and Elaine for transport and so they could conduct a SOG security sweep of the house and the immediate grounds.

W.S. said that once they had moved away from the front porch to the tree line, "I realized there were still unopened beers on the front porch. I went back to the porch, retrieved the beers, and the team shared a couple to celebrate the successful arrests."

The arrest team later told the command post and district leadership that the ruse was a success. "Not a shot was fired, and no one was injured," they reported.

Indeed, the arrest team proved that their reputations were well earned and well deserved.

Word quickly reached the district office "operations room" (formerly the conference room) where Chief DiMartino, Chief LaBier, Marshal Monier, and several deputies were anxiously standing by for word about the arrest operation in Plainfield.

Marshal Monier had briefly stepped away from the operations room to make some notes and a phone call when the word came in that the Browns were in custody and the arrest team was safe.

As Chief Gary DiMartino recalled, "We had our district troops on standby at the office for backup, for transports of the Browns, for protection details, and protective interviews and response, and other missions that could evolve. We had them there, but for operational security purposes, only the command staff had been fully briefed."

As Task Force Commander and Deputy U.S. Marshal Jeff White later said, "'OPSEC' was crucial, and nobody really knew what was going down."

DiMartino continued, "At approximately seven forty-five p.m., when Chief Billy Sorukas called me to say that the Browns were just scooped, I was really pleased, but we now had tons of security to focus on. I told the marshal, and I think he didn't believe it at first, because he asked me to repeat it… like three times!! I then gathered the troops into the conference/operations/war room and made the announcement. 'Two in custody, without incident.' There was some cheering and lots of smiles, and I felt relieved but also really focused on what we had to do next… and it was a lot," Chief DiMartino explained.

Marshal Monier recalled the moment he heard the Browns were in custody and everyone was safe. As he described it, "It was like a great weight had been lifted off our shoulders. Finally… the very long—and very stressful—armed standoff was at an end."

"But I also knew," Monier said, "that a new phase was just beginning. The Plainfield compound was now an active crime scene. It had to be secured and rendered safe because of all the known IEDs and other hazards on the property, and the evidence had to be carefully processed and collected for what I knew would be additional criminal proceedings against Ed and Elaine Brown. And maybe others.

"Fortunately," Marshal Monier said, "we had worked out an agreement with the ATF that once the Browns were in custody, their trained agents would handle rendering all the IEDs on the property safe, and their evidence collection team would handle the collection of evidence, including the guns."

Knowing this, and knowing that the district office had a lot to do for the rest of the evening, the marshal left the individual assignments for the transport of the Browns and the protective details, and other matters, to Chief DiMartino.

Monier got on the phone to make a number of important phone calls to HQ and their sister federal, state, and local law enforcement partners.

To that end, Monier called the ATF special agent in charge to alert them the Browns were in custody and to start mobilizing their teams to respond to the Plainfield property. He called the supervisory resident agent in charge of the FBI, and the special agent in charge of the Criminal Division of the IRS to alert them that the Browns were in custody. He then called U.S. Attorney Tom Colantuono and informed him of the same.

"When I spoke to Tom Colantuono," the marshal said, "I told him that I have good news and maybe not-so-good news from his perspective."

Tom said, "What's the good news?"

"The Browns are safely in custody. Not a shot was fired, and no one was injured."

"That's outstanding, Steve!" Tom exclaimed. "So what's the bad news?"

"Very shortly, you're going to see another government SUV outside your house with a couple of deputy U.S. marshals in it," Monier said. "At least for a time, we're standing protective details back up on you, the judge, and Bill Morse. We need to properly assess the threat environment, and we have a number of interviews to conduct over the next several days to do it. As you know, Ed has said a number of times that he has a 'hit list,' and you and I and others are on it."

"Well," Tom said, "I understand."

"Look at it this way, Tom," Monier said. "You have a ride into the office in the morning all ready to go. I've got to make a bunch of calls, and I'm sure you'll want to report to the main DOJ as well, so I'll let you go."

"Tell everyone I said great job, and congratulations on the arrests, Steve. You guys did good."

"I will, Tom. We'll talk tomorrow," Monier replied.

Monier then called Plainfield Police Chief Gordon Gillens, the director of the New Hampshire State Police, the Lebanon police chief, and the sheriffs in both Grafton and Sullivan Counties to alert them to the news. He kept the conversations brief and said more information would be released in the morning.

Because he knew that news of the arrest of the Browns would travel fast, the marshal also needed to release a statement to the media that night, and plan for a press conference the first thing on Friday morning at the courthouse.

The release, which was faxed to the media outlets that night, read:

For Immediate Release
Contact: U.S. Marshal Stephen Monier (603) 225-1632

October 4, 2007

Headquarters Public Affairs (202) 307-9344

U.S. MARSHALS TAKE CUSTODY OF EDWARD & ELAINE BROWN

In a law enforcement operation marked only by the patience of law enforcement officials, convicted tax evaders Ed and Elaine Brown were taken into custody at their home this evening in Plainfield, New Hampshire. U.S. Marshals made the arrests, without incident, at approximately 7:45 PM (EDST).

Ed Brown, 65, and Elaine Brown, 67, had been convicted on federal tax charges on January 18 and received their sentences, in absentia, during an April 24 court hearing. Since then, the two had refused to surrender. Bolstered by several supporters, the couple remained at their 110-acre residence in Plainfield. Arrest warrants for the Browns had been issued as far back as January 12, when the couple refused to attend their trial. They had continued to possess weapons, even after their felony convictions, and had defied several court-imposed conditions during the proceedings. Dr. Elaine Brown had agreed to wear an electronic surveillance bracelet and not to return to the Plainfield property during the trial. Both conditions were violated.

"The Browns may now begin serving their 63-month federal prison terms," said U.S. Marshal Stephen Monier, District of New Hampshire. "High profile situations like this are always difficult, but they don't have to be tragic. I'm glad no one was injured, and that the community remained safe throughout the operation," said Monier.

Marshal Monier cited a number of reasons for the timing of the arrests. "We had no indication that the Browns intended to voluntarily surrender," said Monier, "so we had to move forward with an operation that promised the safest possible outcome. That day was today."

Monier noted that since the arrests of four Brown supporters on September 12, 2007, there had been a dip in the number of visitors to the house. All factors were weighed by a team of U.S. Marshals Service experts, who have spent several months developing an appropriate operations plan for the arrests should the Browns refuse to turn themselves in. Marshal Monier said that support also came from other federal agencies, as well as state and local law enforcement personnel. The Browns have been turned over to the custody of the U.S. Bureau of Prisons.

A press briefing is scheduled for 10:00 a.m. on Friday, October 5, 2007, at the U.S. District Courthouse in Concord, NH.

For more information about the United States Marshals, please see: www.usmarshals.gov.

∾

It was close to ten p.m. by the time the release was sent out. Monier knew that he had to prepare some talking points for the press conference in the morning. He wanted to give the public as much information as he could about ending the armed standoff in Plainfield, while respecting the rights of the Browns to a fair trial in the likely event they would be indicted on additional criminal charges.

He also didn't want to disclose the names of the undercover deputies and the operative who actually completed the mission, nor did he want to disclose any law enforcement methods, tactics, or techniques that would harm the Marshals Service fugitive-hunting capabilities going forward.

To that end, this operation would be characterized as what it was—one of the oldest tricks in the book—a classic Trojan Horse ruse.

By that time, Chief Deputy Gary DiMartino had meted out assignments to the deputies on hand. First up was transporting Ed and Elaine to a U.S. Bureau of Prisons facility (BOP) to begin serving their sixty-three-month sentences.

As the chief explained it, "The transport teams were briefed. Ed and Elaine would be transported separately. Ed was going to the Donald W. Wyatt Detention Facility in Central Falls, Rhode Island, and Elaine was going to the Federal Correctional Institution (FCI), in Danbury which was located in southwestern Connecticut."

Elaine's transport to FCI Danbury was uneventful. Ed's, however, was not.

On the detail to transport Ed Brown to Wyatt were DUSMs Gene Robinson and Jamie Berry. As Robinson later reported it, "On the night of the arrest, October 4, 2007, Jamie and I were detailed to transport Ed Brown directly to the Wyatt Detention Facility. At about eleven thirty p.m., we loaded him into the district's Astro Van, equipped with the cage separation between the front driver section and the transport section in the back. Truth be told, the Astro Van was aging and should have been replaced by then."

He continued, "We left the courthouse and were careful to ensure that we weren't being tailed by some of the Browns' supporters, as we were certain that word was out by then that the Browns had been arrested. Ed was quiet in the back for the beginning of the trip. We kept all interior lights off, so as not to attract any attention to the van.

"As we got into Massachusetts," Robinson said, "we noticed a state police vehicle pull in behind us. Then the blue lights came on. Jamie said, 'What the heck is this about? Just pull over and tell him we're on the job.'

"So when the trooper came up to the van, we showed him our

credentials, explained we're doing a transport, and asked him why he stopped us.

"'You have no taillights or brake lights on this vehicle. None. It's completely dark,' the trooper told us." Within a few minutes, they got back underway.

"Great," he said, "it's a dark night to begin with, some fog is developing, and we're in a van with no working lights on the rear of the vehicle. To make matters worse, when we got into Rhode Island, the fog was so thick, we had to slow down to ten to fifteen miles per hour to make our way safely.

"When we finally rolled into the detention facility," Robinson said, "and walked into the first holding area, you could tell that the night crew had just finished cleaning the detention cells in that area. There was a strong odor of Pine Sol, the cleaning agent. I knew it well from my time in the Marine Corps. We would use it to clean the barracks. Well, we put Ed into one of the detention cells while we finished the paperwork, and the next thing I see is a rolled-up piece of paper coming out of the bottom of the cell door.

"It was Ed. He was laying on the floor of the detention cell, breathing through the rolled-up paper, and he said to me, 'Gene, they're gassing me, Gene, they're gassing me. They're trying to kill me slowly here.'

"I told Ed," Robinson reported, "'They're not gassing you, Ed. They just disinfected the cell block area.'"

Within a few days, Ed Brown had called one of his supporters from Wyatt and told him that the feds had taken him to a detention facility where they "gassed him" the first night he was there.

This was immediately posted on one of the social media sites following the Browns, with the heading, "Feds are gassing Ed Brown."

Back at the district office in Concord, Chief DiMartino had finished planning the next steps for follow-ups at the Plainfield compound, investigative interviews, and other assignments. At about the same time, Marshal Monier finished making phone calls, and they decided to call it a night. It was almost eleven thirty p.m.

Marshal Monier headed home, while Chiefs DiMartino and LaBier met Chief Sorukas and the undercover arrest team at the Draft Bar and Grill in Concord, New Hampshire, to celebrate and talk over a beer or two.

"The next morning," DiMartino said, "the marshal made the 'official' announcement at the press conference!"

CHAPTER 16
THE PRESS CONFERENCE AND THE AFTERMATH

October 5, 2007

A t ten on Friday morning, October 5, 2007, Marshal Steve Monier, accompanied by Chief Inspector William "Billy" Sorukas, Jr., entered the large meeting and jury room in the U.S. district courthouse to brief the media on the arrests of Edward and Elaine Brown.

The room was filled to capacity with local, state, regional, and national news network people, cameras, and microphones. Marshal Monier took to the podium to make opening statements and answer some questions about the arrest.

What follows is a transcript of that press briefing:

Well, good morning, folks. My name is Steve Monier, United States Marshal for the District of New Hampshire. I'm joined at the podium this morning by Chief Inspector William Sorukas, from our headquarters Investigative Services Division. I want to thank you all for coming this morning.

Obviously, we're here to talk about the arrests of Edward

and Elaine Brown. Last evening, at approximately seven forty-five, a small team of deputy U.S. marshals arrested both Edward and Elaine Brown at their home in Plainfield, in a coordinated and planned operation.

This ended exactly the way we wanted it to end, without a shot being fired and with no one getting hurt.

As determined as Edward and Elaine Brown were, or may have been, to have this dispute end in violence, the U.S. Marshals were equally determined to resolve this situation peacefully, with an emphasis on the safety of our law enforcement personnel involved, the community in Plainfield, and everyone at the residence, to include Ed and Elaine Brown.

We have achieved these objectives. The arrests were accomplished without incident. No one else was at the residence at the time of the arrest.

Throughout this ordeal, the bad news was that the Browns continued to invite supporters to their property. The good news was that the Browns continued to invite supporters to their property.

Last evening, the Browns invited yet another what they thought was a like-minded group of individuals to their home. Unfortunately for them, these supporters actually turned out to be deputy U.S. marshals. By the time Ed and Elaine Brown realized this, they were in custody. Ultimately, this open-door policy that they seemed to have, which allowed the Browns to host some supporters, bring them supplies, welcome followers, even host a picnic. This proved to be their undoing.

They invited us in, and we escorted them out.

Please keep in mind that Ed and Elaine Brown, even though they're now in custody, this remains an active case. We are taking statements, we're gathering evidence, we still have deputies in the field. There's a lot of work yet to be done on this case.

You're aware that just recently, within the past couple of weeks, we took four supporters into custody to face allegations that they aided and abetted the Browns in their continuing obstruction of justice.

Both of the Browns will be turned over to the custody of the U.S. Bureau of Prisons (BOP) to begin serving their sentences of sixty-three months each. They are in transit now, and when they have arrived at their destinations, we will be able to release where they are, at that time.

Before we proceed further, I need to say that the U.S. Marshals are grateful for the support and cooperation that we have received from our law enforcement partners at all levels of government, to include our sister agencies in the Departments of Justice, Treasury, and Homeland Security, as well as our state, county, and local law enforcement partners here in the District of New Hampshire.

We couldn't have done it without all of their support. I just want to say this to make it perfectly clear. I'm the U.S. Marshal here in the District of New Hampshire. I happen to be the face of the U.S. Marshal Service. That's part of my job. But I want everyone to be clear and to understand that this was a team effort on the part of the United States Marshals Service.

I want to thank, in particular, all of the men and women here in the District of New Hampshire first, including our chief deputy U.S. marshal, our deputy U.S. marshals assigned here, our support staff, and our headquarters divisions, our Investigative Services Division, our Special Operations Group, our Judicial Security Division, who have given the support to the district that we have needed for this complex mission, and this complex investigation, which we realized from the beginning had national implications. National implications, because of Ed Brown's ties to militia groups here and around the country. Because of his anti-tax and anti-government rhetoric, and because of his threats toward law enforcement and other public officials.

So I need everybody to understand, this was a team effort.

There are individuals who I mentioned who are in custody for allegedly aiding and abetting the Browns in their obstruction of justice. There are others, not yet in custody, who may also have done so. Their conduct, and the facts and circumstances of their efforts, will be investigated fully, and those investigations will move forward.

I want to thank the United States Attorney's Office, and the people that have been assigned to this case, for all of their assistance throughout this matter, and the Department of Justice.

I think I need to be clear, also, that anyone out there who may be thinking of, in any way, taking action that might impede, interfere with, or obstruct justice as we move forward, they need to think seriously about that before they do it. We will go where the facts lead us in this ongoing investigation.

I'd also like to mention that following their arrests there at the property, U.S. Marshals conducted a protective sweep. During that sweep, we discovered a large number of improvised explosive devices, both inside the residence and out. We discovered a large number of weapons and ammunition inside the residence.

We know, and we've said this before, and we've discovered and confirmed this, that there are booby traps around the perimeter of the house, in the wood line near the house.

Obviously, that property in Plainfield is an active crime scene. It is under court-ordered seizure. We have deputies there who will be working with our sister agencies to process that crime scene. It will take some time. Obviously, no one will be allowed to go onto the property.

Once that is done and everything has been rendered safe, catalogued, and the evidence has been collected, it will be secured and subject to the ongoing forfeiture proceedings.

I think that covers just about everything we needed to say. I'd be happy to answer a few questions.

In response to a question about the undercover deputies:

I'm not going to get into all the details. I will tell you that again, they were there in a capacity where the Browns thought they were supporters, but when they realized that they weren't, it was too late, but I'm not going to get into all of the operational details, nor any of the conversations we may have had with the Browns.

What we've said from the very beginning, when this started, we wanted this to end in the best possible way. The best possible way was to do this quietly from the inside out. That has always been our goal. Of course, we understand that you can control some things, [but] you can't control everything.

All law enforcement operations carry a certain amount of risk. We worked very hard with folks here, in the district, and with our headquarters staff, with Chief Sorukas and his team, and others, to come up with the means and a plan for when the best opportunity existed to carry forward with what we had intended all along. It took a while to get to that point, but that's where patience, I guess, really is a virtue.

In response to a question about the makeup and size of the team:

That's not something I'm going to get into. It's a small team. I don't want to give the exact number, and I'm not going to get into the specifics of exactly how many, but it was a handful.

In response to a question about how this was accomplished:

Well, let me just say this. The planning for this particular operation has been underway for some time. We needed to find the best time, the best means, the best method, with the greatest likelihood of success, and the least likelihood of anyone getting injured, including the Browns. Let me finish. Yesterday was that day. It's when the confluence of events came together where we were able to do that, that there were certain things that led up to it, that helped it along the way.

They were alone last night, I will say, and we said in a release, I think, that we sent out this morning. Following the arrest of the supporters back on September 12th, visitors had dropped off significantly. That worked in our favor. That was part of the plan. This was a plan that came together.

Question: Are the Browns likely to face additional charges?

We've said before that unfortunately the Browns have turned this into more than just a tax case. They were convicted by a jury of their peers on all of the income tax evasion charges and sentenced in absentia, back on April 24th of this year. But, by their continuing actions, allegedly, to obstruct justice, to encourage others to assist them in obstructing justice, by making threats toward law enforcement and other governmental officials, they have turned this into more than a tax case.

There is more work to be done. This is an ongoing investigation. At some point, when all the facts are collected, and the investigation is complete, we will turn that information over to the United States attorneys, who will be handling and looking at those facts and circumstances, and they will decide whether or not additional charges will be brought against the Browns.

Question: The people bringing them food and water...

[inaudible]. Did these people [the Browns] seem to be prepared? How long will the search take?

Yes, they were very prepared. We've conducted a protective sweep. We will be continuing our search of the property and the rendering safe and collection of evidence pursuant to a search warrant, but we don't know how long. And yes, it was confirmed that the Browns have, I think, as you know, they've been preparing for this for some time. They had been stockpiling food, they were equipped to survive "off the grid" through alternative power sources, generators, windmill[s], and solar panels. They constructed their home in such a way, in a remote location of about 110 acres, so that they had good visibility all around the home.

Some have described it in the media as a fortress-like home. It does have an approximately three-story tower with an observation tower on the top that has, and provides, a 360-degree, panoramic view of the property and the open area around the house and the outbuildings. So, yes, they've been preparing for this for some time.

Question: The fact that they were inviting people there was upsetting to many in the community, and you've had some criticism for allowing that.... How long after the deputies were there did it take to get them in custody?

Well, as I said in the beginning, the good news was they were inviting people there. Had we shut it down in the beginning, we wouldn't have been able to accomplish what we were able to accomplish yesterday, obviously, and we were determined to do this the right way. We wanted to do it smarter, not harder. We wanted to work toward the best possible outcome. We achieved that. Not a shot was fired and nobody was hurt.

But I will just say that when a decision was made by the

folks on the ground it was time to move, it went very, very quickly.

Question: Marshal, well obviously the Browns talked a lot about, you know, how they're going out. Could you describe without getting into the details? You say you don't want to talk about [it] right now, could you please describe it a little bit? The intent the Browns had of... being dead... coming out of the house [inaudible]... what they said they wanted. They said they were going to leave dead or alive...

Yes, I would, I guess, I would refer you to the public statements that both Ed and Elaine Brown have made throughout the past eight months. I think their statements speak for themselves. I mean, I don't want to characterize it for them, on how they wanted to go out.

Question: But did they try to do that last night?

Well, they didn't have an opportunity to do that last night. But you're all aware of the statements they have made, that many of you have covered in the press publicly. You have Ed on tape, and Elaine, as well. And you've documented their many statements about the two ways they envision going out. Either as a free man and woman, or in body bags.

Well, they were already convicted felons. Bear in mind that they were already afforded due process on their criminal charges on serious charges of income tax evasion, charges a jury of their peers, after hearing all of the evidence, found them guilty [of]. They were sentenced in absentia on April 24th.

Let me just say this: there was never any doubt on the part of the United States Marshals Service that these warrants would be served. And there was never any doubt that they would serve their prison time.

The only question for us became how can we best accomplish this in a way that would be safest, both for the community, for the law enforcement officers involved, and for the Browns? We're not going to go into… I'm just not going to get into specifics on the operational details. There are security reasons for that. And there are ongoing enforcement reasons for that.

Yes, sir. [points to the press]

Question: Were you prepared in case it didn't go well last night?

We were prepared for many different contingencies. You always have to have preparations, and that involved all of the Marshal Service personnel involved, Chiefs Sorukas' team, the special operations group, and everyone involved. We were prepared for a number of different contingencies, and that's what we worked toward—the best possible outcome.

But, as you know, this is not a risk-free occupation. What police officers and law enforcement officers do every day is filled with risk. And you make certain plans, and you make choices, and you make your best judgment given the facts and the circumstances that you're presented with, and you move forward. We knew, generally, right from the very beginning, how we wanted this to end and what we envisioned was the best way for this to end. It was the process of getting there that took a while.

Moreover, and from the community's perspective, and you brought this up [pointing], it is very frustrating, I'm sure, and has been for the people in the Plainfield community, and the greater Plainfield area, to have to endure a significant event like this for as many months as they've had to put up with it.

We were concerned from the very beginning with the community's safety, with ensuring that the Plainfield Police Department, and the police departments in the greater Plain-field area, had the adequate resources they needed to ensure that the public safety was preserved at all times. We worked closely with them from the beginning to ensure that happened... [inaudible].

We've had consistent contact with our law enforcement partners at the federal, state, and local level, but I don't want to get into characterizing it more specifically than that.

Yes, ma'am. [points to the press]

Question: Are you at all concerned about any sort of action? Now that the Browns have been arrested... that the... [supporters]... anything that they may do?

Well, we're very concerned. You know that certain threats have been made in this case since it started. We're very concerned when that happens, and we will take any threat or any indication that there might be a threat out there very seriously. We will work to follow those leads where they take us and take the appropriate action.

Question: The Browns made statements that if they are taken into custody, they have other people out there that will be able to carry out some of the threats that they've made. Will any added security be placed on any [—] either the federal judges or local law enforcement on... the list, and what will those actions be?

We're aware of those statements, and we're concerned about them. Obviously, we're taking appropriate measures to address those concerns. We're going to monitor and carefully assess the threat environment against any public official, or law enforcement officer, and we will respond accordingly, if the facts warrant it.

Question: Can you... sort of the review the orders... if the federal policy that was discussed... was to go in without any violence being used... in light of other operations like Waco?

Well, that's always the goal. That's always a law enforcement goal. Always to have things go the right way, but to answer your question and as I mentioned, we were aware at the beginning that this case had national significance.

The United States Marshals Service has district offices throughout our nation and its territories. We're the oldest federal law enforcement agency. We've been around for 217 years, and we're charged with protecting the Judiciary and the judicial process, as well as serving warrants. Which is how we got involved in this particular case, even though the original charges, it's a Treasury Department case about their income tax evasion charges, but yes, we were very concerned about doing it the right way.

You know that the Browns and their supporters have used the internet almost from day one. We were concerned about Ed's ties to militia groups and like-minded supporters and the anti-government movement around the nation. So, obviously, we wanted to do it the right way.

Question: My follow-up question is simply how much money was spent by federal authorities making the arrest? This can be a rough estimate. And what's your thought on them still not paying federal income taxes while they're in prison? And furthermore, has your seizure of their property... is it going to justify and get some money back on this?

Okay. That was a lot of questions.

First part of the question, it's been a very expensive operation. I don't have the exact figures, because the investigations are still going on. So we won't have all those figures yet. They're compiled by our management and budget division out of our headquarters... but it's been very expensive. And it will continue to be as we go forward.

You folks know that in June, we executed a seizure warrant on the commercial property that they own, essentially the building that Dr. Elaine Brown's dental offices were in, and the office building in West Lebanon, New Hampshire. That's going through the forfeiture process. We have a seizure warrant and order on the property in Plainfield as well. And yes, the government will seek to satisfy the judgments as to the income tax case, and hopefully, there will be some small part of our operations that can also be recouped.

But that's a Treasury Department issue. We assist in the execution of those seizure warrants.

Question, Marshal, are there lessons to be learned in how the Browns' case was handled as far as the federal government is concerned? Are there other fed agencies... given your situation but... wake up all those situations that evolved into violence, are people going to be looking at what happened here? Look at the Playbook, and find some lessons learned as the federal government... learns lessons from the Waco type of balance and also going forward. Is this going to be significant?

That's a good question. Every significant event is thoroughly debriefed. There are lessons to be learned from every significant event whether it goes well or doesn't go well. And again, in this occupation, which is full of risk, sometimes it doesn't go as planned.

Yes, there will be lessons we've learned from this. We will sit down and we'll analyze what went right and what went wrong, what we could have done better, and that's done in almost every significant case that the Marshals Service is involved in. We have a lot of experience in some of these things.

But let me just say this: analogies are helpful, and lessons learned need to be looked at, but analogies are always imperfect.

Every situation is different. Every situation is unique and has its own set of facts and circumstances and unique twists and turns. So lessons learned are very important. Law enforcement does do that, the federal government does do that, and the Department of Justice does that.

We hope, given the positive outcome in this case, that people will look at what was accomplished here, but let me just say, every situation has its own unique set of facts.

Follow-up: Will you let us peek behind the curtain, so to speak, and just give us a sense of what you believe is the most valuable takeaway lesson learned from this particular case, and how it was handled?

Yes. We'd be happy to do that. But not at this time. This is an ongoing investigation of what could result in more charges… and when things are resolved, bear in mind, that we have supporters that are facing serious allegations, and they are entitled to a full, and fair, and impartial trial, and we don't want to say anything, or do anything, that will interfere with that basic right.

And this is an ongoing investigation into the ongoing matter. We still have a lot of work to do in the field. So, at some point, we can get there, but it's not today.

I'll take two more questions…

Inaudible… their work.

Obviously, this was the best possible outcome. Not a shot was fired and nobody was hurt.

One more question, and this is really the last one.

Was the arrest made inside the house?

The arrest was made on the front porch.

Thank you very much.

With that, the marshal, along with other staff from the district office that were at the press briefing, returned to the Marshals Office on the second floor of the courthouse. The press briefing lasted nearly an hour. Chief Sorukas stayed behind for a few minutes for some follow-up questions from some members of the media.

Generally, the press briefing appeared to go well. Both the print and electronic media filed reports immediately following the press conference. WMUR TV, Channel 9, the ABC statewide affiliate in Manchester, New Hampshire, interrupted their daytime programming to file reports and transmit portions of the press briefing almost immediately. It would be the lead story, with additional sections of the briefing for the next several days, and a link was provided on their website so viewers could watch the entire taped press conference. Several Boston TV stations made it their lead story, and CNN ran stories about the arrest of the Browns throughout the day.

Newspapers throughout the country carried the AP stories that were written about the arrest of the Browns, and the New Hampshire *Union Leader*, the *Concord Monitor*, and the *Valley News*, and local radio stations made it the lead during their news hours. NPR taped the briefing and ran stories both in New Hampshire and nationally about the arrests.

There were three stories on the front page of the New Hampshire *Union Leader* the following morning. One, which led with the headline, "They invited us in, and we escorted them out," opened with this: "After nearly nine months defying law enforcement as convicted felons and fugitives, Ed and Elaine Brown opened the door to their own capture Thursday night."[i]

It continued with quotes from Monier and Chief Sorukas: "William Sorukas, Chief Inspector of the U.S. Marshals Office Investigative Services Division in Washington, said yesterday his bosses recently gave the green light. 'It was a plan that was developed over a period of time and finalized last Wednesday.'"[ii]

Since this was an IRS case to begin with, the IRS Criminal Investigation Division Special Agent in Charge (SAC) Douglas Bricker also issued a statement to the press on the Friday following the arrests of Edward and Elaine Brown. It read in part:

Douglas Bricker, Special Agent in Charge of the IRS Criminal Investigation Division, expressed gratitude and praised the hard work and dedication of the U.S. Marshals and the other federal, state and local law enforcement agencies responsible for the safe apprehension of Ed and Elaine Brown. He noted that, "The arrest was an example of good judgment, patience, and common sense. The safety of the public, law enforcement personnel, and Mr. and Mrs. Brown remained the top priority throughout the entire process, and we are thankful that justice was served in a peaceful manner."

"Moreover," Bricker added, "honest American taxpayers deserve to know that there are consequences for individuals who intentionally evade their tax obligations. In this case, as in all cases, we operate through a system of Justice where facts are presented and applied to the law. Law enforcement reacted to Mr. and Mrs. Brown's decision not to participate within that system. The threat of violence does not and cannot be permitted to deter the United States from enforcing our tax laws. IRS is responsible for and will continue to protect the revenue that our country depends on to operate."

Besides criminal penalties, a variety of other processes exist, including asset forfeiture, civil tax liens, and civil tax penalties. The basic concept is to remove the incentive, profit, and benefit from individuals who do not follow the law. Without repercussions like these, the majority of taxpayers who properly pay their share have to make up the gap for those who think our laws do not apply to them.

The Browns' home and dental building have been seized, secured, posted, and are in custody of the Treasury Department. The property will proceed through the usual asset forfeiture process and may ulti-mately be sold to satisfy the judgment imposed by the court."

In a Sunday, October 7, 2007, article written by Margot Sanger-Katz, a reporter for the *Concord Monitor*, who had written extensively about the Browns during the armed standoff, Sanger-Katz was very insightful. She wrote:

> In many ways, the Ed and Elaine Brown show is over. We will not be able to hear them speak daily on the online Ed Brown *Under Siege* radio show. We will not see fliers for their parties or see the latest video from a "freedom festival" on their Plainfield property.
>
> But Ed and Elaine Brown's story is far from over. The Plain-field tax protesters, who promised their followers an apocalyptic shootout with marshals and were instead arrested quietly Thurs-day, will likely face a raft of new charges and see many of their key supporters prosecuted, said experts who have watched the case.
>
> So far, the Browns have faced no legal sanctions for their behavior, which included issuing explicit threats against judges, prosecutors, and local law enforcement figures, stockpiling weapons, and assembling a barrage of improvised explosives devices, according to court documents and statements from Monier.[iii]

It continued:

> But in a press briefing Friday, Monier suggested that the Browns will face new charges for that conduct. "Unfortunately, the Browns have turned this into more than just a tax case," Monier

said. "By their continuing actions, allegedly, to obstruct justice, to encourage others to assist them to obstruct justice, by making threats toward law enforcement and other government officials, they have turned this into more than a tax case."

Several experts who watch[ed] the tax protest movement said the Browns could face a range of new charges, including conspiring to impede the Marshals, illegal weapons possessions, criminal threatening, obstruction of justice and possession of explosives.

"I don't realistically think they are ever going to see each other again, except in the next trial," said JJ MacNab, a tax evasion expert who has been following the Brown case for a book on the tax protest movement...

The Browns may also live on in the tax-protest movement, which seized the Brown case as a critical example of government injustice. The Browns maintained to the end that there was no law making them liable for federal income taxes, and their stand brought national attention to that perspective. The couple's Myspace page attracted more than 5,000 "friends," many of whom have embraced the Browns' anti-tax views.[iv]

Asked for a comment about the successful arrest of Ed and Elaine Brown, Randy Weaver, a survivor of Ruby Ridge, who had traveled to Plainfield, NH, in June and who held a "press conference" with the Browns on their front porch during the standoff, repeated his claim that U.S. Marshals are "hired guns" for the IRS, and said that Marshal Monier is a "coward."

While the media stories about the Marshals Service Trojan Horse ruse to safely take the Browns into custody were predominantly positive, there was still a lot to do.

DUSM Jamie Berry continued monitoring the websites and blog sites that had been devoted to the Browns and the armed standoff to look for any new or emerging threats. Chief DiMartino and Chief Andre LaBier were following up on the assignments related to the Browns' compound and coordinating with the ATF the rendering safe of the IEDs on the property and the collection and cataloging of the evidence.

The initial reports from the compound were coming in. There were over 200 IEDs—mostly pipe bombs—on the property. There were twenty-two pipe bombs with fuses that were kept on a rack in Ed and Elaine's bedroom closet. In the bedroom were other explosive devices, guns, ammunition, night-vision goggles, a shotgun, a .50-caliber rifle, his-and-hers Scott Air packs, and Kevlar helmets. Some of this was kept near the bed next to Elaine's stuffed animals.

There were several other firearms, including long guns, pistols, and revolvers placed throughout the home, and explosive devices in the laundry room and the cupboard where there were jars of jelly and other foodstuffs.

There were over 40,000 rounds of ammunition stored in the bunker beneath the pantry and kitchen area of the house.

On the outside of the home, among the outbuildings and the tree line of the property, there were dozens more rigged exploding bombs (mostly bags of Tannerite), along with pipe bombs rigged to a trip wire and propane tanks of various sizes hung on trees (which would explode when a round was fired from the house).

The ATF had brought in a team of experts from Boston and Washington, D.C., along with their large mobile command and evidence collection unit from the Boston HQ. It was dangerous and exacting work to render all of the IEDs safe and to photograph, catalog, and collect the evidence. Medics were part of the team at the compound.

Where needed, Chief LaBier's investigative team assisted the ATF to accomplish that. Chief DiMartino worked to ensure that the property —and access to it—was secure. The New Hampshire State Police, along with the Plainfield Police Department and the county sheriff's office, assisted Marshals Service deputies with controlling access to the property.

The search of the property, rendering safe the IEDs on it, and collecting the evidence took two very long weeks.

"It was," Marshal Monier said, "the longest crime scene processing I've seen in my thirty-six years as a law enforcement officer."

Chief LaBier was also working closely with the criminal division chief from the U.S. Attorney's Office, AUSA Bob Kinsella, and with AUSA Arnie Huftalen on any search warrants or subpoenas that would be needed.

The conference room in the Marshals' office, which staff took to calling the district's "Operation Room" and the marshal called the "War Room," was filled with push-pin boards filled with photographs, contact sheets with listings of known Brown supporters, copies of blog postings, and field investigative reports.

The conference room table, which fit twelve people seated, was filled with mounds of Chief Andre LaBier's investigative files, along with several laptops and communication equipment. It would become, for all intents and purposes, Andre's office and home away from home for a long time.

It would stay that way for two more years, until the trials of the Browns' supporters, and the trial on the additional criminal charges brought against Ed and Elaine Brown concluded.

On Friday afternoon, October 5, 2007, Director John Clark's office called the district to alert them that the director would be calling in about an hour to congratulate the staff on the successful ruse to arrest Ed and Elaine Brown. The director's staff said that there would be a "special guest" joining in the phone call, and they would like to be placed on speakerphone so that as many people as possible in the district could hear the message.

At approximately five thirty p.m., Marshal Monier took the call from Director John Clark. The director was joined on the call by Acting

U.S. Attorney General Peter D. Keisler, who was so pleased to hear about the positive outcome of the operation to take the Browns into custody that he wanted to personally congratulate people in the district office.

Marshal Monier took the call in his office and put the director and the attorney general on speakerphone. Unfortunately, there were so many assignments and things left to be done that most everyone was out in the field.

As Monier later explained, "It was an honor to have both the director and the attorney general call us to personally thank everyone, but as I recall, only Chief DiMartino and a few others were left in the office. Everyone else was either up at the crime scene in Plainfield or conducting interviews in the field. Nevertheless, we thanked the director and the attorney general for reaching out."

The following Friday, Director Clark sent this email out to all personnel in the entire U.S. Marshals Service:

From: Director Sends (USMS)
Sent: Friday, October 12, 2007 4:15 PM
To: USMS-ALL
Subject: Message From the Director Re: Recent Events

I wanted to take a moment to give you my perspective about some recent Marshals Service "in the headlines" events.

As many of you are aware, on October 4, 2007, convicted tax evaders Edward and Elaine Brown were safely arrested by U.S. Marshals and one of our own task force officers in Plainfield, NH, at their 110-acre residence where they had been holed-up since January. This lengthy operation required the utmost diligence, professionalism, patience and bravery to bring the Browns to justice. The Browns were safely arrested, but no law enforcement officer or member of the public was injured, despite frequent threats to the contrary made by the Browns. It was the best possible outcome.

Along with United States Marshal Monier, I would like to express my appreciation to all who contributed to this successful operation. The Deputy Director and I both received personal calls from the Acting Attorney General and the Acting Deputy Attorney General lauding our operational plan, measured approach, and successful outcome. The Acting Attorney General was so pleased that he asked to join the Deputy Director and me on a conference call last Friday to thank the employees who participated in the operation, and to compliment all on a "win" for the Justice Department and the American people. Our thanks are extended to not only the District of New Hampshire, but also to the leaders and employees of all of the districts, Headquarters divisions, and other agencies involved. Our teamwork paid off, and this case is a prime example of how well the Marshals Service executes complex operations. I am extremely proud of the bravery and professionalism displayed by all who worked on this potentially dangerous mission.

Of course, while the operation in New Hampshire was going on, the Marshals Service and our task force partners were busy in other parts of the country bringing other dangerous fugitives to justice. On Columbus Day, Deputy U.S. Marshals, along with task force officers, arrested 15 Most Wanted fugitive Anthony Ray Artrip after a lengthy stand-off at a motel near Pittsburgh. Artrip was a convicted bank robber wanted for escape from a detention facility in Kentucky. Once again, Deputy Marshals, task force officers, TOG, SOG, and State and local law enforcement demonstrated the utmost professionalism and bravery during the investigation and arrest.

Every day I review the reports and news clips of all of the

fantastic work being done across the country, and I am constantly impressed by the dedication of all of our employees on the front lines and behind the scenes. To all of you who carry out our operational missions and administer our programs, you are ensuring public safety and homeland security, and your diligence does not go unnoticed or unappreciated by me. Thank you for all you do, I wish you a restful weekend. It is much deserved!

John F. Clark
Director

While the planning to take the Browns into custody and the execution of the Trojan Horse ruse was over, there were several next steps.

The securing of the Browns' compound was well underway. Searching out and interviewing persons of interest who may have, or may know someone who had, made concerning statements toward authorities seeking to enforce the court's orders was also underway.

Given Ed Brown's claims of having "people ready to go" and his statement to an internet radio show within a day of the arrests, where he endorsed the concept of "recruiting assassination squads to target key government agents," the U.S. Marshals Service needed to act. That job fell to the district's and HQ's deputy U.S. marshals brought into the district to conduct interviews, not only in New Hampshire, but in other states around the nation, of those individuals who may know or who may have made direct or indirect threats, concerning statements, or inappropriate communications against any member of the court family, law enforcement officers, or other public officials.

"One thing that was different in this armed standoff compared to those infamous ones of the past, like Ruby Ridge and Waco," Marshal Monier said, "was the Browns'—and their supporters'—extensive use of the internet. The websites [that] stood up to support the Browns, the daily internet radio shows devoted to their cause. All of those things needed to be monitored.

"It was a double-edged sword," Monier continued. "On the one hand, it ramped up support for them, and on the other hand, it gave us a window into what was happening at their property in Plainfield.

"More importantly," the marshal said, "it was the vehicle by which we were able to introduce an undercover operative into the Browns' household. It was a key to the success of the ruse to arrest them."

Accordingly, deputy U.S. marshals fanned out in New Hampshire and a few other states to conduct interviews.

As the New Hampshire *Union Leader* reported a few days after the arrest of Ed and Elaine Brown:

Manchester – Federal marshals are combing New Hampshire and other parts of the country for Ed and Elaine Brown sympathizers suspected of plotting violence in retaliation for the Plainfield couple's arrest last week.

In Manchester, marshals have questioned several members of the Free State Project, a group of small-government activists that includes some of the Browns' most ardent supporters. In one interview that was videotaped and posted online, an agent identified one Free Stater, Rob Jacobs, 42, of Manchester, as a potential threat.

"There's been a lot of talk about once Ed and Elaine Brown were arrested, there was going to be this retaliation," the agent told Jacobs' roommate, Sharon "Ivy" Ankrom, during the filmed interview. "When I've asked people, 'Put yourself in my shoes. Who do I need to be concerned about? Who might actually do something violent?' And they all say Rob."

Jacobs denies being part of any plot to exact revenge for the Browns' incarceration. In an interview yesterday, he said he has been in contact with the agent since last Saturday "and has agreed to answer" questions.

"Their question as to whether I am a threat to anybody is met with a stern answer: No," Jacobs said.

The federal agent's interview at Murphy's Tap Room, a downtown bar frequented by Free Staters, was conducted Friday, one day after U.S. marshals infiltrated the Browns' home and brought the couple into custody."[v]

When asked for a comment about this particular article, Marshal Monier confirmed that the video posted on the internet of that exchange at Murphy's Tap Room was authentic, but he did ask that the identity of the deputy U.S. marshal not be disclosed, due to the "possibility of increased threats against a federal law enforcement officer.

"To their credit, the New Hampshire *Union Leader* did *not* name the deputy conducting that interview," Monier said.

Ultimately, Rob Jacobs retained an attorney and declined to be interviewed by the U.S. Marshals.

This article, however, exemplified what was occurring in many places around the state and in several different states around the nation. Was there a "hit list" out there that Ed Brown had circulated, and were others willing to act on that "list" now that Ed Brown and Elaine Brown had been arrested?

The article continued:

The 13-minute clip focuses mostly on the agent's face as he tells Ankrom why he wants to talk to Jacobs and asks her to tell him where he is. At one point, the video shows, the agent tells her, "I need to gauge for myself, 'Is Rob a threat to people that we're in charge of protecting?'"

Jacobs said he supports the Browns' cause and has visited

their home many times in the past year. He said he has never seen Ed Brown's supposed hit list and said he does not know anyone who might be planning to harm government officials.

Ankrom, 30, a hostess at Murphy's, said she filmed the agent and asked a friend to post the video online because she wanted Jacobs and other people who might be wanted for questioning to know the Marshals were looking for them.

Two other members of the Free State Project—roommates Phillip Allen, 22, and Michael Hampton, 35, of Manchester—said a marshal came to their door last week to ask questions, including whether they know anyone who has threatened to commit violence because of the Browns. Both said they did not.

"I think taxation is slavery," Allen said yesterday. "But I'm not going to shoot anybody."

Keith Murphy, owner of Murphy's Tap Room and a member of the Free State Project, said many Free Staters who already have come to New Hampshire supported the Browns' crusade against the federal income tax. They were turned off, however, as Ed Brown's rhetoric became increasingly violent and after he told reporters all of the world's problems are the fault of Freemasons and Jews.

"We are 'small L' Libertarians," Murphy said of the Free Staters. "We believe violence is inherently wrong. It's not in our nature."

Four people linked to the Browns were arrested last month and have been held on federal felony charges. None was a member of the Free State Project, Monier said."[vi]

During the time that the threat assessment was underway, and these interviews were conducted, the 24/7 protection details continued. After just a couple of weeks, however, the HQ staff from the Judicial Security Division in the district, in consultation with the district leadership team, concluded that the "hit list" was mostly a construct of Ed Brown's mind.

If there was an actual "list," no one had seen it, and none could be found. While there were some supporters in New Hampshire and in other parts of the nation that had made concerning and inappropriate statements online, the decision was made to once again step back the protection details.

As Chief Gary DiMartino and district Judicial Security Inspector Brenda Mikelson said, "We continued to be vigilant in the days that followed, and steps were taken to ensure the continued safety and security of the court family, but we were able to step back the 24/7 details on the protectees."

This was good news to some extent, because the hard work on the part of Assistant U.S. Attorneys (AUSA) Bob Kinsella and Arnie Huftalen—and later AUSA Terry Ollila—and their staff in the District of New Hampshire U.S. Attorney's Office was just beginning. That was, to work with Chief Inspector Andre LaBier, DUSM Jamie Berry, and the New Hampshire staff in the U.S. Marshals Service to prepare for the criminal prosecutions against the four Brown supporters already indicted.

Moreover, the team needed to determine if there was sufficient evidence for a federal grand jury to bring additional indictments against Edward and Elaine Brown for their conduct during the nearly nine-month armed standoff in Plainfield, New Hampshire.

The result would be two very important trials, which consumed the time, effort, and talents of the employees of the U.S. Department of Justice in the District of New Hampshire over the next *two* years. It was an extraordinary effort, and the outcome sent a strong message around the nation to tax deniers, virulent anti-government types, militia members, and many of those who supported the Browns...

CHAPTER 17

THE TRIAL OF THE SUPPORTERS IN 2008

District of New Hampshire AUSAs Robert "Bob" Kinsella and Arnold "Arnie" Huftalen were busy huddling with investigators from the U.S. Marshals Service, the ATF, and other agencies following the arrest of Ed and Elaine Brown. Now that the Trojan Horse ruse had resulted in the successful apprehension of the Browns, the hard work began to prosecute the four supporters. They had been indicted on aiding and abetting the Browns and conspiring with others to impede the U.S. Marshals' efforts to arrest Ed and Elaine.

There are several factors involved in the successful prosecution of a criminal case. Among the most important are good investigators, top-notch prosecutors, lots of preparation, and teamwork.

Fortunately, the U.S. Department of Justice in the District of New Hampshire had all of those things. The chief of the Criminal Division of the District of New Hampshire U.S. Attorney's Office (USAO) for both the 2008 trials of the four supporters and the subsequent 2009 trial of Ed and Elaine Brown on their new obstruction of justice charges was AUSA Robert "Bob" Kinsella.

Kinsella grew up in Newton, Massachusetts, outside of Boston and after high school attended the University of Rhode Island. Villanova Law School followed. Following law school, he was recruited to join the DA's office in Manhattan. He was then lured to join the U.S. Department of Justice in Washington, D.C. After his prosecutorial work in the D.C. office, the U.S. Attorney's Office in Concord, New Hampshire, hired him, where he worked for twenty-nine years, primarily in the criminal division on white-collar cases.

Kinsella was the deputy chief of the Criminal Division when AUSA Bill Morse was handling the tax case against Ed and Elaine Brown. This was when Bob Kinsella first heard about the Browns.

When it came time to prosecute the Browns' four supporters, and Ed and Elaine on the subsequent charges, Kinsella was the chief of the Criminal Division in the Concord, New Hampshire, U.S. Attorney's Office (USAO).

He assigned himself and Arnie Huftalen to handle the trial of the four supporters in 2008 and Arnie Huftalen and AUSA Terry Ollila to handle the subsequent 2009 prosecution of Ed and Elaine on the obstructing justice charges.

Kinsella said that once he heard that Ed and Elaine failed to appear for the remainder of their trial on the original tax case, and later, when Elaine returned to Plainfield and Ed cut off her electronic bracelet, the division started to build a criminal case against their supporters and against both the Browns.

During the nearly nine-month armed standoff, AUSA Bob Kinsella knew that the frequent references to Ruby Ridge and Waco were a rallying cry to sympathetic tax deniers and like-minded militia members around the country. "No one," Kinsella said, "wanted a repeat of either tragedy in New Hampshire. The careful and patient approach the Marshals in the District of New Hampshire adopted to end the standoff without violence was a study in how to do it the right way.

"Once it went on for a while," Kinsella said later, "and Arnie Huftalen, Chiefs Andre LaBier, Gary DiMartino, and Deputy Jamie

Berry identified four people to focus on, that's when we decided we'd had enough with the supporters. I remember that from that point forward, the investigation was seamless. The decision to indict the supporters and pursue a prosecution—there was no disagreement about prosecuting them. The same was true when it came time to pursue new charges against Ed and Elaine."

As the supporters' trial approached, and because of repeated threats against Judge Steven McAuliffe who handled the original tax trial, all of the judges in the U.S. District Court in New Hampshire recused themselves. The case was then assigned to Judge George Singal of the U.S. District Court in Maine.

Judge Singal was a veteran judge who President Bill Clinton nominated to the Maine court on May 11, 2000. The U.S. Senate confirmed his nomination on June 30, 2000. Judge Singal served as the chief judge in Maine from 2003 to 2009 and took senior status on July 31, 2013.[i]

Judge Singal earned his BA degree from the University of Maine and his Juris Doctor degree from Harvard Law School. He served as an assistant county attorney during the 1970s and was in private practice in Maine until his appointment as a U.S. district court judge. Judge Singal traveled from Maine to the District of New Hampshire to handle the trials.

Marshal Steve Monier recalled that, "Everyone who was in his courtroom during the trial of the Brown supporters, and subsequently during the trial of the Browns on the obstruction charges, respected Judge Singal. His knowledge of the law, his demeanor in the courtroom, his rulings from the bench, and the manner in which he conducted the trials.... He was fair to all parties and ruled promptly on both defense and prosecution motions. He was no-nonsense. In a word, he was exemplary."

Originally, there was also a question whether the USAO's office in the District of New Hampshire should handle any of the prosecutions since threats had been made against both U.S. Attorney (USA) Tom Colantuono and AUSA Bill Morse. That was cleared up before the supporters' trial began. The USAO's office in New Hampshire would handle the cases. As USA Tom Colantuono said, "If you allow a defendant to make a threat to get a prosecutor recused, every person would make a threat."

Robert Wolffe, who originally pleaded not guilty to his charges, changed his plea to guilty to aiding and abetting the Browns and conspiracy to impede the Browns' arrests. In the plea agreement, he agreed to testify as a government witness during the trial of Gerhard, Riley, and Gonzalez.

The three remaining supporters' combined trial began on March 24, 2008. Jason Gerhard, Daniel Riley, and Cirino "Reno" Gonzalez were accused of conspiring to assist the Browns with resisting efforts of the USMS to arrest them and bringing and using guns at the Browns' compound in Plainfield. Riley and Gerhard were also charged with making improvised explosive devices (IEDs).

Attorney Cedric Bullock, from the USMS Office of General Counsel, who had assisted the district and worked with the U.S. Attorney's Office during the investigation, flew in from HQ for the duration of the trial. He made himself available to the investigative team and the prosecutors from the U.S. Attorney's Office. As an associate general counsel with the U.S. Marshals Service, his contributions to the case were significant. Cedric earned his J.D. in 1990 from the Widener University School of Law. Before joining the U.S. Marshals, Bullock served as an assistant U.S. attorney in the Criminal and Civil Divisions for the Eastern District of Pennsylvania, as an agency counsel for the DEA, and as a trial attorney for the Department of Justice's Consumer Protection Branch, and was admitted to practice in Pennsylvania and the District of Columbia.

The trial would last ten days. The jury deliberated another four before returning verdicts on all three defendants. There were some dramatic moments during the trial. Originally, Riley, Wolffe, and Gerhard had expressed distrust of lawyers, which, like the Browns, they thought were part of a corrupt court system. Eventually, they accepted court-appointed counsel.

Before he did so, however, Riley filed dozens of *pro se* motions from jail, most of which Judge Singal denied. Riley claimed that he was hamstrung in his own defense by limited access to the jailhouse computer. Eventually, he agreed to be represented by an attorney who had originally been appointed to advise him.

Attorney Sven Wiberg, of Portsmouth, New Hampshire, represented Danny "the Dog Walker" Riley when the trial started. Attorney David H. Bownes of Laconia, New Hampshire, represented Reno Gonzalez, and Attorney Stanley Norkunas represented Jason Gerhard. Norkunas had law offices in Lowell, Massachusetts, but was admitted to practice in the U.S. district courts in Massachusetts, New Hampshire, and Maine.

Several of the defendants listed the Browns and Randy Weaver as witnesses. Weaver, however, was never subpoenaed to appear, and only Elaine was transported from her federal correctional institution to New Hampshire to testify. Like three other witnesses the defense had subpoenaed, however, Elaine took the Fifth after being warned that any statements she might make could be held against her in future proceedings.

On Friday, March 28, 2008, the government called Daniel Tanner, an Oregon-based explosives manufacturer, to the stand to testify about the amount of Tannerite that Daniel Riley had ordered. Tanner, who invented the two-part (binary) exploding target he named "Tannerite," said that while his product was legal and safe when used on shooting ranges as recommended, it could be dangerous in larger quantities when hung in trees and from outbuildings.

"It's a high-order explosive," he told AUSA Huftalen, when he was asked about the placement of Tannerite hung on trees in plastic bags. "It's going to destroy the tree," he replied.

Tanner told the jury that he sent fifty pounds of Tannerite to Daniel Riley and that the two corresponded via email and phone conversations. Tanner produced purchase logs and reviewed shipping labels that had been found at the Browns' compound, which he had sent to Riley's New York address.

Testimony from the ATF explosives expert about the Tannerite found on trees and outbuildings on the property could be detonated by firing a high-powered rifle round at the target, he said. The expert also testified about the dozens of pipe and nail bombs he examined, which were found at the property.

On Tuesday, April 1, 2008, DUSM Ken Nunes described the efforts and planning involved in attempting to arrest the Browns during the nine months. He testified, accurately, that the operation in June involving the Special Operations Group and the New Hampshire State Police SWAT team was an attempt to arrest Ed Brown at the mailbox on Center Town Road.

Nunes told the jury that the Marshals had observed Ed Brown traveling down his driveway on a tractor or his ATV to pick up his mail on a routine basis and that it was an opportunity to grab him using "less lethal" force and then negotiate Elaine's surrender. The plan was abandoned when Danny "the Dog Walker" Riley wandered down the driveway early that morning with Zoe, the dog, in tow.

The *Concord Monitor*, the next day, made this the headline of their coverage of the supporters trial. "Marshals tried to nab Brown in June," the headline read and in the fourth paragraph noted that, "In previous public statements about June 7, U.S. Marshal Stephen Monier has denied that his office had any plans to arrest the tax-protesting fugitive. Instead, he said, the massive law enforcement presence was in Plainfield to provide surveillance of the Browns and their supporters while another team of agents seized a commercial property owned by the couple in West Lebanon."[ii]

Monier was on the defense counsel's witness list and was called as a witness for Daniel Riley. Riley said later from U.S. Bureau of Prisons (BOP) custody that Monier didn't help him at all and probably hurt him. That may have been an understatement.

When Marshal Monier took the stand, Riley's attorney, Sven Wiberg, focused on Monier's statements to the press following the June 7 operation. "You misled the press when asked about the buildup of federal and state law enforcement forces around the Browns' compound on that day, didn't you?" Monier was asked.

Monier explained that everything he said to the media that day was true. "We *were* conducting surveillance that day to determine where everyone was on the Browns' compound. We *did* have a seizure order for the dental office and the commercial building in West Lebanon. We *were* discovered in the woods across from the Browns' driveway when Zoe the dog alerted to our deputies' presence in the woods, and we *did* use non-lethal force to stop and detain Daniel Riley. Every bit of that was true," the marshal said to the jury and the court.

"What I *didn't* do, and what *no responsible Chief Law Enforcement Officer would do*, is talk about what our operational plans were that day to take Ed Brown into custody at the mailbox. Telling the media what our specific plans were to arrest the Browns would endanger law enforcement officers and the public. So no, I didn't talk about that to the press. Nor would I," the marshal said.

The only defendant to take the stand in his own defense was Cirino "Reno" Gonzalez. As Bob Kinsella later related, "He was engaging as he testified. I sensed that he was a sympathetic figure to some of the jurors when he said that he left the compound early in the standoff and that he took his firearms, including the .50-caliber rifle he had purchased, with him when he left. This was different from Riley and Gerhard. The weapons they purchased were found at the compound when Ed and Elaine were arrested. It turned out to be a good move for Gonzalez to testify, as the jury split on a determination of his guilt on some of the counts."

On April 4, 2008, after closing arguments from both the government and each of the defendants' attorneys, the case went to the jury for deliberation. It was a complex case. AUSAs Bob Kinsella and Arnie Huftalen did a masterful job of painting the picture of each of the defendants' involvement in the conspiracy to impede the Marshals and aid and abet the Browns. They brought in and used guns while at the Browns', and in the case of Gerhard and Riley made improvised explosive devices (IEDs).

On April 9, 2008, the jury returned guilty verdicts on Daniel Riley and Jason Gerhard. Both were found guilty of conspiring to prevent the Marshals Service from arresting the Browns, and of aiding and abetting the Browns (accessory after the fact), and the use of a firearm during the commission of a felony. Riley was also found guilty on a charge of handling explosive devices, while Gerhard was found not guilty.

The jury failed to reach verdicts on all the charges against Cirino Gonzalez, and the judge instructed them to continue deliberating. They returned on April 10th, with a split verdict. The jury found Gonzalez guilty on aiding and abetting the Browns, and of conspiring with others to prevent the Marshals from arresting them, but deadlocked on a second conspiracy charge and on the charge of using a weapon in the commission of a felony.

Judge Singal ruled the guilty verdicts stood and declared a mistrial on the two charges where the jury was unable to agree on a verdict. This would allow prosecutors to seek a new trial in the future, if they decided to pursue one.

At sentencing later in the summer of 2008, Wolffe, who pled guilty and testified as a government witness during the trial, received a sentence of thirty months in federal prison.

Gonzalez received a sentence of eight years for his role in aiding and abetting the Browns and conspiring with others during the standoff. Rather than seek a new trial on the charges where the jury had deadlocked, the prosecution asked that those two counts be dismissed.

Gerhard received a sentence of twenty years in federal prison. This was nearly ten more years than the sentencing guidelines recommended. This occurred after he said he had done nothing wrong and called the court a "kangaroo court" when he was offered an opportunity to speak on his own behalf.

Daniel "the Dog Walker" Riley, who helped arm the Browns and helped build some of the IEDs found on the property, was sentenced to thirty-six years in federal prison.

So much for the people who became ensnared in Ed and Elaine Brown's world where you don't pay taxes, defy lawful orders of the court, threaten public officials, build bombs, and obstruct justice.

CHAPTER 18

ED AND ELAINE BROWN ARE BROUGHT BACK TO NEW HAMPSHIRE TO FACE NEW CHARGES

anuary 2009

J On January 21, 2009, a federal grand jury in Concord, New Hampshire, returned an eleven-count indictment charging Ed and Elaine Brown with violations of federal law in connection with the nearly nine-month armed standoff with U.S. Marshals in Plainfield, New Hampshire.

The indictments were kept under seal until arrangements could be made to transport both the Browns from the U.S. Bureau of Prisons (BOP) facilities where they were already serving sixty-three months for their convictions on tax law violations. They were arraigned in U.S. district court on February 19, 2009, on the new charges.

U.S. Attorney Tom Colantuono and AUSAs Arnold Huftalen and Terry Ollila issued the following release to the media at the conclusion of their arraignments. Huftalen and Ollila would handle the prosecution:

EDWARD AND ELAINE BROWN INDICTED

CONCORD, NEW HAMPSHIRE: United States Attorney Tom Colantuono announced the unsealing of an eleven-count indictment charging Edward Brown and Elaine Brown with violations of federal law. The indictment was returned by a federal grand jury on January 21, 2009. The defendants appeared in U.S. district court earlier today and entered pleas of not guilty to the charges.

The indictment alleges that for many months in 2007 "the Browns remained inside the boundaries of the property on which their home was located [in Plainfield, New Hampshire], and they publicly stated their intention to forcibly resist any effort to arrest them." The indictment further sets forth eleven charges against Edward Brown and Elaine Brown (six new charges for Elaine, and seven for Ed). They were:

- conspiracy to prevent officers of the United States from discharging their duties in carrying out the arrests of Edward Brown and Elaine Brown (Count One);
- conspiracy to forcibly resist and impede federal law enforcement officers in the discharge of their duties in carrying out the arrests of Edward Brown and Elaine Brown by means including the use of dangerous and deadly weapons (Count Two);
- carrying and possessing firearms and destructive devices in connection with and in furtherance of crimes of violence (Counts Three, Four);
- possession of firearms after having been convicted of a felony (Counts Five, Six);
- obstruction of justice (Counts Seven, Eight);

- failure to appear for trial (Count Nine—Edward Brown only);
- failure to appear for sentencing in April 2007 following their convictions on tax and other charges in U.S. District Court in January 2007 (Counts Ten, Eleven).

An indictment merely alleges that crimes have been committed. All defendants are presumed innocent until proven guilty beyond a reasonable doubt.

Both Browns, if convicted, faced extensive additional sentences to federal prison. Given their ages, it could be a life sentence for both. In 2009, just one charge—carrying and possessing firearms and destructive devices in connection with and in furtherance of a crime of violence—carried a mandatory minimum sentence of thirty years in jail.

The charges on each of the Browns were identical, except that Ed Brown had two counts of failing to appear in court. He left the original tax trial and failed to return. Elaine did return and did finish that trial. Both, however, failed to appear for their sentencing hearing. Both were sentenced in absentia, while they holed up at their Plainfield compound threatening violence to any who dared arrest them.

The Browns' arraignment on the new criminal charges was held on February 19, 2009. The public seating area in the courtroom was full with employees from the U.S. Attorney's Office, agents from the ATF, and deputies and staff from the U.S. Marshals Office. Members of the print and electronic media were also in attendance.

The arraignment was not without some drama. Magistrate Judge James Muirhead, who three years earlier had handled the first appearance and arraignment of Ed and Elaine Brown, presided.

Having released them on conditions in 2006, Muirhead did not have that option this time. They were not only currently serving sixty-three-month sentences in federal prison, but were facing serious felonies of obstructing justice and using firearms and destructive devices in the commission of a violent crime. They were not eligible for release pending trial.

Deputy U.S. Marshal Steve Bartlett and USMS Inspector Brenda Mikelson brought Elaine Brown to the courtroom first. The Browns had not seen each other since their arrests on October 4, 2007. They were separated in the U.S. Marshals cell block within the courthouse.

Elaine was seated next to Bjorn Lange, the federal public defender who assisted her in the final days of her tax trial in 2007. Elaine told Judge Muirhead that she was "not the person on this indictment." She also said that she did not wish to have an attorney and that she "did not plan to take part in any proceeding on the indictment whatsoever."

She began furiously writing on papers during the arraignment. She wrote out what Judge Muirhead later read at the hearing was an offer of a "promissory bond of $1 billion and a 'private offset' of a $2 billion bond" so she and Ed Brown could go free. Judge Muirhead told Elaine that he could not accept these.

When asked for a plea to the new charges, Attorney Lange told the judge that he recommended that the court enter a plea of not guilty to each of the counts. Lange told the judge, "I'm satisfied that the woman beside me has sufficiently understood" the charges as the court explained them to her.

At the conclusion of Elaine's arraignment, the judge instructed DUSM Steve Bartlett to bring Ed Brown to the courtroom next. After he and Inspector Mikelson brought Elaine back to her cell, he went to get Ed Brown. When he got to Ed's cell, Ed told DUSM Steve Bartlett, "I'm not going."

As Steve Bartlett later told the marshal, "I opened his cell door and stepped in and told Ed that he has to appear in court and that the judge was waiting for him in the courtroom. Ed again said, 'I'm not going.'

"So before I used more hands-on methods to force Ed from the cell block," Bartlett said, "I returned to the courtroom to inform Judge

Muirhead that Ed refused to leave his cell for his appearance. The judge, in turn, told me quite emphatically that he didn't care how we accomplished it, but he wanted Ed Brown in the courtroom for his arraignment.

"Chief Gary DiMartino was notified of the situation," Bartlett said. "When I returned to the cell block area where Ed was, the chief also arrived and talked with Ed.

"Ed told Chief DiMartino that he refused to participate in the proceedings," Bartlett said, "and that he hadn't been able to see Elaine since they were arrested. Of course, Ed and Elaine knew that they were both in the building, segregated by the men's and women's holding areas. Ed told the chief he wanted to see Elaine."

Speaking to Ed Brown, Gary DiMartino said, "Okay, here's the deal, Ed. You go down to the court *first* for your arraignment, and *then* we'll arrange for you to meet briefly up here with Elaine.... That's the deal, and you're going to take it, because the judge wants you in the courtroom."

With that, Ed consented, and DUSM Bartlett and Inspector Mikelson brought him to the courtroom for his arraignment. Similar to Elaine, Ed Brown, now sixty-six years old, rejected the court's authority. At one point during the proceeding, he pointed to the U.S. flag in the courtroom, which was outlined with yellow fringe.

"That's a military flag right there that you're operating under. That's not Constitutional, and it's not the law we operate under," he told Judge Muirhead.

He was seated next to Attorney Michael Iacopino from Manchester, who had been appointed to assist him. Ed rejected the assistance of counsel but at another point said he would accept a "council" of legal advisors. He did not specify what that meant.

Like Elaine, Ed offered the court bonds in exchange for his freedom. Ed's offer was more than Elaine's. He offered $5 billion. The judge explained to Ed that he could not accept that. Brown also lamented to the court that he'd been held in a segregated housing unit and isolated from the general population. He complained that his telephone privileges had been removed for some rule violations and that he didn't know why he was brought to New Hampshire until today.

"I thought it was a hearing to release us," Ed told the court, "and it's just the reverse of that."

Judge Muirhead told Ed that the U.S. Marshals had approved a brief meeting between him and Elaine after the hearing. The court set a preliminary trial date of April 13, 2009.

Because all of the judges in the District of New Hampshire had again recused themselves, Judge George Singal from the U.S. District Court for the District of Maine was assigned the case. As he did for the trial of the three supporters, he traveled to New Hampshire for the Browns' pre-trial hearings and to preside at their trial.

Following Ed's arraignment, DUSM Steve Bartlett and Inspector Mikelson returned him to the USMS cell block and placed him in the cell with Elaine. With some incredulity, Steve Bartlett explained what happened next:

"Ed Brown started talking almost immediately and spent about six minutes telling Elaine that he had been tasered, thrown to the ground, then transported to the Wyatt Center in Rhode Island, where he was placed in a cold cell and gassed.

"He complained about the prison food, his loss of telephone privileges, and being segregated from the general population. Not once did he ask Elaine how she was doing. Not once did he ask about her well-being. It was all about him.

"I was told that their meeting would be brief. So, after about ten minutes of listening mostly to Ed, I told him his time was up. I took him out of Elaine's cell and escorted him back to his cell in the men's detention area.

"On the way to his cell, I said, 'Ed, I listened to you for about ten minutes talk all about you. I never once heard you ask your wife how she was doing.'"

For the purposes of preparing for the trial and any pre-trial hearings, both Ed and Elaine Brown were housed at the Strafford County Jail in Dover, New Hampshire. The Browns initially continued to refuse the assistance of assigned counsel and filed a number of pre-trial motions. One of the first was from Elaine Brown. In her handwritten motion to the Court, Elaine wrote:

> The respondent, Elaine Brown, requests frequent periodic visits with her husband and co-defendant, Edward Brown, also pro se, for the purpose of planning their defense strategy, to begin immediately. As both respondents are currently housed at the same facility, Strafford County Jail, there should be no logistics problem with granting this motion.

In March, the court granted the motion with the stipulation that the U.S. Attorney's Office and the U.S. Marshals Service would work on a plan with the county jail to reasonably accommodate this arrangement. What resulted was the defendants would be allowed to meet privately at least one to no more than two hours a day and would be afforded access to the jail's law library and the government's discovery documents.

The U.S. Attorney's Office prepared thousands of pages of interview transcripts, laboratory tests, videos, and photographs relevant to their case, which they placed on laptops provided to each of the Browns. Jail personnel would visually monitor the Browns but would not monitor their conversations.

It was one of the few *pro se* motions that Judge Singal did grant pretrial. The court deemed most of the motions "frivolous" and dismissed them. The Browns continued to refuse the help of their court-appointed attorneys and refused to review the discovery materials that the U.S. Attorney's Office had delivered to them at the jail.

They also continued to insist to the court that they would prefer not to attend their trial. On March 15, 2009, the judge delayed the trial until late June.

At a hearing on June 1, 2009, Judge Singal tried to persuade Ed and Elaine that they should consult with their court-appointed attorneys and participate in their forthcoming trial. "Your legal strategy," the judge told the Browns, "is almost a suicide pact." He told them that to stay on this course would almost guarantee guilty verdicts for them.

Singal told the Browns that if they continued to insist that they not attend the hearing, he would try to respect their wishes. The court would make arrangements so that the Browns could listen to an audio stream of the proceedings. The judge made it clear, however, that at certain points the Browns would need to be in the courtroom. Those occasions would include their attendance for jury selection and for certain witnesses to identify them.

At the conclusion of the hearing, Judge Singal encouraged them to accept the assistance of their appointed attorneys. Michael Iacopino had been appointed to assist Ed Brown, while Bjorn Lange, the federal public defender, had again been appointed to assist Elaine.

Two days later, on June 3rd, the court received a motion from the Browns saying that they would accept representation from their court-appointed attorneys Lange and Iacopino. It was with certain reservations and began with the following:

> We will agree with reservations, with all rights reserved nunc pro tunc in ab initio [from the beginning], that the court appointed attorneys, Michael Iacopino and Bjorn Lange, may represent the legal fictions, a creation of the state, EDWARD BROWN and ELAINE BROWN, as written on the indictment.

They also said in the motion that their appearance was "without our consent, under duress, and under threat of death."

Jury selection was scheduled to begin on June 29th, and the trial was estimated to last ten days. Once again, Attorney Cedric Bullock from the Marshals HQ Office of General Counsel flew in from D.C. to attend the trial.

Because there had been so much publicity during the course of the Browns' nearly nine-month armed standoff with the U.S. Marshals, the court took extra steps to ensure that the jury selection was both fair and representative. Approximately 230 possible jurors were scheduled to appear that first day, nearly three times the typical number for a trial involving two defendants. It was an acknowledgment that the media had closely followed this case and that it would continue to draw intense interest from the public.

Despite the extensive media coverage of the Browns' 2007 armed standoff with the U.S. Marshals, by the end of the day on June 29, 2009, a jury had been picked. Over twenty-five jurors were dismissed due to their exposure to media coverage. Others were dismissed for a variety of reasons.

On June 30, 2009, Ed and Elaine Brown were transported to the court early from the Strafford County Jail. When they arrived in the USMS cell block within the courthouse, Ed Brown refused to change into a coat and tie for the day's proceedings. He had worn them the day before, during the jury selection, but refused to put them on today.

Inspector Mikelson spoke to Ed and encouraged him to change out of his khaki jail uniform. "The court prefers you to be in civilian clothes, Ed. It's for your benefit, so the jury doesn't see you in your jail-issued clothing," she told Ed.

He refused to change. Judge Singal was made aware of this and told the Marshals to bring Ed to the courtroom in his jail garb. Elaine made no moves to stay in her jail-issued clothing and wore a blazer and slacks into the courtroom.

The first thing that Ed attempted once he was in the courtroom was that he tried to fire his court-appointed attorney. Before the jury had been brought in for opening arguments and instructions from the court, Attorney Michael Iacopino asked to withdraw as counsel "at Ed Brown's request." Iacopino told the court that Ed was displeased with "my representation of him."

When the judge queried Ed Brown about this, he launched into a long and often rambling reply about the justice system, his previous appearances, and his court filings. He said that Iacopino was not able to "properly represent us the way that we should be represented."

Judge Singal denied the request and told Brown that dismissing Iacopino on the first day of trial would be too disruptive. He told both Ed and Iacopino that they needed to work out their disagreements.

The jury was brought in. Both the prosecution and defense attorneys gave their opening statements. When Judge Singal began instructing the jury, he described Iacopino as Ed's attorney. At that, Brown interrupted the judge and shouted, "Objection!"

The court told Ed to "sit down and be quiet!" To the jury, the judge said, "The jury will disregard that last statement from Mr. Brown."

The lead-off witness for the government was U.S. Marshal Stephen Monier. He was called to the stand at approximately eleven fifteen a.m. The prosecution wanted Monier to provide an overview of the Marshals' strategy to arrest the Browns without violence and a timeline of events during the nearly nine-month armed standoff.

He also described the numerous attempts to talk the Browns into surrendering while also working with his leadership team to develop a "ruse" to arrest the Browns peaceably.

At one point, prosecutor Arnie Huftalen asked Marshal Monier if he sent the Browns a letter asking them to turn themselves in.

"I did," the marshal responded.

"Is this a copy of that letter?" Huftalen asked and handed Monier a copy of his first letter that had been sent to the Browns on the 24th of

April, 2007. This was the day they were sentenced in absentia following their convictions on the tax charges.

"Yes," the marshal said, "that's a copy of the letter."

Huftalen asked the marshal to read the letter for the jury, which Monier did. It was then placed into evidence.

Marshal Monier was on the stand for both direct examination by the government and the defense cross-examination for approximately two hours.

Chief Deputy Gary DiMartino, who oversaw the efforts to arrest the Browns, was the second witness to take the stand for the government. In the early phase of the armed standoff, DiMartino spoke regularly with Ed and Elaine in an attempt to maintain calm and have them turn themselves into the Marshals Service.

Following the prosecution's direct examination of Chief DiMartino, Judge Singal ended the first day of trial at two thirty p.m. By three thirty p.m., Ed and Elaine Brown were on their way back to the Strafford County Jail.

The defense cross-examination of DiMartino would begin the next morning on July 1, 2009.

Because they were witnesses for the government, both Marshal Monier and Chief DiMartino were sequestered and were unable to sit in on the trial. Following his testimony, the marshal received periodic updates from Chief Andre LaBier and others on how it was progressing generally.

On July 1st, Chief DiMartino completed his morning testimony after a brief cross-examination by defense counsel. The bulk of the testimony that day was from ATF explosives expert Kenneth Erickson, who described a video played for the court of what the ATF found while inventorying the weapons and explosives in the Browns' home. Erickson told the court that after developing a plan for bomb removal and disposal, they made sure that they had medic support on hand while they were handling any dangerous items. Erickson's testimony continued into Thursday, July 2nd. His testimony—as it had been during the supporters' trial—was impactful.

JJ MacNab, a nationally recognized expert on financial frauds and scams who has testified before several regulatory and legislative bodies on the subject, was the editor of the blog site *Bombs, Taxes, and Red Crayons—The wacky world of tax deniers, right wing extremists, and anti-government domestic terrorists.*

JJ had followed the armed standoff with the Browns extensively and traveled to New Hampshire to attend the entire trial of Ed and Elaine Brown. She was writing a book about the inside world of anti-government extremism in America.[i]

Here is what she wrote on July 2, 2009, about Ken Erickson's testimony on July 1st:

> Mr. Erickson has been an Explosives Enforcement Officer with the ATF since 2001. Prior to that, he worked for the US Army for 18 years, with 12 of those years in explosives. He's traveled to more than 200 bomb scenes with the ATF, most of them "post-blast," where his job is to assess the risk of the situation, and safely collect and dispose of any explosives…
>
> It is a blast to listen to this guy testify. He's an obviously well-qualified witness, he stays on topic, he clearly describes what he saw and did, and he's dealing with a subject matter that is fascinating to everyone in the courtroom.[ii]

He was followed on the stand by SOG Commander David Robertson and several other deputies on the attempt to arrest Ed at the mailbox in June. It was here that SOG team member Edward Recor described that he was one of the two-man sniper teams on June 6 and 7, 2007. And it was here that Recor testified that on June 7, 2007, he had a clear view of the Browns' watchtower and watched Ed appear in the tower holding a .50-caliber rifle. And he saw Ed Brown point it at the driveway.

When Recor was asked by the prosecutor about the effective range of a .50-caliber rifle, Recor said it was "about one mile." When asked about what a .50-caliber round would do to the human body, Recor said, "It would blow a human body apart. It would remove limbs."

Recor then said that when Ed pointed his rifle down the driveway, Recor aimed at Ed's left temple with the safety off on his sniper rifle. He then took up the slack on the trigger (partially depressing the trigger) to the rifle. He told the court that had Ed moved the rifle up to his cheek to aim the rifle and made a "cheek weld," he would have fired and killed Ed Brown.

From her vantage point in the courtroom, JJ MacNab described what happened next when Ed heard this testimony:

Hearing this testimony put Ed into a highly agitated state that lasted the rest of the day. Elaine, in comparison, looked battered. Her posture was slumped, she avoided Ed's eye contact, and she ignored his overly loud commentary to his lawyer.[iii]

Indeed, as JJ described, Ed was agitated following Recor's testimony. He fidgeted in his seat and spoke loudly to Attorney Iacopino at several moments following this testimony.

That same day, witness W.S. Robertson, a member of the undercover arrest team that successfully took the Browns into custody on October 4, 2007, described the events that day leading up to the arrest of the Browns on their front porch. It was riveting testimony and demonstrated to the jury, once again, that the USMS was intent on taking the Browns into custody without the use of deadly force.

All but one of the undercover team members were unarmed. One had a taser and a small pistol hidden on his person. No one else had a weapon.

The Browns, on the other hand, displayed powerful semi-automatic rifles and semi-automatic handguns that evening. Ed Brown pointed the rifle at the undercover team when they first arrived.

Because Friday, July 3rd was the federal holiday for the July 4th weekend, the trial recessed for the weekend at the end of the day. It would resume on Monday, July 6, 2009.

Both AUSAs Arnie Huftalen and Terry Ollila stopped in to the USMS office after the court recessed. From their perspective, the prosecutors said, things were going very well, and they were complimentary of the testimony of the witnesses thus far.

When the trial resumed on Monday, July 6th, the prosecution put more than a dozen witnesses on the stand to identify the firearms found at the property and/or purchased for the Browns by their supporters, and to identify Ed Brown's fingerprints on various items collected by the ATF. The ATF found Ed's fingerprints on the scope of a .50-caliber rifle and on pieces of tape that were part of some of the IEDs recovered at the house.

A New Hampshire State Trooper who had stopped Jason Gerhard for speeding testified about the rifle he saw in the back seat of the vehicle Gerhard was driving. The battalion chief from the Concord, New Hampshire, Fire Department explained to the jury what the purpose of self-contained breathing apparatus was. Ed and Elaine had two of these expensive pieces of equipment.

As they had done for the trial of the Browns' supporters, the prosecution brought back Daniel Tanner to discuss the properties of Tannerite, the binary explosive that he invented and manufactured for long-range target shooting. He explained what a high-velocity round fired from a rifle would do to a bag of Tannerite hung from a tree. Such a detonation, he told the jury, would have a tremendous explosive force and could do a lot of damage to anyone who was nearby.

The last witness of the day was DUSM Jamie Berry who was on the team of deputies and U.S. probation officers who went to the Browns' home in 2006 to retrieve the firearms as part of their bail conditions. He described for the jury seeing a large "shrink-wrapped" block of cash in the gun safe when Elaine opened it.

Deputy Berry also explained that he was assigned to monitor the internet traffic and the websites the Browns and their supporters were using during the armed standoff, including emails between Danny "the Dog Walker" Riley and Reno Gonzalez about the purchase of guns, ammunition, and other materials for Ed Brown.

Before the court recessed, the prosecution said that Jamie Berry's testimony would continue the next day and that the government anticipated resting its case in the morning.

The next morning, on Tuesday, July 7th, DUSM Berry retook the witness stand. He testified about an email that "Dog Walker" Riley had sent to Reno Gonzalez in August of 2007. In it, Riley requested nails, two-way radios, night-vision goggles, scanners, video cameras, prepaid "burner" cell phones, and other materials.

The email ended with his request "for people to come and make a stand, to their death, if necessary."

The prosecution then called Senior Inspector Ken Nunes to the stand. During the armed standoff, Ken was a deputy U.S. marshal with the District of New Hampshire but had since been promoted. Ken Nunes testified that during the time the district was working with the IRS Criminal Division to plan the first ruse and arrest of Ed and Elaine Brown in 2006, he and other deputies conducted surveillance on both Ed and Elaine Brown. During the surveillance, he noted that Ed was always armed with a sidearm and that Ed kept an M1 carbine rifle in his truck. Ed also purchased a lot of his supplies from the Home Depot in Lebanon.

During the months-long armed standoff in 2007, Nunes told the jury he was assigned to work with Chief Dave Dimmitt and help lead a team of deputies brought in from the New York/New Jersey Task Force and SOG, to assist the district with planning an arrest of the Browns. His team was to conduct covert and overt surveillance of the Browns' compound and any activities related to them in the Plainfield and Lebanon areas. As such, he spent a great deal of time in those communities.

He testified to encountering Jason Gerhard in Lebanon and the disturbing nature of Gerhard's conversation with him about having a violent confrontation with the federal government.

With that, the government rested its case.

For the defense, Attorney Mike Iacopino called Ed Brown to the stand.

Ed Brown on the stand was… well, Ed Brown. The one I'm sure the readers will have come to know and love by now in this book. The defiant narcissist who hasn't heard a conspiracy theory about the federal government and the Zionist Illuminati he doesn't know, love, and repeat often to any audience.

Surprisingly, Judge Singal only had to give the jury a couple of breaks during Ed's testimony so he could admonish Ed to stop his antics and answer the questions asked of him.

Ed continued to wear his prison garb to court. He carried a Bible and a copy of the Uniform Commercial Code (UCC) to the stand with him the first day of his testimony. Yes, his cross-examination extended into the next morning, July 8th.

During his testimony on both direct and cross-examination, he said it was "impossible" that he made any threats during his interviews with the media, and it was "impossible" that he pointed a rifle at the under-cover U.S. marshals in the garage, or that he pointed the .50-caliber rifle down the driveway. "Impossible," he said.

He told the jury that he never invited or wanted people to come to the house for the jamboree or the BBQs that were held there.

The defense then called four people to the stand who essentially testified that when they visited the Browns, they never saw any guns or bombs.

The last witness for the defense was Elaine's son, David Hatch-Bernier, with whom Elaine had stayed pending her sentencing on the original tax charges. That is, until she left and went back to Plainfield, where Ed cut off the electronic ankle bracelet.

Hatch-Bernier testified that he helped design the Browns' home in Plainfield, and that it was meant to be eco-friendly, not geared toward a heavily fortified or survivalist structure. He, too, told the jury that he hadn't observed any firearms at the house but admitted that he assumed both Ed and Elaine had some.

Assistant U.S. Attorney Terry Ollila gave the closing argument on behalf of the government. She wove together the evidence and the witnesses' testimony and told the story of Ed and Elaine's initial arrest, the tax trial, and the Browns' nearly nine-month-long effort to thwart the U.S. Marshals from serving the court-issued warrants.

She reminded the jurors of the threats, the guns, the bombs, the supporters, the 50,000-plus rounds of ammunition, the Tannerite hanging in trees, and both of the Browns' many statements about what would happen if the Marshals came to arrest them.

She was brilliant.

The defense followed. Attorneys Bjorn Lange and Michael Iacopino are both very experienced New Hampshire defense attorneys who have been in practice a long time. When it comes to representing defendants in a criminal case, you have no choice but to work with the hand you're dealt.

Given their clients' distrust of all attorneys, Lange and Iacopino did extremely well. With all the accumulated evidence (much of it on display in front of the jury) and the nearly nine-months' worth of statements that both Ed and Elaine had made to the media, on internet radio shows, and to others, it was a tough job.

Attorney Lange's closing argument for Elaine was concise. He asked the jury to separate Elaine from all of the explosive devices sitting on tables in the courtroom and argued that, while she knew of them, she didn't exercise control over them.

As Ed's legal counsel, Attorney Iacopino focused on intent and Ed's fear that he would be killed. He did not *intend* to commit a series of crimes; his *intent* was to live.

Assistant U.S. Attorney Arnie Huftalen gave the rebuttal for the government following the defense closings. The jury heard several things from him of importance.

"Yes, Ed wanted to live," Huftalen said, "but it had to be *his* way." If you attempted to arrest him, or interrupt *his* way, you'd die. As to Elaine, Huftalen argued, a conspiracy is an agreement to do something. Looking at the evidence and using common sense, he told the jury that Elaine was part of the conspiracy.

It was a powerful argument.

Judge Singal then gave the jury his instructions. He was detailed and deliberate as he read each count into the court's record and gave his instructions as to the law. It was approximately 4:20 p.m. when that was done. He asked the jury to begin deliberating and do so until 7:30 p.m.

The jury reconvened the next morning to continue their deliberations. At approximately 1:30 p.m., word spread to return to Courtroom 4 on the third floor of the courthouse. The jury, it turned out, wanted to hear an excerpt of the trial transcript, which was from one of the Browns' media interviews that had been entered into evidence:

Elaine Brown: You've got to use force.
Ed Brown: How?

Elaine Brown: To the death.

Elaine Brown: We don't know how this will end. But there are only two ways we are coming out of here. Either as a free man and as a free woman or in body bags. That has not changed, and that's the stand that everyone must take. Because if we come out in body bags, there's going to be a few more, too. That's not a threat. That's just noticing them that this is the stand that we will take. We have not changed our minds.

After hearing the trial transcript excerpt, the jury returned to their chambers to continue deliberating.

Approximately thirty minutes later, everyone was called back into the courtroom. The verdict was in. The prosecutors and defense counsel took their seats in the courtroom. Deputy U.S. marshals brought Ed and Elaine back up from the cell block.

The spectator seats filled up with members of the media and government employees. There were no known supporters or family members in attendance.

Judge Singal first quietly reviewed the verdict forms for each count of the charges. The verdict was read. It was guilty on all counts for both defendants.

Defense counsel asked that the jury be polled. Each member, when asked, affirmed that the verdict was guilty and unanimous on all counts.

Judge Singal thanked the jury for their service and dismissed them. Sentencing was set for September of 2009. (This would change.) Once the jury left, and the judge departed, Ed and Elaine were brought back down to the cell block for transport back to the Strafford County Jail.

Marshal Monier, Chiefs Gary DiMartino and Andre LaBier, and the members of the USMS office were all pleased with the verdicts, as were the members of the U.S. Attorney's Office. This case had occupied significant resources from both organizations—and other federal agencies—for more than three years. And there was still the sentencing to go.

There were no "high fives" or "celebrations" within those offices, only the somber acknowledgment that dedicated U.S. DOJ employees had upheld their oath of office and done their jobs to the best of their abilities.

JJ MacNab remarked on this in her "Post-Trial Housekeeping" posting on her *Red Crayons* website on July 11, 2009:

A note to the US Marshals

Ed Brown gloated and taunted and smirked at you for 9+ months. You guys didn't even gloat for 30 seconds. You kept your cool in and around the courtroom—no high-fives, no simmering looks at the guy who wanted to kill you during the standoff, not even so much as a whispered "yes" when the first guilty verdict was read aloud. It was pretty chilling for me to see all of the guns and bombs in the courtroom, and I wasn't Ed and Elaine's intended target. You guys were, and your professionalism rocked. The U.S. Marshal Service should be proud.[iv]

That afternoon, Acting U.S. Attorney Michael Gunnison, Assistant U.S. Attorneys Arnold Huftalen and Terry Ollila, and U.S. Marshal Stephen Monier issued a press release about the jury's verdicts in the matter of Edward and Elaine Brown. It read:

EDWARD AND ELAINE BROWN CONVICTED

CONCORD, NEW HAMPSHIRE: Acting United States Attorney Michael J. Gunnison and United States Marshal Stephen Monier announced that a federal jury convicted Edward Brown and Elaine Brown of Plainfield, NH on the following obstruction and weapons-related charges following a 7-day trial:

- conspiracy to prevent by force, intimidation or threats officers of the United States from discharging their duties in carrying out the arrests of Edward Brown and Elaine Brown (Count One);
- conspiracy to forcibly resist and impede federal law enforcement officers in the discharge of their duties in carrying out the arrests of Edward Brown and Elaine Brown by means including the use of dangerous and deadly weapons (Count Two);
- carrying and possessing firearms and destructive devices in connection with and in furtherance of crimes of violence (Counts Three, Four);
- possession of firearms after having been convicted of a felony (Counts Five, Six);
- obstruction of justice (Counts Seven, Eight);
- failure to appear for trial (Count Nine—Edward Brown only);
- failure to appear for sentencing in April 2007 following their convictions on tax and other charges in U.S. District Court in January 2007 (Counts Ten, Eleven).

U.S. District Judge George Z. Singal scheduled a sentencing hearing for September 3, 2009.

On January 21, 2009, a federal grand jury indicted Edward and Elaine Brown on multiple obstruction and weapons-related charges. The indictment alleged criminal conduct which began in January 2007 during the Browns' federal criminal trial on tax and other financial charges. The indictment detailed how the Browns obstructed justice, conspired to forcibly resist arrest, and possessed firearms and destructive devices at their heavily-fortified compound in Plainfield, NH, until an undercover team of Deputy U.S. Marshals arrested them at their home on October 4, 2007.

The evidence at trial included testimony of officials including the United States Marshal and Deputy United States Marshals who participated in the effort to take Edward and Elaine Brown into custody after Edward Brown failed to appear for his January 2007 trial, and after both Edward and Elaine Brown violated their bail conditions and failed to appear in Court for their sentencing hearings on April 24, 2007. The Browns were each sentenced *in absentia* on that date to 63 months in prison on the financial charges.

During the during the Summer and Fall of 2007, the Browns remained at their Plainfield compound, where they received supporters, issued militant and threatening statements, and stockpiled weapons and explosives until their October arrest. As detailed at trial, these included pipe bombs, improvised explosive devices made of gunpowder cans with nails and screws taped to the outside, and a large assortment of handguns and rifles, including extremely powerful .50 caliber rifles.

Some of the Browns' supporters were also charged with weapons offenses and other charges relating to the standoff at the

Plainfield compound. Jason Gerhard of Brookhaven, New York, and Daniel Riley of Cohoes, New York, were convicted of charges including using and possessing a firearm and a destructive device in connection with a crime of violence. Gerhard was sentenced to a prison term of 20 years, and Riley to a prison term of 36 years. Additionally, Cirino Gonzalez of Alice, Texas, was convicted of conspiring to forcibly interfere with the U.S. Marshals Service's efforts to arrest the Browns, and was sentenced to 8 years in prison.

Each of the charges on which the Browns were convicted today carry the following maximum penalties: Count One - 6 years; Count Two - 8 years; Counts Three and Four - life [mandatory 30 years minimum]; Counts Five and Six - 10 years; Counts Seven and Eight - 10 years; Count Nine - 5 years; Counts Ten and Eleven - 5 years.

Commenting on the verdict, Acting U.S. Attorney Michael J. Gunnison stated: "Today's verdict affirms that no one is above the law. By rejecting the rule of law, and substituting a personal code involving weapons, explosives and threats, the defendants committed increasingly serious crimes. Their conduct has no place in a civil society, and the jury's verdict brings the prosecution to an appropriate end. I would like to commend the trial team on a job well done, and thank all of the federal, state and local law enforcement officials who met each challenge during the investigation with patience and professionalism, and without incident."

United States Marshal Stephen Monier said, "The United States Marshals Service is pleased with today's verdict. Significant resources were dedicated to bringing a peaceful end to a serious—and potentially explosive—stand-off with Ed and Elaine Brown and their co-conspirators. We are grateful that no law enforcement officer, member of the public, or the Browns were harmed. I am proud of the brave members of the undercover team who took the Browns into custody, our leadership team, Deputy U.S. Marshals, and the many federal, state, and local law enforcement officers who assisted us during this difficult operation."

This case was investigated by the United States Marshals Service with substantial assistance from the Bureau of Alcohol, Tobacco, Firearms and Explosives, the Internal Revenue Service, the FBI, the New Hampshire State Police, the Plainfield, NH Police Department, Lebanon, NH Police Department, and the Sullivan County Sheriff's Office. The case was prosecuted by Assistant U.S. Attorneys Arnold H. Huftalen and Terry Ollila.

If you're the head of a U.S. government agency responsible for prosecuting an important criminal case, or cases, you'd want an office filled with talented assistants available to handle those cases when they went to trial. Then you'd want the best support staff possible assisting with the trial preparation and the presentation of photographic, video, and the other physical evidence needed in the courtroom.

Fortunately for the District of New Hampshire, the U.S. Attorney's Office had that and more when it came time to try Edward and Elaine Brown, first, on the initial tax-related charges, then the Brown supporters for aiding and abetting and weapons charges, and the Browns again for their obstruction of justice and use of firearms and destructive devices.

Because in the end, Assistant U.S. Attorneys Bill Morse, Bob Kinsella, Arnie Arneson, Terry Ollila, and their staff did a masterful job of prosecuting the Browns and their supporters. As AUSA Bob Kinsella told U.S. Marshal Steve Monier, it was "seamless" from beginning to end.

CHAPTER 19
THE SENTENCING OF ED AND ELAINE BROWN

October 2009

The sentencing of Ed and Elaine, which had originally been scheduled for the end of September 2009, was delayed. Ed Brown's attorney had moved for a thirty-day psychiatric evaluation of Ed Brown to assess whether he was capable of understanding the court's proceedings moving forward.

Judge Singal ordered the evaluation, and Ed was moved to a U.S. Bureau of Prisons (BOP) facility where the evaluation could be performed.

The issue of competency had come up before during the approach of Ed and Elaine's criminal trial. Judge Singal ruled they were competent, and the trial would proceed.

In this case, with respect to Ed at the time of sentencing, he ordered the evaluation at the request of his court-appointed attorney.

On October 2, 2009, Elaine was brought into the court for sentencing while Ed Brown was being evaluated. A U.S. Probation Office pre-sentencing report had been prepared for the court with their recommendations as to a sentence within the sentencing guidelines.

Those guidelines, for the six counts on which Elaine was found guilty, the report noted, resulted in a sentencing range of 495 to 528 months in federal prison (forty-one to forty-four years).

Elaine's defense attorney entered his objections to the pre-sentencing report into the record. Attorney Lange requested a sentence of 361 months (thirty years—which was the minimum mandatory sentence for the use of a firearm in the commission of a crime of violence).

The prosecutor endorsed the sentencing range within the guidelines outlined in the pre-sentence report, which was a sentencing range of 495 to 528 months (forty-one to forty-four years).

When Elaine was allowed to speak, she said that she and Ed chose to go down the path of denying the validity of the tax laws to "awake the public to the corruption of the U.S. government." She told the court that the standoff was an act of "civil disobedience" and talked about the New Hampshire Constitution's right to revolution and New Hampshire's state motto of "Live Free or Die."

She also said that she would continue to expose the fraud of the federal government from prison. She "will always resist," she told the court. Two supporters in the courtroom were escorted out when they clapped at the end of Elaine's elocution to the court.

Judge Singal didn't buy any of her explanations for the nine-month standoff where she and her husband engaged in criminal conduct and where she "wanted to kill without trial… or the protection of the law."

Pointedly, in his remarks, the judge noted that "when Mrs. Brown was talking earlier, she excused herself politely when she paused for a drink of water but gave no excuses for her crimes."

The judge also found it difficult to reconcile "a person who sleeps near both stuffed animals and explosive devices." It was impactful stuff.

The judge then sentenced Elaine to 420 months in federal prison. Elaine would be in jail for thirty-five years, which was on top of the sentence of sixty-three months for her convictions on the earlier income tax–related charges.

At the time of sentencing, Elaine Brown was sixty-eight years old.

Ironically, had she accepted the plea deal offered to her at the original trial for the tax-related charges, she would have been eligible for release a few weeks after this sentencing date.

January 2010

On Monday, January 11, 2010, Ed Brown was brought back in to Judge Singal's courtroom in the U.S. district court in Concord, New Hampshire, to hear first the outcome of his competency hearing that had been requested by his defense attorney and then to hear his sentence on the jury's findings of guilty on all counts.

Ed Brown had been transported to a BOP facility where he could be evaluated by a forensic psychologist. The doctor spent more than the usual amount of time with Ed. In addition to his interviews with the psychologist, Ed had taken a 300-plus-question written exam.

The doc said that "Ed only wants to talk on his terms" and that he eschewed the usual question-and-answer type of interview, "so I let him talk and gathered information that way."

The doctor ruled out mental illness and determined that Ed met the criteria for narcissistic personality disorder. He said that Ed "suffered from grandiosity, and believed he was superior in many ways." At one point during the doctor's testimony about a narcissistic person believing they were "smarter than those around them," Ed blurted out, "That sounds about right," or words to that effect.

Accordingly, the psychologist said that Ed understood the charges against him, understood the role of a prosecutor, the defense attorney, and the duties of a judge.

In the end, Judge Singal found Ed Brown competent to participate in his sentencing hearing. So the court proceeded with the sentencing.

Following the prosecution's argument about the bombs, guns, and other dangerous devices found at the Browns' compound in Plainfield, the government said that they agreed with the pre-sentencing report's recommended sentencing range of 570 to 622 months (forty-seven to fifty-one years) in federal prison.

When it came time for Ed to give his allocution to the court, he said many things. He said he thought the U.S. Marshals "were pretty good dudes... and women." He pointed out that the Zionists were responsible for much of the world's problems and that he was referring to "Zionists," not "Jews."

Ed Brown said that all the research he did was to expose the "cell within the criminal government that will murder Americans..." and that the cell doing this within the government was the U.S. Attorney's Office. "They orchestrate everything... along with the Illuminati, the Knights Templar, the Jesuits, the Moose Lodge... and the Freemasons."

Judge Singal asked, "Did you say the Moose Lodge?"

Ed said, "Yes, I did."

Ed also said that the U.S. Attorneys' Offices were responsible for Waco, Ruby Ridge... Oklahoma City, and 9/11.... He stated that the judge was "filthy rich." Ed Brown said that he (Ed Brown) had been told he was "anti-government."

"I am not anti-government, sir. I am the government," he told the court.

With that, Ed sat down and the judge began with an opening statement about the purpose of sentencing following a finding of guilty. Among other things, Judge Singal explained that a sentence must promote a respect for the law.

Hearing that, Ed jumped up and insisted that he be removed from the courtroom. The judge agreed and told the Marshals to escort him out. They did so.

When he continued, Judge Singal said that he found Ed Brown to be completely unrepentant for his criminal conduct and noted that

many people who sided with Brown had their lives ruined as a consequence. Not once did Ed Brown express that he cared about those lives
or the lives of anyone around the Browns, the judge noted.

Judge Singal then sentenced Edward L. Brown to 444 months
(thirty-seven years) in federal prison. Ed's fate was sealed, just as that of
his supporters' and his wife Elaine's had been.

The Marshals, who Ed had vowed to kill should they dare to try
and arrest him, escorted him back down to a nondescript jail cell in the
courthouse, in the likes of which he would probably spend the
remainder of his life.

Steve Monier, whose tenure at the U.S. Marshals had ended at the
beginning of November 2009, attended Ed's sentencing hearing on
January 11, 2010, as a civilian. He sat in the public seating area within
the courtroom. Steve was accompanied by his wife, who had stood by
him throughout his thirty-eight years as a law enforcement officer and
who had listened to the threats levied against her husband—and her
and their children—during the time the Marshals Service was dealing
with the armed standoff in Plainfield, New Hampshire.

As it was with many other law enforcement officers and *their* families during the long saga in the hills of Plainfield, it was a stressful
period for the Monier family.

The truth is that the families of law enforcement officers also serve.

CHAPTER 20

PRESENT DAY: PLAINFIELD, NEW HAMPSHIRE

The Town of Plainfield, New Hampshire, was "first settled by a group from Plainfield, Connecticut. It was one of the towns incorporated by colonial governor Benning Wentworth in 1761, at the beginning of the reign of King George III."[i] Like many New Hampshire communities incorporated during this period, Plainfield was settled because of its geography, its natural beauty, and its location near a navigable river.

Plainfield is bounded on the west by the Connecticut River, which separates New Hampshire and Vermont. Grantham Mountain is the highest point in Plainfield at 2,660 feet above sea level.[ii] In 2010, the population of Plainfield was 2,364, with 684 families residing in the community, according to the census.

A part of Plainfield lies on the northern edge of the Cornish Art Colony, which was an art colony with its center in Cornish, New Hampshire. It was a popular enclave that flourished from approximately 1895 through WWI. Artists, sculptors, writers, and architects flocked to the area, especially during the summer months. The central figure of the Cornish Colony was Augustus Saint-Gaudens, who attracted the summer crowd to the colony.[iii] Today, the Saint-Gaudens Cornish Colony is a National Historic Site.

In 1898, artist Maxfield Parrish, one of the most successful American painters and illustrators of the first half of the twentieth century, moved his family to Plainfield, New Hampshire. No doubt he was drawn to the area because of its natural beauty and the Cornish Art Colony. By 1900, Parrish was one of the most successful illustrators in the United States, and took many commissions for commercial art for the next two decades. "Parrish was earning over $100,000 per year by 1910, when homes could be bought for $2,000."[iv]

Aside from living for a brief time in "Saranac Lake, New York, and Castle Hot Springs, Arizona, from 1900 to 1902," for health reasons, Parrish spent sixty-seven years of his life in Plainfield, New Hampshire.[v] He was well known in the community and mixed in well with the farmers, educators, and townsfolk. Parrish painted the stage backdrop in the Plainfield Town Hall. Maxfield Parrish died in Plainfield on March 30, 1966, at the age of ninety-six.

This was the town that Ed and Elaine Brown bought property in and decided to build their home on the 110 acres they purchased there. As the U.S. Marshals heard many times from residents who had lived their entire lives in Plainfield, it was a great place to live, work, and raise a family. To those who have visited the Connecticut Upper Valley area in New Hampshire, or lived there, you know it's part of God's country.

So no one wanted the attention brought to Plainfield, New Hampshire, that Ed and Elaine Brown brought to it in 2007. The anti-government conspiratorial rantings, the militia members, the guns, the bombs, the attraction to like-minded tax deniers and hangers-on—they could go elsewhere, thank you, the people of Plainfield said.

More importantly, no one in Plainfield—or the State of New Hampshire—wanted this peaceful community to be equated with Ruby Ridge, Waco, Oklahoma City, or other well-known flashpoints for violence. In 2007, for nearly nine months, it appeared that could be a possibility. The U.S. Marshals Service in the District of New Hampshire worked hard to ensure that it didn't become the reality.

When the Browns' supporters and Ed and Elaine Brown were finally sentenced to federal prison by January of 2010, and the story started to fade from the headlines, things in Plainfield began to settle down. The traffic to the compound, the threats, the militia members, tax deniers, Free Staters, and others who had inserted themselves into the armed standoff were no longer traveling to and from the community.

Folks in town wondered aloud what would become of the property off Center Town Road now that it had been sealed, gated, shuttered, alarmed, and subject to forfeiture by the Treasury Department, but they didn't miss the drama or the danger. The same was true in neighboring Lebanon, New Hampshire, with the commercial building.

When then-former U.S. Marshal Steve Monier attended Police Chief Gordon Gillens' retirement celebration in 2010, a resident and native of Plainfield told him, "Things are finally settling down and getting back to normal. Some folks were sad that the Browns had forced the situation to the point they did and may die in jail. Others feel they got what they deserved. There's no doubt they created a very dangerous standoff that could have been a spark for violence in our town. Thank God you guys handled it well."

Monier replied, "It was a team effort. We couldn't have done it without the support of Chief Gillens and your PD and the many others who helped. It's why I'm here today. To show my respect for Gordon, and help honor his many years of service."

When a member of the Rotary Club in Goffstown, New Hampshire, who had known Steve Monier for many years, asked him to reflect on the armed standoff several years later, Monier said, "I knew that there were tax deniers out there and had read a bit about them, but until the Brown case started, I had no idea how prevalent the belief was across the nation, that you didn't have to pay your federal income taxes. Frankly, it was an eye opener."

Just one other contemporaneous and prominent example of this was the actor Wesley Snipes. Snipes was at the top of his acting game after making the three vampire-slaying *Blade* films (the last having been released in 2004) and having starred (ironically) alongside Tommy Lee Jones as the character Mark Sheridan in the 1998 hit movie *U.S. Marshals*. It was the sequel to the mega-hit movie *The Fugitive*, which starred Tommy Lee Jones and Harrison Ford.

In April of 2008, however, Florida U.S. District Court Judge William Hodges sentenced Snipes to three years in federal prison for willfully failing to file tax returns over a three-year period. They were misdemeanor charges. But Snipes had been tried in Florida alongside co-defendants Douglas Rosile and Eddie Ray Kahn for using some of the same fringe arguments common to "tax deniers" to say the government had no legal right to collect taxes on income from individuals. Snipes was found not guilty on the felony charges but guilty on the three misdemeanor charges.

His co-defendants were not so fortunate. Rosile was a former accountant who had lost his licenses in Ohio and Florida and had prepared Snipes' paperwork. Eddie Kahn was the founder of American Rights Litigators and another successor group that purported to help their members "legally" avoid paying taxes. Rosile and Kahn were both found guilty on felony charges. Kahn was sentenced to ten years in prison, while Rosile received fifty-four months (four and a half years).

Apparently, Snipes, who during the three-year period in question made $13.8 million from his movies, bought into this nonsense. He owed the government $2.7 million in back taxes.

The federal judge was not amused by any of this and, even though these were three misdemeanor charges, noted that "in my mind these are serious crimes, albeit misdemeanors." The judge emphasized that Snipes exhibited a "history of contempt over a period of time" for the

U.S. tax laws. Judge Hodges accepted the prosecutors' recommendation of one year in prison for each conviction.

"When I read about the talented actor Wesley Snipes getting caught up in this 'tax-denier' propaganda," Steve Monier told his friend, "I knew that it was a larger movement than I originally thought.

"Then," Monier continued, "there was the militia and sovereign citizen aspect to the case since Ed Brown was the 'so-called' head of the U.S. Constitution Rangers. This is where the guns, the bombs, and the anti-government 'we don't recognize the jurisdiction of this court' rhetoric came in. It was sovereign citizen and militia rhetoric."

In the 1990s, the "patriot-militia" movement was often discussed in the media. According to some, the growth of militias probably reached its peak about 1996. This was after the tragic 1992 eleven-day standoff at Randy Weaver's cabin in Ruby Ridge, Idaho; after the fifty-one-day standoff that ended on April 19, 1993, when the FBI tried to inject tear gas into the Branch Davidian compound outside Waco, Texas, and it burst into flames; and after the April 19, 1995, bombing of the Alfred P. Murrah Building in Oklahoma City, Oklahoma.

On March 25, 1996, a group of sovereign citizens calling itself the Montana Freemen began an eighty-one-day standoff in Montana after its leaders were arrested and charged in a multimillion-dollar fraud case. In the end, the standoff ended peacefully.

The Southern Poverty Law Center (SPLC) issued a report in May of 1997 saying that the patriot and militia movement "count" showed that it reached its peak in 1996 with 858 militia-type groups, up from 224 in 1995. According to follow-up reports thereafter, the number of groups began a steady decline through 2000.

There was evidence the SPLC said, however, that by 2009 when the Browns were being sentenced, the militia groups were on the rise once again. And it wasn't just groups from the far right.

A "left-leaning radio station" in Los Angeles in 2009, they reported, aired a weekly talk show where callers and the show's hosts ranted about the Jewish control of media and the "new world order" controlled by "Zionist Occupied Government." The show railed against the then-mayor of Los Angeles for "supporting Israel" and "dancing around with a yarmulke on his head." A co-host said that descendants of European Jews in Israel should leave the Middle East and go live in Europe.[vi]

On December 13, 2022, *USA Today* ran an article trying to dispel the notion that there is no law requiring American citizens to pay income taxes. This was in response to a video being widely circulated on social media (which appears to have originated on TikTok) featuring interviews with three people claiming to be former IRS agents who say that there is no law or statute that says ordinary Americans must pay federal taxes on their income.

When it originally appeared on TikTok on November 19, 2022, it "garnered more than 100,000 likes. Versions of the claim have been widely shared on Facebook and Instagram."[vii]

While the tax-denier movement appears to have abated from its zenith, it is, unfortunately, still out there. So are those that adhere to the movement's beliefs. They are "out there."

It's unfortunate that some Americans are being drawn into the belief that there is no law requiring individuals to pay their federal income taxes. It's hard to understand that people who live and work in the United States wouldn't know that our taxes pay for our military and national defense, for Social Security, for Medicare as we age, and any number of things that we benefit from by paying taxes.

Granted, we can get upset with many of the things that our federal taxes shouldn't be spent on. The examples are numerous and need not be enumerated here, but the response to those things shouldn't be an armed standoff with those charged with enforcing existing law. Rather, it should be with peaceful demonstration and with working to elect federal representatives who wish to spend federal dollars on only those things necessary.

Unfortunately, this was lost on Ed and Elaine Brown and their supporters. They paid the price for their ill-conceived response to the court proceedings. The judicial system found the Browns guilty of felony income tax violations and their subsequent conspiracy to obstruct justice, among other things.

Following their sentencing, all of the supporters and Ed and Elaine Brown were remanded to the custody of the U.S. Bureau of Prisons (BOP). They served time at various federal correctional institutions (FCIs) throughout the United States.

In 2019, because the U.S. Supreme Court in *United States v Davis* invalidated part of the statute that had to do with the minimum mandatory sentence of thirty years for using a firearm in connection with a "crime of violence" (*18 U.S.C. § 924(c)*) as unconstitutionally vague, the Browns and their supporters were brought back to the U.S. district court in New Hampshire for a resentencing hearing.

Following those resentencing hearings in front of Judge George Singal, here is where those principal players are now:

- Daniel "the Dog Walker" Riley, of Cohoes, New York, was released from BOP custody on January 31, 2020. Riley served approximately twelve years in federal prison.
- Jason Gerhard, of Brookhaven, New York, was released from BOP custody on January 30, 2020. He is now living in Belmont, New Hampshire. In November 2022, he was elected to the New Hampshire State Legislature representing the Merrimack 25th District. One of the first bills he sponsored in the New Hampshire Legislature was to restore firearm ownership rights to ex-felons (which would

have no impact on his federal felony convictions). Gerhard served approximately twelve years in federal prison.

- Robert Wolffe, from Randolph, Vermont, who had changed his plea to guilty and testified at the trial of Riley, Gerhard, and Gonzalez, was sentenced in 2008 to thirty months in BOP custody. With time served pre-trial, Wolffe was released on November 16, 2009.

- Because Cirino "Reno" Gonzalez, of Alice, Texas, had a split verdict and had been found not guilty on the second conspiracy charge and the charge of using a firearm in connection with a violent crime, Gonzalez was released from BOP custody on August 29, 2014. Gonzalez served approximately six years in federal prison.

- Randy Weaver, the principal actor in the 1992 armed standoff with federal law enforcement at Ruby Ridge, died at age seventy-four, on May 11, 2022. At the news conference he held with the Browns on their front porch on June 18, 2007, he declared, "I ain't afraid of dying no more. I'm curious about the afterlife, and I'm an atheist." By now, his curiosity has been satisfied.

- Elaine Brown was released from BOP custody on February 28, 2020. She appeared for her resentencing hearing in front of Judge Singal by video from a prison medical center in Texas. The judge said he believed that Elaine Brown had rehabilitated herself and would not be a risk to the public. He noted that she had written an apology to her local paper in Plainfield in 2014 before she had any hope of a sentence reduction and that Elaine was deeply repentant. Elaine served approximately eleven years in federal prison.

Elaine had sued for divorce from Ed Brown while in prison. The divorce was made final in 2022. According to her daughter Bethany

Hatch, "She is doing well and moving forward with her life." As of the time of this writing, Elaine Brown is eighty-two years old.

- Ed Brown, who continues to file frivolous motions and showed no repentance to the court, is not scheduled for release from BOP custody until June 9, 2034. In 2034, Ed Brown will be ninety-two years old.

In an odd twist to the story of Ed and Elaine Brown, "Sonny," the spiritual guru who had shown up at the Browns' compound in mid-March of 2007 to give "divine guidance" to the Browns may have reappeared at the compound seven months later on Sunday, June 15, 2008.

But was it him?

After the Browns had been arrested on October 4, 2007, the ATF and Marshals worked to collect evidence and render the property as safe as possible from the IEDs and booby traps they discovered there. This took several weeks. The Treasury Department then secured the house and had ADT install an alarm system (more on this later).

Should anyone break into the house, the alarm would trigger a first response from the Plainfield Police Department. That happened at 10:27 on Sunday morning, the 15th of June, 2008, months after the Browns had been arrested on their front porch. Chief Gordon Gillens and Corporal Anthony Swett responded. The chief was the first to arrive.

When he got to the gate to the driveway, Chief Gillens noted that it was still locked and the "No Trespassing" signs were intact. He radioed dispatch that he would be checking further, unlocked the gate, and drove up to the house.

There, he found a man with a mostly white beard, dressed all in white, sitting on the front porch to the home, with a white shoulder bag hanging from around his neck. He quickly noted the forced entry through the front door. Concerned the white bag might contain a handgun, the chief ordered the unknown male to the ground. The man did as directed.

The chief also saw there were handmade signs at the house posted in place of the "No Trespassing" signs. The handmade signs read, "House of Prayer."

Shortly thereafter, Corporal Swett arrived as back up. They placed handcuffs on the man, who would only identify himself as "Son of Man" when asked for his name. He refused to give them any other name. A quick search of the property disclosed the break-in and trespass and an air mattress that had been set up just inside the entranceway. Later, the police determined that the white bag contained three Bibles, some vegetable seeds, and other personal effects.

He was arrested and transported to the county jail for processing. "Son of Man" later said his name was Israel Sonneosman, but he carried no identification and refused to submit to fingerprinting or having his photograph taken. "Son of Man" was held at the jail, pending an arraignment in the Claremont District Court.

At arraignment, "Son of Man" or "Sonneosman" continued to refuse to disclose his real name to the officers or to the district court judge. The judge was not amused and found him in contempt of court.

"Son of Man" served thirty days before he would submit to processing and providing his real name to authorities. He was Mark Anthony McDaniels, age fifty-two, from Hawaii. After pleading not guilty to the criminal charges, he was held until his trial in the Claremont court, on August 13, 2008.

His mother, Barbara McDaniels, flew to New Hampshire to attend her son's trial. McDaniels took the stand to testify in his own behalf. He told the court that he had been sent by "God to claim *His* property and be a steward of *His* house, the House of Prayer." McDaniels referred to himself as "the comforter."

The judge found McDaniels guilty of criminal trespassing and receiving stolen property but not guilty on a third charge for refusing to cooperate with the booking process. He sentenced McDaniels to serve sixty days in the House of Correction, which McDaniels had already completed. He also gave McDaniels a six-month suspended sentence, which would be dismissed in two years on the condition that McDaniels not return to the Browns' former property. McDaniels agreed.

Barbara McDaniels said that her son had been caught up in what she termed a "group of religious extremists" beginning about 2004. She believed they were called the "House of Israel." Since that time, she said, her son had limited communication with his family and had given up most of his possessions. According to the mother, Mark Anthony was often homeless.

The "Sonny" who traveled to Plainfield in mid-March during the armed standoff had stayed with Ed and Elaine Brown for more than a week. That "Sonny" was also dressed in all white, had a long, very white beard, and also carried a white bag over his shoulder. He offered the Browns his "guidance" on his views of Christianity and his interpretations of the "laws of man." When that "Sonny" left the compound, he flew back to Hawaii from the Manchester-Boston Regional Airport. The Londonderry Police approached him and spoke with him and took some surveillance photographs of him for the U.S. Marshals, but they had no reason to detain him. He was in possession of a boarding pass.

Was the Mark McDaniels arrested and convicted of trespass in 2008 the same "Sonny" as had visited the Browns in March of 2007?

The Plainfield Police Department didn't believe so. When asked about the similarities by members of the press, Plainfield PD Corporal Paul Roberts said that "despite the similarities in attire, the surveillance photographs of 'Sonny' at the Manchester airport show a stockier man with a fuller and much whiter beard."

Chief Gary DiMartino agreed. When he compared the photographs of the "Sonny" from during the standoff to that of Mark McDaniels that Plainfield PD arrested seven months later, he surmised they were two different people.

"I don't believe they're the same person," DiMartino said. "However, it is quite a coincidence that two similarly attired people from Hawaii, professing a similar form of Christianity, would show up at the compound in Plainfield.

"Moreover," Chief DiMartino added, "we were told that McDaniels had only one phone number in the prepaid cell phone he had with him. It was the cell phone number of one of Ed Brown's supporters from New Hampshire. How he got that name and that phone number, we don't know. When the Brown supporter was contacted, he told us he didn't know anything about Mark McDaniels or why he was at the former Brown property. By that time, we were elbows deep into our investigations and the preparations for the upcoming trials."

Marshal Steve Monier added, "It's possible they were from the same religious group that McDaniels' mother talked about and that they knew each other in some manner. We'll never know for certain, but in any case, it's very unlikely that either 'Sonny' or 'Son of Man' McDaniels will ever again return to the Plainfield property."

After clearing the property of IEDs and booby traps, the Treasury Department took steps to secure the compound by installing a locked gate at the end of the driveway, posting government "No Trespassing" signs, and shuttering and alarming the house. They hired ADT to install an alarm system at the home to alert law enforcement of any break-in, such as when "Son of Man" Mark McDaniels broke in.

Given the large square footage and unique attributes of the house (a bunker, an escape tunnel), the installation took some time. An IRS agent accompanied the technician during the install. At one point some hours into running some of the wiring to the alarm system, the technician called the agent over.

"I think you need to see what's hidden in this shaft," the technician told the agent.

He directed the agent's attention to what looked like a small elevator shaft running from the ground floor to the top floor. Hanging near the top was a pouch or a bag, which had something in it.

The agent was able to retrieve the bag, and when he opened it, he found gold and silver bullion and gold and silver coins. Apparently, the safe where Ed and Elaine Brown had kept shrink-wrapped packets of cash wasn't the only place they kept some of their monetary assets. They decided to squirrel away hard currency as well.

Marshal Steve Monier later recalled that after the gold and silver was inventoried and appraised, "It had an approximate value of $60,000 and was subject to the same forfeiture proceedings as the real property."

The other question often asked in connection with the Brown case is, "Where is the sovereign citizens movement today?" Does it still exist, and can the people who identify with the movement still be a threat to law enforcement?

The movement is alive and well. In fact, it has spread around the world, and some sovereign citizens can still pose a threat to law enforcement. The FBI has described the movement as "domestic terrorism" in the U.S. and calls its followers "anti-government extremists who believe that even though they reside in the U.S., they are separate or 'sovereign' from the United States."

Mark Pitcavage, a researcher at the Anti-Defamation League (ADL), who has followed the movement for more than twenty years, has said that the "ideology hatched in the 1970s and grew out of Posse Comitatus, a U.S. anti-government group that contained many followers who were anti-Semitic and believed governments were controlled by Jews."[viii]

The movement rose to prominence in the 1990s alongside the militia movement and then spread to Canada through anti-tax groups and later to Australia, the UK, and Ireland, according to Pitcavage.[ix]

Following the horrific Oklahoma City bombing, the movement lost much of its appeal to people who might otherwise have been sympathetic, but it did not die. Today's sovereign citizens may go by other names such as freemen or common law citizens. While some have ties to a militia group, you are more likely to see sovereign citizens filing frivolous legal pleadings in courts when they have an unsatisfactory encounter with a government agency that they believe to be illegitimate.

But other encounters with law enforcement have turned deadly. In 2010, two Arkansas police officers stopped sovereign citizen extremists Jerry Kane and his sixteen-year-old son, Joseph, during a traffic stop on Interstate 40. One officer attempted to frisk Jerry Kane outside of the van they were driving, and a struggle ensued. Joseph Kane then jumped out of the van and opened fire with an AK-47 rifle, killing both officers.

Approximately two hours later, police shot both the Kanes in a second encounter at a Walmart Supercenter. In that confrontation, two more officers were wounded and hospitalized with serious injuries. Both Kanes died at the scene.

Unfortunately, law enforcement is a profession filled with risk.[x] There is no doubt that extremist groups of all stripes can pose a threat to law enforcement officers nationwide.

EPILOGUE

The author and contributors hope that there are some enduring lessons to be learned from the armed standoff in Plainfield, New Hampshire. When this situation first developed, the district took a go-slow, less adversarial approach and opened lines of communication with both the Browns immediately.

It also developed the outline of a strategy early on that the best way to end this without violence would be to conduct another ruse—in this case a Trojan Horse strategy. The thought was, "We arrested them successfully on a ruse the first time; let's do it again."

There were several factors that worked in the district's favor. One was the remote location of the Browns' compound in a sparsely populated area of Plainfield, New Hampshire. The second was that the Browns said they weren't leaving their property, and they didn't.

The other huge factor in this standoff, unlike others that preceded it, was the use of the World Wide Web. Needless to say, this changed the landscape for law enforcement and, as discussed in the book, was a double-edged sword. Many of the threats and inappropriate communications were being sent back and forth on the internet.

The district was fortunate enough to have people in New Hampshire working with other agencies and USMS HQ to monitor the blog sites, websites, Myspace, and other pages in real time to gather important intelligence, but it took some doing. The law enforcement community, particularly at the federal level, needs to be nimble when it comes to situations like the Ed and Elaine Brown case going forward.

The "go-slow approach" was not without some controversy. There were times that the pressure to "arrest them now" came from within the agency, as well as from outside. The leadership teams debated, found consensus, and moved forward. Ultimately, this approach led to the successful conclusion of the longest armed standoff in USMS history. No one was injured or killed, and the Browns and their key supporters were brought to justice.

As to what happened with the key players from the USMS involved in this case, each year, the Attorney General of the United States recognizes Department of Justice employees and teams for exceptional law enforcement service and remarkable achievements in policing.

Here are some snippets of the recognition afforded to some of those USMS members and one of their local partners:

In recognition of their outstanding leadership and management of the investigation and apprehension of dangerous armed fugitives Ed and Elaine Brown, without incident or injury, the 2007 *Attorney General's Award for Distinguished Service*, went to (USMS) *Gary R. DiMartino*, Chief Deputy U.S. Marshal, District of New Hampshire; from the USMS Investigative Operations Division, Regional Field Chief *David M. Dimmitt*, Chief Inspectors *William J. Sorukas Jr., John M. Cuff, Joseph M. Parker*, and *Andre J. LaBier*; Inspector *Wayne S. Warren*; Commander *David K. Robertson*, Special Operations Group, Technical Operations Division; Special Deputy U.S. Marshal *Jeffery M. May*, Southeast Regional Task Force; Supervisory Deputy U.S. Marshal *W.S. Robertson*, Middle District of

Georgia; and from the Plainfield, N.H. Police Department, Chief *Gordon A. Gillens*. The team was recognized for their outstanding service and leadership to the American people.

The U.S. Marshals Service also conducts an annual awards ceremony to recognize outstanding performance by a district office, group, or individual for service "above and beyond."

To that end, for the year 2007, the District of New Hampshire received its second *"District of the Year"* Award for its handling of the Browns' armed standoff. The district's first ever *"District of the Year"* award, for 2004, was also achieved during the tenure of U.S. Marshal Stephen Monier and Chief Deputy U.S. Marshal Gary DiMartino.

In 2007, Chief Deputy U.S. Marshal Gary DiMartino and U.S. Marshal Steve Monier received the USMS Director's Award for "*Leadership Beyond the Standard.*"

Judicial Security Inspector Brenda Mikelson received the USMS Director's "*Special Act Award*" for her leadership and management of the protection details. When Chief DiMartino retired from the USMS in January of 2011, Brenda Mikelson was promoted to Chief Deputy U.S. Marshal in the District of New Hampshire. Brenda retired from the USMS in 2023 after thirty-one years of distinguished service as a law enforcement officer.

DUSM Jamie Berry received the 2007 USMS "*Employee of the Year*" Award for his investigative work on the Ed and Elaine Brown case and his work during Jason Gerhard's arrest at Ft. Leonard Wood, Missouri.

Chief Gordon Gillens, from the Plainfield, New Hampshire, Police Department, also received the 2007 USMS "*Law Enforcement Officer of the Year*" Award for his work with the U.S. Marshals during the armed standoff.

Chief Gillens, a decorated USMC Vietnam combat veteran, retired from the Plainfield PD in 2010. Most of the community turned out to a BBQ at the fire department that summer to honor his twenty-five years of service as the Plainfield police chief. The then-*former* U.S. Marshal Steve Monier attended the BBQ. Sadly, Chief Gillens, a long-time Plainfield, New Hampshire, resident, passed away unexpectedly on Tuesday afternoon, January 17, 2023. He was seventy-seven years old.

In addition, the Department of Treasury, IRS Criminal Investigation Division presented an award to Chief Deputy Gary DiMartino for his work on the Browns' case. It was inscribed:

> *In recognition of your leadership, patience, and sound judgment concerning the safe apprehension of Ed and Elaine Brown and the Law Enforcement Mission of IRS Criminal Investigation Division, October, 2007.*

In accepting the award, Gary said he was grateful, but that the award belonged to the District of New Hampshire, U.S. Marshals Service office, and everyone that worked on this case.

USM Stephen Monier spent a total of thirty-eight years as a law enforcement officer. When former New Hampshire Attorney General Kelly Ayotte became U.S. Senator-elect Kelly Ayotte in November of 2010, she asked Steve to serve as her Special Assistant for Homeland Security, Military, and Veterans Affairs. He served in that position until his (final) retirement from government service in 2017.

Steve continues to reside in New Hampshire with his wife, Sandi, where their children and grandchildren also live. Steve and Sandi enjoy spending the coldest months of winter in Florida.

This is Steve's second published non-fiction. The first, titled *Crime of the Century: The Lindbergh Kidnapping Hoax*, was published in 1993 with his co-author and friend, Attorney Greg Ahlgren of Manchester, New Hampshire.

Chief Deputy U.S. Marshal Gary DiMartino retired in January of

2011 after a twenty-seven-year career with the United States Marshals Service, and thirty-one years as a law enforcement officer.

After retirement, Gary founded Innovative Safety Concepts, LLC, a safety and security consulting company that provides services to both government and private sector clients. Innovative Safety Concepts is still in operation today.

Gary and his wife Lisa continue to reside in New Hampshire with their son, where they remain active in their community. They also enjoy traveling to Hawaii when they can, to visit their daughter and her husband, an active-duty member of the military.

Following retirement from the USMS, Chief Dave Dimmitt taught criminal justice for five years at a career technical center in Hudson, New York. He is now retired and spends time with his family. He enjoys fishing, reading, and corn hole tournaments. Chief Dimmitt splits his time between his home state of Iowa and New York. While in Iowa, Dave belongs to the Mayor's Youth Advisory Group in his hometown and volunteers his time mentoring young people in the local community high school.

A few years after the Ed and Elaine Brown armed standoff, Chief Dimmitt was diagnosed with cumulative Post Traumatic Stress Disorder (PTSD), a mental health issue that affects far too many of our law enforcement officers and first responders. As Dave says, "Cumulative PTSD in the law enforcement community is a *real issue* and needs to be recognized by the profession and addressed in a more comprehensive way."

The National Alliance on Mental Illness (NAMI) is the nation's largest grassroots mental health organization dedicated to building better lives for the millions of Americans affected by mental illness. There are more than 600 NAMI state organizations and affiliates across the country. Many NAMI affiliates offer an array of free support and educational programs. You can locate them by going to their website at: www.nami.org/findsupport.

AUTHOR'S NOTES

What happened to Zoe the dog and Amelia the cat?

Right after the undercover marshals arrested Ed and Elaine Brown on the front porch of their fortress-like home, I started receiving phone calls, emails, and other messages (sometimes in person while picking up my mail) asking, "What happened to Zoe the dog?"

I'm a dog lover. I understood it.

Zoe was a wonderful young female German Shepherd that the Browns had acquired during the armed standoff. At several points, I'm sure Zoe was very stressed. Having owned dogs all my life, it broke my heart. Dogs get spooked when there are loud noises, like gunfire and things going *boom*. Sadly, Zoe was exposed to that and more.

It wasn't very well known at the time, but the Browns also had a cat named Amelia. Cats aren't very fond of things that go *boom*, either.

Working with the Plainfield Police Department, we contacted the Upper Valley Humane Society. They responded and rescued both Zoe and Amelia. It was not long before both of them were placed in good homes, hopefully where they wouldn't have to worry about guns, bombs, and scary people.

The second question I often get asked is, "What became of the

Browns' 110-acre hilltop compound and the dental office?" Pursuant to the Treasury Department's forfeiture proceedings and orders from the court, both properties were sold at auctions overseen by the U.S. Marshals Service. Under the skillful supervision of Chief Deputy Brenda Mikelson, it took a great deal of work.

There were no bidders at the first attempt at an auction in August of 2014. It probably had something to do with all the disclaimers warning that, despite an exhaustive search, there may still be booby traps and explosives on the property.

In October 2015, a Plainfield resident successfully purchased at auction both the former Brown residence on Center of Town Road and the commercial property on Glen Road in Lebanon, paying $205,000 and $415,000 respectively for each. The properties have since been resold.

I would be remiss if I didn't take a moment to thank the incredible people I worked with throughout my thirty-eight-year career in law enforcement, the last eight of which were with the U.S. Marshals Service. A special thanks to those I served with at the Goffstown, New Hampshire, Police Department, where I learned what it meant to *serve* the community and *protect* life. Goffstown was a wonderful community for the thirty years I helped police it, and it still is today.

U.S. Marshals don't get to pick a new team after their appointment to the office. I was blessed, in the District of New Hampshire, to walk into an office filled with dedicated men and women. In comparison to many of the other ninety-four "districts," we were a small office. But, to a person, they were very, very talented. A big thank you to every one of them. You will not be forgotten.

To USMS Director John Clark (now retired) and the many senior people at USMS HQ, and others we worked with throughout 2007, before and after, you all added to the storied history of the U.S. Marshals. There's a reason the U.S. Marshals are legendary. It's the people who have worn the Star and served so well for more than 234 years. You have added to the Star's luster, and for good reason. Thank you.

To Plainfield PD Chief Gordon Gillens and his team, Lebanon PD Chief Jim Alexander and the members of his team, the Sullivan and Grafton County Sheriff's Offices, the New Hampshire State Police, Governor John Lynch and his office, New Hampshire Attorney General Kelly Ayotte and Deputy Attorney General Bud Fitch, the New Hampshire National Guard: you all did your communities, your state, and the nation proud. Thank you for the support and cooperation.

My parents taught me that public service to our neighbors and the nation is a worthy calling, and faith in God and family maintains us. To my partner and best friend in life, my wife Sandi, and our wonderful children and grandchildren, no one could ask for more. You are *always* there for me, and your love and affection has *always* sustained me.

While I have tried to accurately summarize the salient points and timeline(s) of the original tax trial, the supporters' trial in 2008, and that of Ed and Elaine Brown in 2009, this is not a book about the criminal proceedings. It's about the efforts of the USMS to successfully end a dangerous, 266-day armed standoff in Plainfield, New Hampshire.

Any mistakes as to those trial summaries, or any other facts and circumstances set forth in this book, are mine.

Stay well, and stay safe.

Steve Monier

September 2023

ACKNOWLEDGMENTS

Many people helped in the researching and writing of this book. A special note of appreciation is due to my contributors, retired USMS Chief Deputies Gary DiMartino and Dave Dimmitt. You were there when it happened, and you've been there for this book. Thank you!

To our research assistants Kate Renaud and Denise Roberge, the problem wasn't a shortage of information about this case, it was organizing the most important information about the case. To our readers, Ken Monier, Susan Monier, Ashley Methot, Chad Monier, and Denise and Kate again, thanks for taking the time and for your help with the project!

To the *many* people who played a big role in ending the standoff, or seeing that justice was done, and agreed to be interviewed for this book, *thank you* for taking the time to speak with us via Zoom or in person. You know who you are. Your memories of what took place when, where, and how, and the "inside" stories, made this a fun project at times, even though the topic is quite serious.

Laughter is necessary even in the darkest of times. Thank you for the hours of conversation and your contributions to this book.

APPENDIX

Show me the Law...

"The Sixteenth Amendment authorizes Congress to establish an individual income tax. 26 U.S.C.§ 1 imposes and sets rates for a tax on the income of every married individual, head of household, unmarried individual, estate, and trust. 26 U.S.C. § 6012 requires the filing of income tax returns, and 26 U.S.C. § 6151 requires payment of income taxes."

In addition, the question of whether the federal income tax laws are constitutional or whether they are applicable to individuals has been well litigated. Here is a sampling of some of the most commonly mentioned claims that tax deniers will cite as to why they need not pay federal income taxes on earned income, the response from the IRS, and the case law addressing each issue:

Contention: The federal income tax laws are unconstitutional because the Sixteenth Amendment to the United States Constitution was not properly ratified.

This argument is based on the premise that all federal income tax laws are unconstitutional because the Sixteenth Amendment was not officially ratified or because the State of Ohio was not properly a state at the time of ratification. Proponents mistakenly believe that courts have refused to address this issue.

The Law: The Sixteenth Amendment provides that "Congress shall have the power to lay and collect taxes on income, from whatever source derived, without apportionment among the several states, and without regard to any census or enumeration." The Sixteenth Amendment was ratified by forty states, including Ohio (which became a state in 1803); *see Bowman v United States*, 920 F. Supp. 623 n.1 (E.D. Pa. 1995) (discussing the 1953 joint Congressional resolution that confirmed Ohio's status as a state retroactive to 1803), and issued by proclamation in 1913. Shortly thereafter, two other states also ratified the amendment. Under Article V of the Constitution, only three-fourths of the states are needed to ratify an amendment. There were enough states ratifying the Sixteenth Amendment even without Ohio to complete the number needed for ratification.

Furthermore, after the Sixteenth Amendment was ratified, the Supreme Court upheld the constitutionality of the income tax laws; *see Brushaber v Union Pacific R.R.*, 240 U.S. 1 (1916). Since then, courts have consistently upheld the constitutionality of the federal income tax.

In Rev Rul. 2005-19, 2005-1 C.B. 819, and in Notice 2010-33, 2010-17 I.R.B. 609, the IRS discussed this frivolous argument in more detail and warned taxpayers of the consequences of attempting to pursue a claim on these grounds.

Relevant Case Law:

Sochia v Commissioner, 23 F.3d 941 (5th Cir. 1994): The Fifth Circuit held that defendant's appeals, which made Sixteenth Amendment challenges to income tax legislation, were frivolous and warranted sanctions.

Miller v United States, 868 F.2d 236, 241–42 (7th Cir. 1989) (per curium): The Seventh Circuit imposed sanctions on Miller for advancing a "patently frivolous" position, stating, "[w]e find it hard to understand why the long and unbroken line of cases upholding the constitutionality of the sixteenth amendment generally, *Brushaber v Union Pacific Railroad Company*... and those specifically rejecting the argument advanced in *The Law That Never Was*, have not persuaded Miller and his compatriots to seek a more effective forum for airing their attack on the federal income tax structure."

United States v Stahl, 792 F.2d 1438, 1441 (9th Cir. 1986): The Ninth Circuit, upholding Stahl's conviction for failure to file returns and for making a false statement, stated that "the Secretary of State's certification under authority of Congress that the sixteenth amendment has been ratified by the requisite number of states and has become part of the Constitution is conclusive upon the courts."

United States v Foster, 789 F.2d 457 (7th Cir. 1986): The Seventh Circuit, rejecting Foster's claim that the Sixteenth Amendment was never properly ratified, affirmed his conviction for tax evasion, failing to file a return, and filing a false W-4 statement.

Knoblauch v Commissioner, 749 F.2d 200, 202 (5th Cir. 1984): The Fifth Circuit rejected as "totally without merit" the contention that the Sixteenth Amendment was not constitutionally adopted and imposed monetary sanctions against Knoblauch based on the frivolousness of his appeal.

Other Cases:

George v United States, No. 5:21-CV-01187-EJD, 2022 WL 562758 (N.D. Cal. Feb. 24, 2022); *United States v Moleski*, Crim. No. 12–811 (FLW), 2014 WL 197907 (D. N.J. Jan. 13, 2014); *Banister v U .S. Dep't of the Treasury*, 110 A.F.T.R.2d (RIA) 2012-6790 (N.D. Cal. 2011); *United States v Benson*, 2008 WL 267055 (N.D. Ill. Jan. 10, 2008); *United States v Schulz_PDF*, 529 F. Supp. 2d 341 (N.D.N.Y. 2007); *Stearman v Commissioner*, T.C. Memo. 2005-39, 89 T.C.M. (CCH) 823 (2005).

Contention: The Sixteenth Amendment does not authorize a direct non-apportioned federal income tax on United States citizens.

Some individuals and groups assert that the Sixteenth Amendment does not authorize a direct non-apportioned income tax and, thus, U.S. citizens and residents are not subject to federal income tax laws.

The Law: The constitutionality of the Sixteenth Amendment has invariably been upheld when challenged. Numerous courts have both implicitly and explicitly recognized that the Sixteenth Amendment authorizes a non-apportioned direct income tax on United States citizens and that the federal tax laws are valid as applied. In Notice 2010-33, 2010-17 I.R.B. 609, the IRS warned taxpayers of the consequences of attempting to pursue a claim on these grounds.

Relevant Case Law:

Young v Commissioner, 551 F. App'x 229, 203 (8th Cir. 2014): Rejecting as "meritless" and "frivolous" Young's arguments that the income tax is an unconstitutional direct tax, the 8th Circuit imposed $8,000 in sanctions.

Taliaferro v Freeman, 595 F. App'x 961, 962–63 (11th Cir. 2014): The Eleventh Circuit rejected as frivolous the taxpayer's argument that the Sixteenth Amendment authorizes the imposition of excise taxes but not income taxes and ordered sanctions against him up to and including double the government's costs.

In re Becraft, 885 F.2d 547, 548–49 (9th Cir. 1989): The Ninth Circuit, rejecting the taxpayer's frivolous position that the Sixteenth Amendment does not authorize a direct non-apportioned income tax, affirmed the failure to file conviction.

Lovell v United States, 755 F.2d 517, 518–20 (7th Cir. 1984): The Seventh Circuit rejected the argument that the Constitution prohibits imposition of a direct tax without apportionment, upheld assessment of the frivolous return penalty, and imposed sanctions for pursuing "frivolous arguments in bad faith" on top of the lower court's award of attorneys' fees to the government.

United States v Jones, 115 A.F.T.R.2d (RIA) 2015-2038 (D. Minn. 2015): The court rejected as frivolous the taxpayer's arguments that individual income tax is unconstitutional because it is "a direct tax which must be apportioned among the several states," noting that "[i]t is well-established that the Sixteenth Amendment authorizes the imposition of an income tax without apportionment among the states."

Maxwell v IRS, No. CIV 3090308, 2009 WL 920533, at *2 (M.D. Tenn. Apr. 1, 2009): The court characterized the taxpayer's arguments that there is no law that imposes an income tax, nor is there a non-apportioned direct tax that could be imposed on him as a supposed non-citizen as "routinely rejected."

Other Cases:

Broughton v United States, 632 F.2d 706 (8th Cir. 1980); *George v United States*, No. 5:21-CV-01187-EJD, 2022 WL 562758 (N.D. Cal. Feb. 24, 2022); *United States v Troyer*, 113 A.F.T.R.2d (RIA) 2014-387 (D. Wyo. 2013); *United States v Hockensmith*, 104 A.F.T.R.2d (RIA) 2009-5133 (M.D. Pa. 2009); *Stearman v Commissioner*, T.C. Memo. 2005-39, 89 T.C.M. (CCH) 823 (2005).[i]

Contention: The Internal Revenue Service is not an agency of the United States.

Some argue that the IRS is not an agency of the United States but rather a private corporation, because it was not created by positive law (*i.e.*, an act of Congress) and that, therefore, the IRS does not have the authority to enforce the Internal Revenue Code.

The Law: Constitutional and statutory authority establishes that the IRS is an agency of the United States. Indeed, the Supreme Court has stated that "the Internal Revenue Service is organized to carry out the broad responsibilities of the Secretary of the Treasury under § 7801(a) of the 1954 Code for the administration and enforcement of the internal revenue laws." *Donaldson v United States*, 400 U.S. 517, 534 (1971).

Pursuant to section 7801, the Secretary of the Treasury has full authority to administer and enforce the internal revenue laws and has the power to create an agency to enforce such laws. Based upon this legislative grant, the IRS was created. Thus, the IRS is a body established by "positive law" because it was created through a congressionally mandated power. Moreover, section 7803(a) explicitly provides that there shall be a Commissioner of Internal Revenue who shall administer and supervise the execution and application of the internal revenue laws.

The IRS warned taxpayers of the consequences of attempting to pursue a claim on these grounds in Notice 2010-33, 2010-17 I.R.B. 609.

Relevant Case Law:

United States v Fern, 696 F.2d 1269, 1273 (11th Cir. 1983): The Eleventh Circuit declared that "[c]learly, the Internal Revenue Service is a 'department or agency' of the United States."

Nevius v Tomlinson, 113 A.F.T.R.2d (RIA) 2014-1872 (W.D. Miss. 2014): The court granted summary judgment in favor of the government, rejecting Nevius's claim that the IRS is a private corporation, rather than a government agency.

United States v Provost, 109 A.F.T.R.2d (RIA) 2012-1706 (E.D. Cal. 2012): The court rejected the taxpayer's arguments and stated that the United States is a sovereign, not a corporation, the IRS is a government agency, and that arguments to the contrary are "wholly frivolous."

Salman v Dep't. of Treasury, 899 F. Supp. 471, 472 (D. Nev 1995): The court described Salman's contention that the IRS is not a government agency of the United States as "wholly frivolous" and dismissed his claim with prejudice.

Edwards v Commissioner, T.C. Memo. 2002-169, 84 T.C.M. (CCH) 24 (2002): The court dismissed the argument that the IRS is not an agency of the United States Department of Treasury as "tax protester gibberish" and stated that "[i]t's bad enough when ignorant and gullible or disingenuous taxpayers utter tax protester gibberish. It's much more disturbing when a member of the bar offers tax protester gibberish as a substitute for legal argument."

ABBREVIATIONS

AD Assistant Director
AFIS Automated Fingerprint Identification Systems
ASAC Assistant Special Agent in Charge
ATF Alcohol, Tobacco, and Firearms
AUSA Assistant United States Attorney
BOLO Be On the Look Out
BOP Bureau of Prisons
CBP Customs and Border Patrol
CDUSM Chief Deputy United States Marshal
CID Criminal Investigative Division
CSO Court Security Officer
CST Civil Support Team
DEA Drug Enforcement Agency
DOJ Department of Justice
DUSM Deputy United States Marshal
FBI Federal Bureau of Investigations
FCI Federal Correctional Institution
FIST Fugitive Investigative Strike Team
FLETC Federal Law Enforcement Training Center

HIDTA High Intensity Drug Trafficking Area

IACP International Association of Chiefs of Police

IG Inspector General

IOD Investigative Operations Division

IRS Internal Revenue Service

JFTF Joint Fugitive Task Force

JSD Judicial Security Division

MSP Massachusetts State Police

NCIC National Crime Information Center

NHNG New Hampshire National Guard

NHSP New Hampshire State Police

OCDETF Organized Crime Drug Enforcement Task Force

OGC Office of General Counsel

PIO Public Information Officer

RFTF Regional Fugitive Task Force

SA Special Agent

SAC Special Agent in Charge

SDUSM Supervisory Deputy United States Marshal

SOG Special Operations Group

SPLC Southern Poverty Law Center

SSA Supervisory Special Agent

TIGDA Treasury Inspector General for Tax Administration

TOG Technical Operations Group

USA United States Attorney

USM United States Marshal

USAO United States Attorney's Office

USDC United States District Court

USMC United States Marine Corps

USMS United States Marshals Service

NOTES

PREFACE

i. United States Constitution Rangers Handbook.
ii. Ibid.
iii. "Defense Militia Builds NH Base," *NH Sunday News*, October 9, 1994.

1. NOT JUST ANOTHER DAY...

i. Front cover of *Forging the Star*, University of North Texas Press, 2016.

2. THE 2006 IRS INDICTMENTS

i. "Defense Militia Builds NH Base," *NH Sunday News*, October 9, 1994.
ii. Ibid.
iii. "Militia Leader Says Feds Did It," by Jeanne Morris, *NH Sunday News*, April 22, 1995.
iv. Ibid.
v. *Wikipedia*, "The Oklahoma City Bombing."
vi. In a meeting with Bob Schultz, founder of *We the People Foundation*, January 21, 2007.
vii. "Westboro Man Fights Filth, 'Buster' Brown Uses Sex Appeal to Zap Pests," by Diane Derby, *Sunday Telegram*, October 21, 1984.
viii. "ARMED & DANGEROUS: MILITIAS TAKE AIM AT THE FEDERAL GOVERNMENT," The William and Naomi Gorowitz Institute on Terrorism and Extremism, Fact finding report of the Anti-Defamation League (ADL), pg. 20, 1994.
ix. Admin post, *Red Crayons Blog*, April 6, 2008.

3. THE FIRST RUSE: OPERATION JOINT TRUST

i. "How U.S. Marshals used Redskins tickets to bust fugitives in 1985 sting," by Scott Allen, *The Washington Post*, December 18, 2015.

4. THE BROWNS' ARRAIGNMENT AND RELEASE

i. 'Jesuit Masonic Zionists' targeted by billboard, by Aaron Nobel, *Connecticut Valley Spectator*, June 5, 2003.
ii. Ibid.
iii. Ibid
iv. Ibid.
v. Ibid.
vi. Ibid.

5. THE TAX TRIAL

i. "The Sixteenth Amendment: The Historical Background," by Arthur A. Ekirch, Jr. *Cato Journal 1* (Spring 1981), p.173.
ii. "Best of Both Worlds" (an interview with Milton Friedman), *Reason*, June 1995, p. 33.
iii. "Wife makes a deal; husband digs in," by Kate Davidson & Margot Sanger-Katz, *Concord Monitor*, January 17th, 2007
iv. Ibid
v. *Associated Press*, January 18th, 2007.
vi. Ibid
vii. "Tax evader says he will fight capture; Wife convicted, stays with son in Worcester" Philip Elliott, *The Associated Press*, January 18, 2007
viii. Ibid

6. THINGS HEAT UP IN THE COLD HILLS OF PLAINFIELD

i. Report from the Office of the Inspector General, *A Review of the Allegations of a Double Standard of Discipline at the FBI*, November, 15, 2002.
ii. "The Tragedy of Ruby Ridge," Christopher Godsick's *Chasing Evil* podcast, August 2022.
iii. Ibid.
iv. *Ruby Ridge*, Wikipedia.
v. Monier's stock statement to the press in the initial stages of the Plainfield standoff. February, 2007. Monier would give variations of this statement, depending on the particular day, and what question was being asked, but this was his "theme" to "downplay" references to Waco and Ruby Ridge throughout the standoff.

7. NEW HAMPSHIRE FREE STATERS...
AND OTHERS GET INVOLVED

i. Chief Kenneth Nunes would continue to be promoted to increasing positions of responsibility. He has served as the Chief Deputy U.S. Marshal for the Northern District of NY and the District of Massachusetts. He currently serves as a Chief Inspector in the Office of Emergency Management Branch of the Tactical Operation Division.

ii. "Brown requests aid, weapons on Myspace, Wife, meanwhile, has broken her silence," by Margot Sanger Katz, *Concord Monitor*, February 10, 2007.

iii. Ibid.

iv. "Brown has polite offer to end 'Little Alamo' impasse," by Kristen Senz, staff reporter, *Connecticut Valley Spectator*, January 25, 2007.

v. Ibid.

vi. Ibid.

vii. Ibid.

viii. "The Early Years of the Free State Project" Free State Project website, www.f-sp.org/history.

ix. Ibid.

x. "The Mission: Liberty in Your Lifetime!" Free State Project website, www.f-sp.org/mission.

xi. RidleyReport.com

xii. Ibid.

8. MORE CHARACTERS GET INVOLVED

i. "Browns call the police for friend – Tax protesting couple treated his cancer" by Margot Sanger-Katz *Concord Monitor*, March 22, 2007

ii. Ibid

iii. Ibid

iv. Ibid

v. "Browns get five years," by Margot Sanger-Katz, *Concord Monitor*, April 25, 2007.

vi. Ibid

vii. "They don't exist to me," by Kristen Senz, *NH Union Leader*, April 25, 2007.

viii. Ibid

ix. Ibid

x. Ibid

xi. "Nabbing tax protesters not worth loss of life," *Concord Monitor*, April 29, 2007.

xii. Ibid

xiii. Ibid

9. JUNE 2007: A FIRST OPPORTUNITY PRESENTS ITSELF... AND ED BROWN NEARLY DIES

i. "Trojan War," *Encyclopedia Britannica*, updated April 7, 2023.

ii. Ibid.

iii. Ibid.

iv. David K. Robertson spent thirty-seven years serving in local, state, and federal law enforcement. The many high profile events David worked and/or commanded during his career include missions in Iraq and Afghanistan, Ground Zero after 9/11, Hurricanes Andrew and Katrina, the Timothy McVeigh execution, first World Trade Center bombing trials, the Ed and Elaine Brown case. After retirement, David went back to work in law enforcement in Louisiana and served in various roles at the Office of Inspector General, State Police, and Alcohol Tobacco Control.

v. A ghillie suit is a type of camouflage clothing that is designed to blend in with the natural environment and conceal the wearer from detection.

vi. *"Feds gather; Browns unscathed,"* by Maddie Hanna and Margot Sanger-Katz, *Concord Monitor*, June 8, 2007.

vii. Ibid

viii. Ibid

ix. Ibid

x. Ibid

10. THINGS GET WEIRDER

i. Prison Planet, "Naïve to believe Ed Brown events were not Preparation for future siege," Paul Joseph Watson & Alex Jones, *InfoWars.com*, June 7th, 2007.

ii. Ibid

iii. "$1B Judgment Against Alex Jones Not the Final Word," *Associated Press*, October 13, 2022.

iv. "Browns commended for civil disobedience," by Margot Sanger-Katz, *Concord Monitor*, June 26, 2007.

v. Ibid.

vi. "Tax resisters finding allies in cyberspace," by Raja Mishra, *The Boston Globe*, June 22, 2007.

vii. Ibid.

viii. Ibid.

ix. Ibid

x. Ibid.

xi. Ibid.

11. THE BROWNS HOST A PICNIC/CONCERT

i. "Freedom Concert Held at Brown's NH Home Amidst IRS Standoff," by David Deschesne, Editor/Publisher, *Fort Fairfield Journal*, June 23, 2007.

ii. Ibid.

iii. Ibid.

iv. Ibid.

v. Ibid.

vi. "Browns throw themselves a party" by Maddie Hanna, *Concord Monitor*, July 15th, 2007.

vii. Ibid.

12. THE LONG SUMMER CONTINUES

i. "Police: tax evaders' supporters clogged 911 lines," AP report, *Concord Monitor*, July 30, 2007.

13. THE SEPTEMBER 12TH ARRESTS

i. "Camp Casey, Crawford, Texas" Wikipedia.

ii. The rifle signed by both Randy Weaver and Ed Brown was turned over to HQ for inclusion into the U.S. Marshals Service Museum, which opened in July of 2023. It's a must-see museum in Ft. Smith, Arkansas.

iii. "2 plead innocent in helping N.H. tax-evading couple," *Associated Press*, September, 14, 2007.

iv. The term "extradition hearing" in federal court is inaccurate as used in this AP article. Since this was a federal court pertaining to federal crimes, it was simply the defendants' appearance in the U.S. District Court where the defendant was arrested, for him/her to be remanded to the custody of the U.S. Marshals for transfer to the district where the criminal charges were brought.

v. Ibid.

14. NOT THIS TIME...

i. "Prosecutors: Browns' supporter left evidence trail on Internet," by Beverley Wang, AP Writer, September 17, 2007.

ii. Chief Billy Sorukas retired from the USMS after serving in law enforcement for thirty-one years. In 2021, his book *Chasing Evil: Pursuing Dangerous Criminals with the U.S. Marshals* was published by Author House, July 2021.

15. THE INTRO, A BURGLARY, THE SOLDIER LEFT BEHIND, AND THE TAKEDOWN

i. Being "drive stunned" with a Taser refers to the process of using the Taser as a pain compliance technique. It is a mode of operation where the Taser is held against the target without firing the projectiles, and is intended to cause pain without incapacitating the target [1]. The term "drive stun" is used to describe the process of using the EMD weapon as a pain compliance technique [2]. When an attacker has been "Tasered," the muscles in their body involuntarily contract, making them virtually helpless and may experience pain [3].

16. THE PRESS CONFERENCE AND THE AFTERMATH

i. "They invited us in; we escorted them out," by John Whitson, *NH Union Leader*, October 6, 2007.
ii. Ibid.
iii. "Experts: More charges likely for Browns; The couple publicly threatened officials," by Margot Sanger-Katz, the *Concord Monitor*, October 7, 2007.
iv. Ibid.
v. "Feds seek Brown sympathizers," *NH Union Leader*, October, 2007.
vi. Ibid

17. THE TRIAL OF THE SUPPORTERS IN 2008

i. "*George Z. Singal,*" Wikipedia.
ii. "Marshals tried to nab Brown in June," by Margot Sanger-Katz, *Concord Monitor*, April 2, 2008.

18. ED AND ELAINE BROWN ARE BROUGHT BACK TO NEW HAMPSHIRE TO FACE NEW CHARGES

i. *The Seditionists: Inside the Explosive World of Anti-Government Extremism in America*, St. Martin's Press, 2018.
ii. "Brown Trial: Wednesday, July 1, 2009," by JJ MacNab, www.redcrayons.net, July 2, 2009.
iii. "Brown Trial: Thursday, July 02, 2009," by JJ MacNab, Bombs, Taxes, and Red Crayons, July 2, 2009.

iv. "Brown Trial: Post-Trial Housekeeping," by JJ MacNab, Bombs, Taxes and Red Crayons, July 11, 2009.

20. PRESENT DAY: PLAINFIELD, NEW HAMPSHIRE

i. "Plainfield, New Hampshire," Wikipedia.
ii. Ibid
iii. "Cornish Art Colony," Wikipedia.
iv. "*Maxfield Parrish*," Wikipedia.
v. Ibid.
vi. "Left-leaning Station Airs Anti-Semitic Rants," Intelligence Report, Southern Poverty Law Center, 2009 Fall Issue, August 30, 2009.
vii. "Fact check: The Constitution requires American citizens to pay income taxes," by Hannah Hudnall, USA *Today*, December 13, 2022.
viii. "What is the 'sovereign citizen' movement?", by Max Matza, BBC News, Washington, August 5, 2020.
ix. Ibid.
x. According to the accounting from the National Fraternal Order of Police, 331 law enforcement officers in the United States were shot in 2022. Of those, 62 officers were killed. Another 185 officers lost their lives in the line of duty due to accidents, illnesses, or assaults with vehicles (14).

APPENDIX

i. From the IRS Tax publications, "*The Truth About Frivolous Tax Arguments — Section I (D to E)*" See: The Truth About Frivolous Tax Arguments — Section I (D to E) | Internal Revenue Service (irs.gov)
Showing Plainfield, NH on the Vermont border and its relationship to Concord, NH, the Capital City.

www.ingramcontent.com/pod-product-compliance
Lightning Source LLC
Chambersburg PA
CBHW062113020426
42335CB00013B/950